Ru may 05

DELUSIONS OF
POWER

DELUSIONS OF
POWER

VANITY, FOLLY AND THE
UNCERTAIN FUTURE OF
CANADA'S HYDRO GIANTS

WAYNE SKENE

Douglas & McIntyre
Vancouver / Toronto

Douglas & McIntyre Ltd.
1615 Venables Street
Vancouver, British Columbia
V5L 2H1

Canadian Cataloguing in Publication Data

Skene, Wayne, 1941–
    Delusions of power

    ISBN 1-55054-589-2

    1. Electric utilities—Canada.   2. Electric utilities—Canada—
Management.   3. Electric power production—Canada.
4. Hydroelectric power plants—Canada.   I. Title.
HD9685.C32S53 1997   333.793'2'0971   C97-910496-3

Editing by Brian Scrivener
Jacket design by Peter Cocking
Jacket photograph by A. Breakey/Tony Stone Images
Typeset by Brenda and Neil West, BN Typographics West
Printed and bound in Canada by Friesens
Printed on acid-free paper ∞

The publisher gratefully acknowledges the support of the Canada Council for the Arts and of the British Columbia Ministry of Tourism, Small Business and Culture.

Contents

Preface and Acknowledgements   v

1   Prometheus Meets the Common Sense Revolution   1

2   The Magic of the Electricity Marketplace   11

3   Prometheus Bound   31

4   Power at Cost   55

5   Maîtres Chez Nous   92

6   Nothing More Free than Free   126

7   Wrestling with the Ghost of Betty Furness   173

8   The Words of the Prophets   206

Bibliography   223

Index   228

This book is dedicated to my mother, Jean Skene, who taught me, among other things, that there never was a prophet born who should not be questioned.

Preface and Acknowledgements

If there is an industry where change is now the only constant, it is the nation's electricity business. For generations we expected our provincial power utilities to provide us with cheap, reliable electricity. By and large they came through, often in a pace and fashion about as exciting as daily milk deliveries. We flipped the switch and the light was there. That was what we wanted out of the relationship. But those days of complacency are disappearing as the public power utility business begins to go through the most dynamic and indeterminate period of change in its history. The scope and velocity of the conversion now taking place in the public power industry is stunning, occasionally distressing and very often perplexing.

One day we read that Hydro-Québec has for years adamantly refused to renegotiate its lucrative contract for Churchill Falls electricity with Newfoundland. The next day we read that because Quebec wants permission from an American regulatory agency to sell its electricity into the United States, it is now prepared to discuss renegotiation with Newfoundland; negotiate with Newfoundland to get access to the U.S. market?

One day we hear that B.C. Hydro has just sold its downstream benefits to the Columbia River Treaty to an American public utility for billions of dollars. The next thing we hear the deal is off, then it is on again, and B.C. Hydro is either caught up in a scandal in Pakistan or using the huge surpluses in electricity it now holds to lure business to British Columbia with cut-rate prices.

The evening TV news told us Ontario Hydro was making strides in finally putting its financial and technical house in order, with huge expectations for paying down its massive debt from a three-decade binge of nuclear plant construction, and suddenly the sombre faces at the corporation's media conference inform us that our largest power utility must now spend up to $8 billion to repair nuclear reactors because they no longer meet minimum standards. Bad management is blamed. Bad management in nuclear power? A thought begins to circulate: The Pickering nuclear facility is closer to Toronto than the Chernobyl facility was to Kiev.

The elements of transformation in our once dull and comfortable electricity business are now coming at us so swiftly that in the two years it took to research and write this book, the text had to be significantly re-written at least twice—the last time over three days following Ontario Hydro's shocking announcements about its nuclear predicament on August 13, 1997.

What *is* happening out there? How did we get into this mess? Who is in charge? What will this industry look like in five years, never mind two decades from now? Who will provide me with that safe, reliable and inexpensive supply of electricity my family needs? These are questions that this book attempts to answer.

Foreboding thoughts aside, this is still a grand story to tell. Where power comes from and how it has affected out lives is an immensely important topic, one that offers access to a magnificent sweep of the years covering our nation's development, the men who guided and propelled that advancement and the damaging paths of folly and vanity they often led us down—to our collective cost and peril.

The dimensions put to their stories are stunning. These men built an industry that employed tens of thousands of Canadians. Ontario Hydro once had more employees than Yukon had citizens. They built immense power corporations worth billions of dollars in both revenues and assets, often rivalling Canada's largest banks and corporations in size and economic clout. And in moments of high public purpose, they often undertook to build generating plants and transmission systems that no private-sector power company on earth would have contemplated. In that sense, they were hugely motivated by the ethic of public progress. They seemed fearless.

But their manipulation of consumer demand and the errors in forecasting the public's need for electricity also added billions in unnecessary debt to our collective fiscal burden. That burden, and the use of their institutions as "blunt instruments of public policy," as my publisher, Scott McIntyre, once put it, inhibited the proper and necessary social developments that could have made us an even more equitable and charitable nation.

They also often conducted themselves in ways that seriously and unforgivably damaged the environment. They totally ignored the impact their visions had on native peoples, leaving them open to charges of being blatantly racist. At times, they followed their polestar of electric power and public purpose with an arrogance and unaccountability toward the public good that reached the scandalous, and often bordered on the criminal.

Deferring as we too often do to authority, many Canadians assumed the actions of our public power utilities and their executives were being watched over assiduously by provincial authorities and prudent regulatory regimes. In fact, the reverse was true. Too often the watchdogs of public purpose lacked the bite necessary to nudge these powerful monopolies in the proper direction. This lack of scrutiny allowed the utilities to move easily in and out of trouble under lax regulation and run up billions in unnecessary expansion in dams, fossil-fuel generating plants and nuclear power facilities.

Still, until I began delving into issues currently affecting the industry, I was not totally aware that the giant public utilities we had relied upon for so long were now being ripped apart by forces, both technological and global, that even these titans could not master. As I peered into their past, I found myself watching them coming to the end of their time.

The entire world electrical power industry—all one trillion dollars' worth of it, not just Canadian public power utilities—is on the verge of an unprecedented restructuring. It could turn out to be as profound an event as the moment of our evolution from agricultural existence into the state we know as the Industrial Revolution.

That said, this is a book less about electricity than it is about power. It began as an inquiry into the histories of our major provincial power utilities and ended up being an essay, putting it perhaps a bit too awkwardly, on the ethics of technology and the belief that growth can always be a solid basis for that ethic. It cannot, for growth, as we know by now, can be as evil and damaging as it is good. The illusion that we become "good" by progressing each day, as Rollo May once put it in *Power and Innocence*, "is a doctrine bootlegged from technology and made into a dogma in ethics where it does not fit."

Power has two dimensions. It can cause or prevent change. Most often we use it, we would hope, as a door to possibilities, like the Latin root *posse*, from which that term comes. It means "to be able." In that sense, the power we are talking about here—that the histories of electricity development in Canada most often represent—has really been a century-long battle between our urge to use it as a means to enhance ourselves, as Nietzsche would put it, and a simple striving to exist, as Darwin might have phrased it. Strangely enough, that is roughly what the stories of electricity development in Canada come down to—Nietzsche versus Darwin.

These stories, these brief time-cells of power being put to use in delivering electricity to the public, are largely a matter of man searching, pitting himself against elements, seeking to overcome challenges and difficulties and at the same time attempting to grow and, hopefully, to generate more life. In that sense, when we attempt to explain where we have been on the electric journey—and where we might be heading—we are talking about power both as an expression of narcissism and life process for as many of us as can possibly benefit from it.

To me, there are three very important lessons buried in the heart of Canada's electrical utility experience. First, because we face such uncertainty in the future, we might be wise to take our guidance from a culture we admire for its stability. The Greeks—in particular, Plato and Aristotle—taught us to be extremely suspicious of sweeping social change, particularly precipitous and not well reasoned change, the kind not terribly different from the addled symphony we hear these days from too many corporate leaders, right-wing governments and neoconservative zealots. It is not that the Greeks were an early manifestation of the Luddites. They just believed, based on their experiences, that the more radical the change, the more chaos and social disintegration we suffered. I suggest the Greeks as the most appropriate prophets for our future because I have much more faith in the words and thinking of Aristotle than I do in those of the Business Council on National Issues, the Conference Board of Canada or the Fraser Institute.

A second lesson to be learned is that the growth and the development our modern societies pursue are not infinite. At current velocity, they certainly are not sustainable. If we are not careful, our pursuit, as technically admirable and socially desirable as it might appear, will only accelerate our journey in a finite direction.

The final lesson is that power often can be more acquisitive and regressive than beneficial—more Darwinian and less Nietzschean. Like all power held and applied, whether it be technical mastery or political dominion over others, some of it is good, some of it is bad, some life enhancing and some utterly foolish.

There are many people I must thank for assisting me with this project. But I will begin by expressing my appreciation to the Canada Council for graciously awarding me a grant that allowed me to explore my topic in greater scope and depth than would have normally been the case. And, of course, were it not for my publisher Scott McIntyre and his passions, it is highly unlikely a book about Canada's power utilities would exist at this very important juncture in the industry's history and development.

There were a number of people who went out of their way to provide me with research materials and access to interview subjects. Pat Crawford and Elizabeth McClaren at B.C. Hydro's library service were exceedingly pleasant and helpful in my search for information, as were Mary McLaughlin, Mary Rowe and Terry Young at Ontario Hydro. As in my other book ventures, my son Cameron and his wife, Pauline Pelletier, provided me with vast and necessary quantities of research findings and impeccable transcriptions of the many interview tapes. And thanks as well to Brenda Lum, who diligently and reliably provided me with research and background material on the electrical industry.

This is not a history book so much as it is a book of stories about histories, some provided by historians and journalists, but a large number offered to me by people who gave graciously of their time, their recollections and their experiences associated with the world of electricity and power. I had the pleasure of interviewing a number of people on a wide variety of subjects. All were cheerful, accommodating and forthright in their recollections. Among them were Arthur Dickinson, Stephen Probyn, Bud Wildman, Mario Germani, Marv Daub, Bern Brenner, Mark Huggins, John Robinson, Conrad Guelke, David Austin, John Laxton, Janet Craig, John Hall, Andrew Wilson, Bill Tieleman, Mark Jaccard, Marvin Shaffer, Dick Gathercole and John Sheehan. In particular, I owe Dr. Allan Kupcis, Rod Taylor and Paul Burke at Ontario Hydro a debt of thanks for their time and their candour.

The number of people who volunteered their time and insights is long and I apologize to those I may have inadvertently overlooked. But there were others I met who went out of their way to ensure I had the information, materials and sources I needed. In that respect, I must express my appreciation to those who spent so much time helping me interpret the colourful political and organizational tapestry that each provincial power utility represents; in particular Ralph Torrie, Paul McKay, Neil Freeman, Tom Adams, James Wilson, John Murphy, Bob Menard, Professor Myron Gordon and former Premier of British Columbia, Mike Harcourt.

I should point out that once again I have tried to write a book that challenges conventional wisdom and common interpretation of time and circumstance. That is always a risky task. It can lead to conclusions, however well-intended and ardently pursued, that sometimes are not shared by those who agree to be interviewed. I have made every effort to ensure that what was related to me was used only in proper context. I accept full responsibility for wandering off into those differing conceptual fields and hope the deviations and occasionally revisionist interpretation of events have not lost me too many friends.

I must sincerely thank my editor, Brian Scrivener, for once again putting on display his editorial mastery of the rules of zestful non-fiction writing, as well as exhibiting a sense of tact and patience that should place him on the spectrum of forbearance just to the left of Job.

And always there is my thanks to Connie. She has put up with this particular brand of journalistic folly for many years now and has always been there to offer encouragement, probing insight and splendid moments of distraction. I am not at all sure these bookish excursions would be even worth the effort if she were not there beside me.

Wayne Skene
Surrey, B.C.
August 1997

1 / Prometheus Meets the Common Sense Revolution

Ah! but the world is large
in the light of lamps!
But in memory's eyes, Ah! but
the world is small.

— Baudelaire

PICTURE THIS: The Beaches district of Toronto. It is a Saturday morning in November, just before dawn. You have been awakened by the sound of winter's first storm. Waves of freezing sleet off Lake Ontario beat against the window panes. Snow begins to gather in drifts on the front lawn. You open the door to retrieve the morning paper and watch with anxiety as the wind whips the large elms in the front yard, bending them ominously back and forth against the power lines leading to your home. You close the door and try to ignore the sounds of the storm blowing outside.

You move to the kitchen and turn on the coffee machine. You check the TV Weather Channel. You switch on the radio for the latest storm report. You listen for the reassuring hum of the furnace. You open the children's bedroom door just a crack to make sure they are covered and warm. You log on the Internet for more storm information. You run through a mental checklist of things to do if the power goes out, but you cannot remember where you put the flashlights or the emergency candles. You cannot even recall the last time electricity was not there for you. You turn on the reading lamp. A sudden gust of wind shakes the house. The light dims, flickers and then returns to normal.

You relax into your favourite chair with the thought that the one thing in life you seem able to rely upon is electricity—that marvellously economical commodity that over the years has provided your home and your family with light, heat and comfort—with little or no interruption. You open the morning newspaper ...

Harris Government Ready to Sell Ontario Hydro

Toronto/November 27, 1999—Less than three weeks after winning re-election by the thinnest of margins over a resurgent Liberal Party in a late-term election, Premier Mike Harris's Progressive Conservative government once again rattled the province's political scene with the surprise announcement that Ontario Hydro would be sold off to private shareholders.

The decision came a little over two years after a shocking internal report cited bad management in the utility's nuclear power division as the reason for shutting down seven of the corporation's nuclear reactors at a cost of up to $8 billion. That report, tabled in mid-August of 1997, led to the resignation of Ontario Hydro's president and chief executive officer and refuelled the Harris government's determination to sell the public utility.

During the 1995 election campaign that led to the defeat of Bob Rae's New Democratic government, the Conservatives had targeted Ontario Hydro for "privatization." In late 1997, the Harris government waffled on that promise when they passed legislation breaking the province's power utility into two publicly owned companies—one to run the transmission system and the other to generate electricity.

Critics claimed the move was simply a prelude to privatization, pointing out that other provinces were heading in the opposite direction and making every effort to gain competitive advantage by keeping their utilities in public hands.

However, with a fresh but narrow mandate to govern, and with more than four years to pacify irate Ontario voters and electricity ratepayers, selling off the province's power utility operations was quickly put back on the Harris government's policy agenda.

Yesterday's news has been labelled as the start of the "Common Sense Revolution—Phase II." It stunned public power supporters, elated privatization exponents, but triggered widespread concern across the province as to what the sell-off might mean for household electricity prices and reliability of supply.

It also set the scene for what next week will be a mad scramble of investors and Bay Street financial institutions as they queue for multi-million-dollar pieces of the share offering action.

The sale of Ontario Hydro could turn out to be one of the largest utility privatizations ever undertaken. It is estimated it will bring as much as $12 billion to government coffers and could mean millions of dollars in fees and contracts for Canadian and foreign financial institutions.

The debate over who should own the province's electrical power utility—government or private shareholders—began in earnest yesterday when various consumer groups and privatization critics argued that the Ontario Hydro sell-off will end up *costing* ratepayers and taxpayers billions of dollars. It also raises serious questions about reliability of service with the generation and distribution of provincial power now destined for private-sector hands.

"Going 'private' will cost Ontario taxpayers a bundle," said one noted University of Toronto economist. "Even with its debt load, Ontario Hydro saves the people of Ontario over a billion dollars a year. Putting this public utility in private-sector hands will inevitably mean higher electricity rates.

"The only way higher rates can be avoided would be for the province to absorb about $10 billion of Ontario Hydro's long-term debt—effectively passing the higher costs caused by privatization from Ontario ratepayers to Ontario taxpayers," said another angry critic.

Many do not agree with that assessment. Large industrial and commercial customers, who have been lobbying heavily for years for their electricity rates to be reduced, applauded the move to privatize Ontario Hydro and force it to compete for customers.

"Yes, it will mean lower electricity rates for us," the head of the industry's lobby association admitted. "But it will allow our members to be more competitive. That means more investment, more jobs and more tax revenue for the government."

The move by the Harris government will also be a boon to independent power producers. With the elimination of Ontario Hydro's monopoly status, the gates to the province's electrical marketplace have been thrown wide open.

"Allowing us to sell our electricity into a market that was once controlled by Ontario Hydro will provide consumers with more choice," said the executive director of the province's independent power producers' association.

Some senior executives within Ontario Hydro had already been pressing the Harris government to open the Ontario market to competition and privatize the public utility. Even before he was appointed to his position by the Harris government, the utility's chairman was a well-known champion of private ownership. As one critic pointed out, it should be no surprise that senior management are eager to sell the corporation. If the British "privatization" experience is any model, their salaries will sky-rocket.

"The British experience also had a further troublesome caveat for taxpayers," another industry watcher claimed. "When the Central Electricity Generating Board was broken up between 1988 and 1991, the juicy parts were privatized while the highly controversial nuclear generating power plants were left in public hands. Evidently, they were too hot to handle for private investors, who got to keep the valuable assets. The public got stuck with the bad assets. Guess who will pay the bill for all those radioactive nuclear facilities in Ontario when they are finally decommissioned?"

According to one very senior Hydro official, the key to survival in today's continental marketplace is competitiveness. "The private sector is inherently more efficient and better able to compete than government-run operations. Not only that, thanks to technological change, electricity is now just another commodity in the marketplace. This service no longer needs government ownership."

Critics and many academics maintain that the claims about efficiencies and savings gained by private ownership are exaggerated and unsupported. One economist even goes so far as to refer to the information and studies provided by private-sector exponents as "almost entirely B.S.!"

"The belief that market forces will keep rates low and make Ontario Hydro more efficient is based more on naive faith than science, or even experience," she concluded.

However, a number of large industrial users argue that open competition for electricity will cause rates to come down—for them, at least—by twenty percent over five years.

"If the justification for privatizing Ontario Hydro is cheaper electricity rates, where is the proof?" asks the president of the 15,000-member Power Workers' Union. "We won't find it in the U.S. where privately owned utilities charge their customers, on average, thirty percent more than public utilities, and still do not provide the same reliability of service that we do."

Please See Hydro sell-off / A2

The lights suddenly dim. Another gust of wind shakes the house. Through the window you can see the shadow of a large limb breaking free from the elm tree and striking the garage roof. The baby cries out from the bedroom, babbles for a moment, then falls back to sleep. You pick up the newspaper again.

Who can you believe? Everybody seems to be throwing numbers and theories around, talking ominously about the threat of "competition," about "change," about "choice." Choice? What does that mean? Will I have to go shopping now for the best buy in electricity? And why all the urgency to this?

The lights dim once more. The power surges and dies. Black. The wind continues to howl outside. Unaccountably, the power returns. The lights come on. Now, you think, I'll have to re-set all those cursed digital clocks ...

Hydro sell-off

From page A1

Supporters of deregulation and privatization most often couch their enthusiasm in buyer-friendly terms, talking about "customer-driven competition," the "need" for deregulation, "more consumer choice," and "competitive market forces" as an alternative to public monopoly control.

"The issue is not just privatization of a public monopoly," said one Harris government cabinet minister. "The issue is the inevitability of change in the North American power industry. We are moving very quickly from a monopoly environment to open competition. And you cannot have really effective competition—with all its benefits for consumers—without privatizing and breaking up the monopoly provincial utilities have held for decades."

Competition exponents like the cabinet minister point to three basic factors influencing change in the electricity business: the surplus of electrical generating capacity that now exists; the introduction of new, cheaper generating technologies that can compete with the provincial utilities using hydraulic, coal or nuclear power; and the dramatic change in the size, scope and velocity of change in the electrical marketplace after the Free Trade Agreement and the NAFTA were signed with the United States.

The marketplace we once recognized and enjoyed—familiar Canadian public monopolies providing cheap, reliable electricity for their provinces, seldom competing among themselves—has been blown apart by the reality that the market is now North America-wide.

"And we are not just talking about Ontario being subject to these new continental forces of competition," said the cabinet minister. "The whole world of electricity is being turned upside down. The days of public monopoly ownership are over. It's happening right across the country.

"Quebec, British Columbia, Manitoba, Nova Scotia, even Newfoundland—all these provinces are having to face new business realities and gear up for competition with U.S. electricity suppliers. In a few years, people in B.C. or Quebec will not even recognize their old, protected monopolies. Competition, not monopoly control, is the new reality in electrical power."

"That is so much balderdash," says one Ottawa power consultant. "The exact opposite is true. If there ever was a time when we needed strong, well-regulated monopoly generators and deliverers of electricity in each province, it is now."

The Ottawa consultant—considered an international expert in sustainable power development—argues that bigger is both better and inevitable. He claims the best way to compete in the future with large American power corporations is to have our own power utilities with economies of scale large enough to take them on.

"If we believe this open competition guff, we will just weaken ourselves, and the Americans will gobble us up, one by one," he said. "What will happen is what is already happening in the United States. Large corporations are buying up their smaller competitors so they can control the marketplace. If anything, in the United States, the industry is aggregating, not disassembling.

"Our publicly owned provincial utilities—Ontario Hydro excepted, as of yesterday, of course—already have good competitive size advantages. Selling them off now would be the height of folly. The smart thing to do is hold on to the advantages we already possess—keep large power utilities that can take on the likes of Consolidated Edison and Pacific Gas & Electric."

In terms of installed generating capacity, Ontario Hydro is the largest electric utility in North America. It currently generates more than ninety percent of the province's electricity and serves, directly and indirectly, 3.9 million urban, rural and corporate customers.

Despite the latest move by the Harris government, most Ontario consumers—voters as well as electricity ratepayers—are not convinced that competition and privately operated power utilities will mean cheaper electricity rates for them.

In fact, an Environics Research Group poll conducted in the province in the summer of 1996—just before the Harris government began backing off their first privatization promise—revealed that two-thirds of those polled were opposed to any sale of Ontario Hydro to the private sector. Less than one-quarter were in favour of privatization.

"As people hear more about the issue, their opposition to privatization actually grows," said one pollster. Other polls confirm that a majority of small consumers has become more or less comfortable with the cost of electricity provided by their public utility.

Concerned ratepayers point to their monthly telephone bills to show deregulation and market competition do not guarantee lower costs for small consumers. The first thing that happened when the Canadian Radio-television and Telecommunications Commission opened the local phone business to competition in May 1997 was that home owners' telephone bills rose by $3.

And when Canadian-owned Unitel ran into financial trouble from new competition, it was immediately eaten up by the U.S. telecommunications giant AT&T.

A 1995 study by Mississauga Hydro concluded that electricity rates for its customers could rise by as much as thirty percent if Ontario Hydro were to be privatized. A similar London Hydro study reported roughly the same results.

In fact, it has been reported that an internal Ontario Hydro study concluded that same year that rates could climb by as much as thirty-two percent. Shortly thereafter, the study, and its controversial findings, so it was said, mysteriously disappeared from Ontario Hydro's publicly available records.

Consumers living in rural regions of Ontario fear that a privately operated Hydro would not provide the kind of service they have become accustomed to under a publicly owned utility. Critics claim that in the interests of ensuring high profits for investors, maintenance and overall system reliability would inevitably be compromised.

Ontario Hydro was originally responsible for providing Ontario with "power at cost." But the utility has been the subject of intense debate and public scrutiny for more than two decades now. Much of the pressure has come from the changing nature of the electricity marketplace. But many of Ontario Hydro's problems stem from corporate decisions made in the past, including over-estimating future demand for electricity and undertaking costly expansion in controversial nuclear generating facilities.

When the troubled, $14 billion Darlington nuclear facility came on stream in the early 1990s, its roughly 3,500 megawatt capacity was considered totally surplus to consumer needs.

By 1992, Hydro's long-term debt had climbed to $34 billion (representing about thirty percent of the province's total debt) and electricity rate increases in Ontario homes were averaging over nine percent a year.

Throughout North America, many large monopoly utilities like Ontario Hydro found themselves caught in an electricity "death spiral," according to one economist. "Demand fell, leaving the utilities with huge power surpluses. Falling revenues made it difficult to service the massive debts they carried from two decades of capital expansion. Increasing competition from independent power producers—now using cheap natural gas to generate electricity—only magnified the problem."

By the mid-1990s, the major fear for large public and private monopoly utilities was the possibility of "stranded assets"—another term for virtual bankruptcy, where revenue does not cover massive debt payments. It is estimated that in the United States, the stranded assets problem could eventually saddle American taxpayers with a $300 billion bill.

Up until the board of directors decided in August 1997 to spend $5 to $8 billion to bring their nuclear division up to acceptable standards, Ontario Hydro was in better financial health than it had been for decades. The utility was forced to go through a major structural reorganization in 1993. Its workforce dropped by 12,000 employees, or more than one-third of its staff. Capital spending

8

plans were slashed by $24 billion. Operating budgets were cut by $1 billion and electricity rates were frozen.

That year, Ontario Hydro declared a fiscal year net loss, after charges for the restructuring, of $3.6 billion—the largest corporate loss in Canadian history. Despite a further write-off of $2.5 billion in 1996 related to its nuclear-generating program, Ontario Hydro seemed to have turned things around.

"Ontario Hydro saves billions of dollars for the province," claims one government critic. "It gives us economic strength. Harris is asking the citizens of Ontario to take part in a costly economic and social experiment that will one day end up costing taxpayers billions of dollars."

After the radical cost-cutting and restructuring of 1993 was finished, Ontario Hydro began eating into its debt. "If we had been a private company turning itself around that dramatically," said one Hydro manager, "we would have been applauded for being so 'entrepreneurial'."

The announcement of the Harris government's decision to sell Ontario Hydro, and end a ninety-three-year span of public ownership, came in the form of a late-afternoon press release from the office of the Minister of Environment and Energy. It came on the heels of two years of government vacillation over whether or not to privatize the utility.

A Power Workers' Union spokesperson points out that what they suspected all along is happening: the Harris government intended to privatize Ontario Hydro from the start. "The PC government was just waiting until the political coast was clear before making the controversial move," he said.

Other critics suggest that the move was motivated more by practical considerations than ideological ones. According to some sources, the move to privatize Ontario Hydro is a clear indication that Conservatives have failed in their promise to control spending and reduce the provincial debt.

Under the PCs, provincial deficits have been averaging $6 billion a year since 1996 and the debt has risen roughly $24 billion to $120 billion since the Harris government came to office. Going into 1997, Ontario's deficit was the highest in the country as a percentage of gross domestic product. A series of much-vaunted Reaganomics tax cuts failed to generate badly needed revenue and there is little chance the Harris government will reach its stated goal of a balanced budget by fiscal year 2000–01.

Privatizing Ontario Hydro may provide the Harris government with the cash it needs to meet the promises it has been making to eliminate deficits and bring down the province's debt ...

The driving sleet and snow has now turned into freezing rain. It coats the barren limbs of the elm trees and the power lines to your home. The cold wind swirls and smacks against the house. The bulb in the reading lamp flickers, dims and goes out again. The Weather Channel picture on your television set surges, then dissolves into a dark, grey mass. The furnace motor dies, the red light on the coffee maker vanishes and the colours and lines on your computer screen shrink into a brief, glaring dot, before disappearing altogether.

Who are you going to call?

2 / The Magic of the Electricity Marketplace

The best way to get rich is to have a monopoly.

— Cable king Ted Turner, *Maclean's* magazine, May 26, 1997

SOMEWHERE OUT THERE, just beyond the horizon of life's daily challenges and experiences, a giant wave of change is building in strength and severity. Like a mammoth *tsunami*, triggered by some unseen seaquake or undersea volcanic eruption, this continent-wide tidal swell carries with it the potential to change forever the relaxed relationship we have had with one of life's most important elements—electricity.

We know something is happening "out there" with this electrical wave of change, but many of us are not sure what it might mean when the high tide finally arrives on our doorstep. Most are confused not only about the current state of affairs surrounding this essential service, but also about how seriously future circumstances will affect our lives and our pocketbooks.

We hear and see media stories about our public electrical utilities being bloated with debt and headed for bankruptcy. We are bombarded with evidence that our once-trusted power monopolies have been damaging the environment at a shocking pace with decades of dam and transmission line construction. They've poisoned northern waters with mercury pollution, destroyed valuable fish habitat and filled the atmosphere with greenhouse gases.

Ontario, in particular, wrestles daily with the question of whether the decision years ago to rely largely on nuclear power for electrical generation was a wise or a foolish move for Ontarians. Each story that appears about a corroded pipe or coolant spill at the Pickering generating facility, only about thirty kilometres east of Toronto, triggers, in some minds, thoughts of Chernobyl and Three Mile Island.

We read snippets of stories in newspapers and magazines about the fight over who will eventually control the generation and distribution of electrical power in Canada. We listen, with no particular comprehension, to the arguments for and against this massive, looming structural change in the electricity business. We hear stories about the speed with which change is coming at us. We have a rough idea of when it might hit. But we have no idea of what the damage might be. After all, the lights still go on when we flip the switch.

But the details—Who will provide me with electricity in the future? Will electricity cost the average consumer more? Why? Will there be blackouts?—are so confusing and often contradictory that most of us are left with nothing more than a growing sense of trepidation, a feeling that once again the average consumer is being asked to play guinea pig in what is a potentially damaging ideological free-for-all in the guise of economic restructuring.

Except for oxygen, water and food, nothing—not even sex—is as important to members of modern society as electricity. The average North American adult reportedly has sex sixty-seven times a year. Yet we need electricity every minute of every hour of every day.

Those marvellous electrons, protons and other charged particles that provide us with light, heat and power have so pervaded our lives that we often do not acknowledge their existence. Electricity, and all it mysteriously does for us, has become an essential part of our life's rhythm, like plasma—a quiet, reliable substance we would find difficult, if not impossible, to live without.

Our whole world is wrapped with this essential need for electricity. It heats our homes and apartments while we sleep. It keeps the alarm clock ticking and ready to roust us for work. One flip of a light switch in the morning triggers a series of services we simply take for granted, from the perking coffee pot on the kitchen counter to the automatic opening of the garage door, from accessing E-mail on the Internet to the day's-end relaxation before the television set, or those peaceful hours with a good book. We have long passed the point where it might be argued that without electricity civilization would regress. Without electricity, there would be no civilization as we know it.

With little real intrusion in our lives, electricity always seems to be there for us. It is stable, inexpensive and generally reliable. It silently supports us, making life unbelievably comfortable. It drives the economic and industrial engines of resource extraction. It helps manufacture goods we buy. It provides transportation and trade and is the pulse that gives us the modern health care we relish. Through computer science and the research tools it provides, it allow us to keep pushing out the boundaries of science and education in the search for the opportunity to make life even better than it is.

But there is a fierce battle outside raging, as the poet put it, for control of what has been termed "this most politicized of fuels." In Canada, it is not just a battle over who should own and manage an almost thirty-billion-dollar a year industry. It is also a contest that could fracture the expectations Canadian consumers have held about their province's electrical utility business. It will inevitably be a test to see what price we will have to pay in the future—both in dollars and in terms of damage to the environment—for this marvellous gift from the proton gods.

And we are not alone. The future structure of electrical power generation and distribution is indeed part of a global wave of change. In the United States of America, where the generation and distribution of electrical power produces revenues in the hundreds of billions of dollars annually, the forces of deregulation and competition in the electrical generation and transmission industry are being unleashed with no certainty of where the industry is going and what the costs and benefits to the consumer might be.

The problem facing Canadians is partly a matter of economics and partly a matter of political ideology. But a lot of it is purely hyperbolic. To listen to many energy analysts and newspaper columnists one would have to assume that the entire energy world just finished radically altering the structure and nature of its business, with huge successes marked up by one nation after another. Canada had better hurry up and change the way it does electricity generation and distribution or we will be stuck in the dark ages, goes the current wisdom. But that is not what is happening.

Change in the energy business has been going on around the world for years now. Some of that change is coming to Canada; some of it is already here. Canadians and their power utilities will inevitably have to modify the way we do the business. But to say that we as a nation are "behind" or that we are not adapting "properly" or "quickly enough" to what has already been accomplished in other countries, and therefore is *ipso facto* what we should be doing because everything being done beyond our borders has all been such a massive, consistent success, is pure rubbish.

Between 1988 and 1991, Britain deregulated and privatized most of the parts of its once vertically integrated electrical power industry. Even though there is much debate and controversy about whether it was a good or a bad move for ratepayers and taxpayers, the British example has been cited, mostly by privatization advocates, as a model for other nations to follow.

Yet there are any number of academic studies showing that Britain's experiment in privatization has not at all been the success its advocates claim, and it certainly has not achieved the reductions in price and improvements in service that were promised. To be sure, the ratepaying public did not do as well as eager investors.

In July 1997 the new Labour government slapped a windfall profit tax on former state-owned companies like British Energy PLC. It was the Blair government's way of getting back some of the vast profits investors in British utilities reaped when the Thatcher government sold them off at ridiculously low prices. Privatized dirt cheap, the utilities then realized large operating profits which were passed on, not to the Exchequer, but to shareholders through larger than usual dividends and to executives through embarrassingly huge salary increases.

In 1990, Norway deregulated its electricity utility industry and opened the door to competition, but did not move to privatize. Rates for industrial customers declined by as much as twenty-six percent, but by 1995 residential and commercial rates had, on average, not fallen. And the Norway deregulation experience carried with it two very serious implications for energy supply and the environment.

As University of Manitoba associate professor George Chuchman wrote in a 1995 study of regulation, competition and privatization for Ontario's Power Workers' Union, Norway's deregulation seemed to have eliminated incentives for demand-side management of electricity (finding ways to conserve electricity rather than finding new means of generating more electricity) and integrated resource planning, or planning the most efficient, sustainable and environmentally sound applications for all sorts of energy, not just electricity. In that sense, the Norway experience seemed to prove a deregulated market can lead to an environmentally unfriendly energy market.

Countries like Argentina, Brazil and Chile were motivated to deregulate electricity and make radical change in the industry to reduce debt, cut deficits and try to attract more foreign capital to shore up those countries' struggling economies. This does nothing but stimulate demand for electricity. None of this is compatible with sustainable development, or the idea that we should be planning resource use so there is something left for our children and their children.

As Chuchman put it in his 1995 study, as confusing and inconsistent as the evolving state of the world's electricity business happens to be, there are some valuable lessons to be learned. "The most important one is that a headlong rush into privatization prior to exploring the alternatives offered by incentive regulation, is likely to be misguided and fraught with financial danger."

The generation of electricity is big business. In the United States, the industry has revenues twice as large as the airline and telecommunications businesses *combined*. It is probably no exaggeration to say that access to cheap and reliable electrical power is considered by Americans to be one of their fundamental freedoms.

It was in America where the electricity *tsunami* began to roll, triggering once again what could be a prolonged period of instability— near-bankruptcies, multi-billion-dollar mergers, the possibility of stranded public assets, increased taxpayer debt and uncertain power service. Years of dubious regulation of both public and privately owned electrical utilities, combined with rising costs of construction for highly questionable nuclear generating capacity, plus the inflation caused by energy supply shocks triggered by Organization of Petroleum Exporting Countries (OPEC) oil pricing, set the stage for popular demands for deregulation of the U.S. power industry.

In 1978 the Carter administration and the U.S. Congress responded with the Public Utility Regulatory Policies Act (PURPA) as a means of encouraging improvements in energy efficiency through cogeneration, and to take advantage of alternative sources of electrical power other than nuclear and fossil fuels. PURPA opened a Pandora's box. It required electric utilities to offer to buy electricity at prices reflecting their avoided cost (of not building new plants to generate their own electricity) from small cogeneration and renewable power producers.

Independent producers began flooding the U.S. electricity market with cheaper, more environmentally friendly power, primarily using new fuel-generated sources such as natural gas in a process referred to as combined-cycle gas turbine generation, just as consumer demand began to slacken. The sudden supply of independently generated power capacity was much larger than expected. As prices fell and competition increased, a drop in consumer demand caught traditional monopoly utilities with surpluses of energy and mounting debt left over from decades of constructing expensive nuclear and coal-fired generating plants.

The growing band of independent power producers also demanded access to the monopoly utilities' transmission grids to deliver their cheaper electricity, not just to the monopoly utilities, but to customers. "Competitive open access" to utility power grids became the battle cry around which the non-utility generators, and large industrial users looking for cheaper electricity, now rallied. From there it was not a large leap to demand that the entire system of monopoly control over the generation, transmission and distribution of electricity be deregulated and the market opened to competition, not unlike the situation in telecommunications.

In 1992 the Energy Policy Act gave the Federal Energy Regulatory Commission (FERC) the power to order the utilities to provide wheeling services (electricity trade transactions over interconnected transmission facilities) for wholesale distribution of electricity between the producers, local distribution companies, and large industrial customers. The call now was for "retail wheeling"—the ability to sell your electricity directly to consumers using the utilities' grid and distribution systems.

The call for retail wheeling was the call for the ultimate in deregulation—a demand for the disassembling (or "unbundling") of the generating, transmission and distribution elements of vertically integrated power utilities. These once-powerful monopoly utilities were now under intense pressure to share the market with independent electricity producers, not unlike telephone long-distance resellers when those markets were deregulated.

The American experience quickly spilled over the 49th Parallel, putting pressure on provincial governments to follow the American example, to deregulate the industry and open up their electricity markets to competition. But the development of the Canadian electrical power industry differed significantly from the U.S. experience.

In the United States, a substantial portion of the generation, transmission and distribution of electricity was historically left in the hands of shareholder-owned private power utilities. These utilities were subject to regulation by state or federal regulatory bodies. An equally large portion of the U.S. electrical utility business remained in public hands. Two of the most prominent examples are the legendary Tennessee Valley Authority and the Bonneville Power Administration, the largest electricity generator in the U.S. Pacific Northwest.

But regulatory control did not always ensure that the customers' best interests were being attended to. Very often the relationship between the customer and the privately owned monopoly utility was a strained one. The utilities, in particular the privately held ones, were often seen by critics as too fat, too rich, too protected by eager regulators and too unyielding to the demands for cuts in electricity rates or improvements in service.

In many instances these utilities were allowed rate-of-return increases simply based on the amount of capital spending they promised for the construction of new generating capacity. This almost predictably increased revenue and dividends for their shareholders. The argument, of course, was that "risk-taking" shareholders deserved to be looked after. They were looked after so well for decades that power utility stocks and bonds became the most lustrous of blue chip investments.

On the other hand, Canada's experience has generally been the history of how large, publicly owned utilities controlled, in the name of their provincial governments, the supply and price of electricity. Unlike the experience in the United States, where the rules of free enterprise and open competition were muted early on in this century in favour of regulated private and public monopolies, Canadians —after first tasting the bitter fruit of private monopoly ownership and control—largely chose to put their faith in the hands of publicly owned corporations.

Despite what some critics might say, Canadians were, by and large, comfortably rewarded for their faith in these provincially controlled, public-sector giants: rewarded with the power we always needed to light and heat our homes, at a price that has most often been seen as a bargain in relative terms.

It is generally conceded that throughout this century the primary instrument for industrial development in our largest and most robust province was the publicly owned Ontario Hydro. Ontario Hydro grew to become one of the largest power utilities in the world. Yet even though it was a large public bureaucracy, it seemed capable of functioning like it was a friendly neighbour.

As Keith R. Fleming wrote in *Power At Cost: Ontario Hydro and Rural Electrification 1911–1958*: "Few institutions had a more lasting or pervasive influence on the lives of Ontarians than has Ontario Hydro." Over the nine decades of its history, Ontario Hydro has been considered "a beacon for public enterprise," "a successful building block in the social fabric of Ontario," and, in terms of its orthodox importance to largely Presbyterian Ontario, "something similar to the United Church" in the manner in which it kept the faith of providing "power at cost."

In Canada more so than in the United States, electricity evolved into less a service providing electricity to homes and businesses than an extremely valuable tool provincial governments could use for economic development. It was so attractive in that respect that it often distorted political philosophies to the point where one could not tell a "conservative" from a "liberal" from a "social democrat," when it came to running the province's power utility.

In 1961 British Columbia Premier W. A. C. Bennett, along with his free-enterprise Social Credit government, shocked investors and ideologues across the continent when he nationalized the obdurate and lacklustre private utility, the B.C. Electric Company. The move fired off the starter's pistol for one of the most impressive economic growth spurts in Canadian history. As David J. Mitchell wrote in *W. A. C. Bennett and the Rise of British Columbia*, Bennett "realized that the control he needed to exercise over power development in the province could not be achieved if he left matters in the hands of the private sector." By putting its faith in public power, Bennett's British Columbia shifted almost immediately from a struggling coastal province, with great resource potential in its interior, into a modern, diversified economic force, confidently facing the competitive trading forces along the Pacific Rim.

In Quebec, the wizardry of public hydro power included a magical way of entwining vast economic development with the province's move toward cultural and linguistic sovereignty. "Find me another business capable of inspiring a song on the hit parade," then-Liberal cabinet minister, René Lévesque, challenged those critical of the

Lesage government's 1963 decision to use Hydro-Québec as the foundation for its nationalist aspirations.

According to Lévesque, Hydro-Québec would henceforth be "the goose that laid the golden egg" for modern Quebec—the province's "flagship of development." During a planning session for the 1963 election, an election called by the Lesage Liberal government to seek a mandate for the nationalization of Quebec's electrical utilities, it became clear that the power to drive the province toward economic self-sufficiency and cultural sovereignty—perhaps independence—could only come about through the public ownership of hydro-electric power. It was in that very session that the prophetic term, *maîtres chez nous*, was coined.

The force of public power in Quebec would help propel francophone culture into a soaring orbit, as Lévesque would later put it, "when the people of Quebec set their clocks to the time of the twentieth century"—until late 1994, that is, when then-Premier Jacques Parizeau was forced to put an indefinite hold on Quebec's massive Great Whale hydro-electric project.

The mid-1990s seemed a time when all of a sudden Canada's perpetual-motion machine called electrical power generation was, if not coming to a stop, at least beginning to wear down. The preceding three decades had been an era of huge investment in dams, coal-fired generating stations and nuclear reactors. No project seemed too large or too expensive to undertake. Once among the largest and healthiest of this nation's corporations (a decade and a half ago no private corporation could rival Ontario Hydro in asset wealth and profitability), these power giants began to come under attack from a number of sources in a suddenly changing world of electricity production and demand.

All the contributing factors seemed to cross reticularly, catching each monopoly member of the power sector in their sights. The rate of growth in consumer demand for power had begun falling in some areas as early as the 1970s, but more spectacularly in the 1980s, thanks to recessionary forces and conservation measures like more energy-efficient appliances. Cheaper alternative fuel sources began making their way on to the power market.

The 1980s were also a period of a growing antipathy toward mega-project development. In the case of nuclear-generated electricity, antipathy was replaced by anxiety and widespread public antagonism.

The megaproject era spawned large debt loads that hampered plans for new borrowing for expansion of electrical supply. Public criticism began increasing notably over the burdensome debt-load megaprojects incurred but also over the vast environmental damage caused by hydro projects—destruction of fish stocks, destruction of wildlife habitat, flooding of arable land and dislocation of native peoples from their traditional lands.

At the time, North American utilities began reporting an unsettling and persistent series of costly nuclear reactor accidents and plant failures. Also, in Canada in particular, that embarrassing history of treatment of native peoples by our public power monopolies became as important an issue to some potential customers, like New York state, as the future price of the megawatts of electricity they were negotiating.

These factors converged, less than celestially, on the battered and reeling North American electric power business, helping to put all monopolies, private as well as public, under the microscope of intense public scrutiny, sparking debate that now occasionally reaches highly questionable ideological tones on the issue of who could best run the electricity industry—the private or the public sector. Into this confusing debate over the effectiveness of our continent's electric power industry, riding the high roller we know lies just beyond the horizon, come the "Electric Surfers"—organizations who can only profit from the demise of the existing electric power order.

One of the most vocal critics of monopoly power are those, quite naturally, who will profit hugely from the introduction of a deregulated power industry. Large industrial business users, some of them already generating their own power using the cheaper natural-gas-fuelled, combined-cycle system, have been demanding—and receiving—rate reductions from power suppliers. They also want access to the general electricity market for their generated power surpluses. They want to play in the Big Leagues with the utility generators, and they want a large hand in setting the rules to the game.

"Regulation has never reduced [electricity] prices," said Arthur Dickinson, executive director of the Association of Major Power Consumers of Ontario (AMPCO) in September 1995. AMPCO represents Ontario's largest electricity users. "All it does is try to create an artificial market. But if you open the market to competition you'll find people there to supply whatever is needed. That's the nature of a competitive marketplace. A monopoly cannot function efficiently in today's electricity market environment in North America."

The threat from large industrial electricity users (in Ontario they buy roughly one-third of Ontario Hydro's output) is real and persistent: If you do not open the electrical marketplace to competition and allow us to shop for cheaper power, we may opt out as buyers of monopoly electricity and use new technologies to produce our own electricity. Or we will put more pressure on the political system to allow us to buy electricity at a lower price from the growing number of independent, non-utility generators (NUGS). Either way, the result could be large and potentially fatal cracks in the monopoly status—and financial health—of the continent's public and private power utilities.

Independent producers face immense legislative, regulatory and operational barriers to entry into the regimes of the traditional monopoly utilities. Still, that has not dissuaded them. Backed by the demands of the large corporate electricity customers, the NUGS have been moderately effective in pressing some provincial governments to begin easing monopoly regulations on the generation, transmission and distribution of electricity.

But for the moment, the demands being made for dramatic structural change in the electricity business in Canada have only served to confuse and distress the average consumer. The Big Surfers know what they are after—the cheapest source of electricity possible. But average Canadian electrical ratepayers have little clear idea of what the outcome will be for them when the wave hits.

"If you look at what the average ratepayer cares about, they care about two things," says John Murphy, president of Ontario's Power Workers' Union. "They care about the cost they are paying for their electricity and they care about reliability. Those are the primary issues for the people out there."

Beyond those criteria, all most consumers know is that change is coming to how electricity is made and delivered to their light switch. Most also know that if past experience with deregulation is any guide, there is a better than fifty-fifty chance the result will end up being confusing, more costly and, perhaps, unnecessary as far as the average ratepayer is concerned.

Even if one is able to dissect the many arguments for and against the way the Canadian electrical power industry is organized, and how it should operate, it is difficult for average consumers to sort out the hyperbole and make sense of what they are being told.

On the one hand, we read that we must urgently (there is no time to waste!) ready ourselves (deregulate the power industry, privatize and sell off those "costly, inefficient and imperious" public utilities) and make the remaining power generators more "efficient"—today's common business euphemism for cutting costs, jobs and investment. This will allow us to ready ourselves for continental competition in the electricity marketplace. The Americans, so the argument goes, are gearing up to sell us huge amounts of cheap electricity.

But with the odd exception, provincial power utilities are once again making money, paying their bills and looking after their debt payments. As well, Canadians—including large industrial users—enjoy some of the lowest electricity rates in the world. Americans living in Los Angeles or New York would envy the electricity rates even Ontarians pay.

We are told we need customer-driven competition to get the jump on competition, lower electricity rates and be ready to stand strong when the moment of decision comes to the level playing field of continental power competition. We need to do all this to keep our electricity prices as low as possible so we can be industrially competitive under the Free Trade Agreement and the NAFTA.

We are told electricity customers are demanding more choice, that electricity rates are too high and have to come down, but it is seldom clear who those demanding customers are. Are they average home owners? Or are they large industrial and commercial operations fishing for just another way to get their costs down? After all, there are data showing that except in specific industries like smelting, heavy manufacturing and some resource extraction and processing, electricity costs are not a significant factor in a business's cost equation.

"The large consumers like an aluminium plant or a big automobile factory would like to buy power at a lower price—below the cost normally charged by the public utility," said the University of Toronto's Myron Gordon, a professor emeritus of finance. "If you have 'competition,' what you'll have is large users will get the lower price because they can shop around. Small users like you and me will pay higher prices."

When doubters trot out statistics and data countering much of the hype generated by competition supporters, we are asked to have faith that the private sector is inherently more efficient than the public sector and therefore will bring us all better service and cheaper power rates and, as a consequence, bring greater profitability for Canadian-based businesses fighting it out in the global marketplace.

"A lot of people talk as if you have a competitive environment in California and it's sweeping across the United States," says Professor Gordon. "There is competition, mandated by the federal government, at the wholesale level. Large utilities like Pacific Gas & Electric, or independent power generators, can sell anywhere they want to industrial customers or municipal utilities. But there is no competition anywhere at the retail level." States such as California are moving toward a more open market more aggressively than others, with promises to implement retail wheeling, but no jurisdiction on the continent is yet at that point of being a fully competitive retail marketplace.

The enchantment of cheaper electricity as part of the road map to an industrial Holy Grail is a strange one to many Canadians. On the one hand, Canadians already enjoy the second-lowest electricity rates in the world. Even factoring in Ontario Hydro's relatively high 5.7 cents per kilowatt-hour for fossil-fuel generated electricity and 5.5 cents per kilowatt-hour for nuclear power (a kilowatt-hour is the amount of electricity needed to run ten 100-watt lights bulbs for one hour), the cost of Canadian electricity is a whopping forty percent cheaper, on average, than electricity in the United States.

So why would we try to emulate the American model for electrical generation and distribution? Why hurry to dismantle the Canadian public monopoly system?

We are told public monopoly utilities are inefficient, poorly managed and loaded down with long-term debt. On the face of it, that seems to be true. Together, the indebtedness of Canada's public power monopolies adds up close to one hundred billion dollars. Most monopoly utility critics would also say that if there was a dollar for every act of arrogance and public indifference performed by these power giants over the past few decades, their social debt might be substantially higher than their financial debt.

According to some critics, Ontario Hydro has been a financial basket case for a number of years now. In 1993 the utility declared a $3.6 billion loss, the biggest annual loss in Canadian history, perhaps one of the largest in the world. Ontario Hydro is one of the world's largest borrowers of money. It paid $3.2 billion in interest on debt in 1996. In the same year it carried short- and long-term debt totaling $31.8 billion.

But the nation's oldest public utility also holds almost $40 billion in assets. Granted a significant portion is in questionable nuclear facilities, but Ontario Hydro still generated almost $9 billion in revenue in 1995 and 1996. In 1995, the utility had net income of $628 million. Net income for 1996 would have been close to $600 million had not the board of directors decided to take a $2.5 billion write-off related to nuclear facilities. Given the uncertainty in today's electricity market, the move made sense for the future.

Had it not been for the fateful news about the shaky state of its nuclear division tabled by the internal investigation team on August 13, 1997, Ontario Hydro could have expected net income of $740 million in 1997, rising to $900 million by 1999. But the August announcement that the utility would need from $5 billion to $8 billion over the next four years to repair and upgrade existing nuclear facilities put a quick halt to that revenue march.

For the foreseeable future, the revenue Ontario Hydro would normally have directed toward debt reduction would, at least until 2001, be paying for all those nuclear chickens coming home to roost.

Given the churning state of the marketplace and the move toward greater consolidation of utilities in the United States, a privatized Ontario Hydro would probably be American-owned in a short time. After all, to an American utility flush with cash, Ontario Hydro would not be a particularly bad buy. It carries substantial amounts of surplus power—cheap power by U.S. price comparisons. It has a generating capacity of roughly thirty thousand megawatts. Its unit costs are lower than those of most U.S. utilities. As unsatisfactory as its financial numbers might look to some Canadians, they are insignificant to a multi-billion-dollar company intent on getting a leg-up on competition in a North America–wide market.

What about those questionable nuclear assets? If worst comes to worst, you can always pull a Margaret Thatcher—leave them for the public sector to figure out what to do with them. And what would the average taxpayer lose if the decision were made to sell off most or even part of Ontario Hydro's more valuable assets?

Well, added to its present book numbers is the fact that each year Ontario Hydro, as a provincial public entity, pays no federal taxes on its income (an indirect saving for ratepayers and taxpayers) and in

1996 put into the coffers of the Province of Ontario $282 million in water rentals and debt guarantee fees. It has averaged deposits to the public purse of $278 million a year for the past five years.

Although the cries to privatize Ontario Hydro echo less persistently these days, there is still pressure to dismantle or "unbundle" it. In May 1997, the Harris government announced it would issue a white paper and hold public hearings over the summer to decide how best to break it up, at least into two publicly owned corporations. The government was not prepared at the moment to privatize, but it was prepared to dismantle or dismember. Why? Why now? To many Ontario ratepayers, there seems to be no clear evidence that radical and massive change is necessary, or would be beneficial for all concerned; it seems that a wait-and-see approach would be the prudent strategy to take.

To listen to critics in British Columbia (such as large independent electricity producers, the provincial Liberal Party and the right-wing Fraser Institute), B.C. Hydro is not that far behind Ontario Hydro in the race for last place in the public utilities sweepstakes. But looked at another way, B.C. Hydro is arguably one of the most efficient and profitable utilities on the continent. Thanks to access to plentiful hydro-electric power, recent corporate reorganizations and more employee downsizing, B.C. Hydro can claim a respectable AA+ credit rating from Standard and Poor's. B.C. Hydro, like Ontario Hydro, pays no federal taxes, an indirect saving for B.C. taxpayers. In 1995, the provincial utility also put an impressive $600 million back into provincial tax coffers from rate returns on equity ($198 million) and on water rentals and taxes ($402 million). In the last fiscal year the total was $523 million.

Thanks to the foresight and wisdom of W. A. C. Bennett, beginning in 1998 British Columbia will receive 1,400 megawatts of free electrical power—enough to supply electricity for 500,000 households—over the next thirty years. This power is the province's contracted "downstream benefits" from the Columbia River Treaty signed with the United States in 1961. It is estimated this downstream benefit represents an additional lump of power to British Columbia equal to more than twelve percent of the utility's present output. It could be worth as much as $2 billion at today's low prices. If prices rise over the next thirty years, it could be worth as much as $5 billion.

The extra 1,400 megawatts of power could also mean that B.C.

Hydro will not have to accrue any large capital debt building new generating capacity for decades to come. B.C. Hydro's long-term debt, as reported for 1996, was a relatively modest $7.6 billion. British Columbia should, in effect, be basking in cheap power for years to come.

The downstream benefits from the Columbia River Treaty now make the province's public power utility—already the healthiest in the country—one of the most envied monopoly utilities on the face of the earth. B.C. Hydro remains one of the lowest-cost utilities in North America. Over the past decade, electricity rate increases were less than the cost of inflation. In real terms, the cost of electricity for British Columbians declined by twenty percent over the same period.

Yet, in January 1997 the province's New Democratic government announced it will formulate a policy over the next year to end B.C. Hydro's virtual monopoly over the province's electricity business. The government claimed it was taking this initiative to prepare B.C. Hydro for the future challenges expected from a North American system "moving slowly, inexorably towards this more competitive, more deregulated environment."

No doubt some British Columbians scratched their heads at the news. Many wondered aloud why an NDP government would be prepared to make life tougher for B.C. Hydro when, on the face of things, it now seems to be a relatively healthy public utility.

Daily newspapers and supperhour TV news shows reported that forest and mining firms loudly applauded the government's intentions, saying they could see themselves saving millions of dollars in power costs in a competitive market, but, the Vancouver *Sun* admitted, "there are fears residential rates could rise." More heads were scratched.

Even with the loss of a series of lucrative long-term export contracts signed with U.S. northeastern states worth as much as $24 billion, gnawing reports of monopoly excesses like thirty-four vice-presidents on staff and the shocking costs of "going away" parties for former executives, Hydro-Québec provides the second-cheapest electricity in Canada for its ratepayers. A bill for a 1,000 kilowatts of power in Montreal is roughly half what one would pay in Toronto and one-third that of New York City.

At the moment, if revenue from Churchill Falls in Labrador is factored out, Quebec's struggling utility is not as profitable as the two other major power utilities. But it does carry substantial surpluses of cheap, hydro-generated power—the very commodity that provides a utility with a large competitive advantage in a continental marketplace.

The pressures for privatization are not as acute in Quebec as they are in other parts of the country. And the question about the merits of competition within the province are nowhere near as pronounced as they are in Ontario or British Columbia. But the Bouchard government is opening its transmission system—and therefore its domestic market—to generation competitors in the United States and Canada. Why would that be? Why do you "open" a market when you already possess some of the cheapest power on the continent?

Critics of Canada's public power utilities point out that the U.S power industry is "shaking itself out." This shake-out would seem to be resulting in slightly more elements of competition and lower rates for large electricity users. But it also includes potential bankruptcies of the more uncompetitive utilities and the inevitable merging of competitors. Some consumers might ask, is that not going in the opposite direction? Won't that mean, in the long term, less competition rather than more?

If we believe the hype, American electricity producers are at this moment pacing back and forth along the 49th Parallel, anxiously waiting the opportunity to storm Fortress Canada and beat up our provincial utilities. But others would argue that given the present price advantage enjoyed by most Canadian power utilities seeking to sell power to the U.S. market, America looks like a market ripe for the picking by Canadian utilities and independent power producers.

"The fact of the matter is that Ontario Hydro, with its excess capacity, is more competitive than utilities in the States," says Myron Gordon. "But what they advocate—going down to the States and try to take business away from the privately owned utilities there—is the most dangerous thing imaginable.

"As soon as you have free trade in power, all the power utilities in the U.S. will go to work and use NAFTA to advance their interests by saying: 'Ontario Hydro is being subsidized [by its government], just the way they talk about the lumber industry.' So it would be a disaster to get into this competitive trap."

A unique problem faced by Ontario Hydro is that as much as seventy percent of its sales are at the wholesale level—electricity sold to municipal utilities. Most large, vertically integrated utilities in the United States sell only about ten percent of their power at wholesale. Consequently, under the regulations imposed by FERC, Ontario Hydro has a very limited wholesale market in the United States, whereas the American utilities have a very large wholesale market in Ontario. "This difference in industry structure," says professor Gordon, "puts Ontario Hydro at a very severe competitive disadvantage."

For Canadians, the most ominous failures occurring in the United States are those in the public-utility field. Certainly, many U.S. investor-owned power monopolies will face a substantial dose of competitive reality over the next few years. By comparison with Canada's provincial power giants, their U.S. counterparts are already being shredded by deregulation and competition.

The federally owned Bonneville Power Administration (BPA), which currently provides service to Washington and Oregon, is the largest electricity generator in the U.S. Pacific Northwest. Born in the days of the Great Depression, the BPA trades more electricity than any other federal agency. It provides forty-two percent of the power consumed in the U.S. Northwest and generates about three percent of all power generated in the United States. Now the BPA is a target for breakup and privatization (or a candidate for the stranded assets category), thanks to the heavy financial damage done by competition from the private sector over the last few years.

The BPA debt payments to the U.S. Treasury alone register about $1.4 billion a year. In the first six months of 1995, the BPA lost roughly $700 million as industrial customers drained away to cheaper electricity sources. In early 1995, the cash-strapped BPA had to renege on the first contractual understanding for the return of British Columbia's downstream benefits under the Columbia River Treaty. The original agreement called for the BPA to pay British Columbia an initial $250 million fee along with 950 megawatts of power until 2024. The BPA walked away from the understanding when competitive forces kept driving down the price for electricity. Prices that so affected BPA solvency had fallen dramatically for industrial and some business users but were heading up for residential customers.

Is the BPA example what B.C. Hydro and many nervous customers and taxpayers have to look forward to—in terms of industry chaos, service instability and the price of electricity for residential users—in that future open, competitive marketplace?

Some supporters of independent power production offer up the NUGS's power potential as the ultimate replacement for what they consider ailing and moribund public monopolies, going so far as to cite the possibility of future power shortages unless the independents are given a chance. Yet, we are living in a period of immense surpluses in electrical generating capacity. It will be years—perhaps as far away as 2010—before current surpluses are used up. According to its own officials, Ontario Hydro, the national utility "basket case," does not require any new electrical generating capacity until 2009 at the earliest. So where is the panic to break up the public monopolies? Where is the rationalization to privatize? Why all the confusion and contradiction?

Granted that over the decades, Canada's public utilities have not exactly been their own best public-relations representatives. These monopolies too often exhibited a bureaucratic arrogance that turned "power at cost" into a depressing social distortion. They turned that slogan into "power at immense social and environmental cost."

Hydro dam systems, constructed all across the country, destroyed vast fish spawning areas and wildlife habitat. Reservoirs became contaminated with mercury poisoning. Native communities were forced to move to make way for reservoir flooding and their rights to their land were repeatedly ignored for decades by hydro officials and provincial politicians. Not until the imperial hydro development aspirations of the Province of Quebec were brought to a halt in 1994, with the decision to shelve Great Whale, was it finally recognized that aboriginal people had a legal and binding claim to the land they lived on—and not even a multi-billion-dollar government hydro project could take that away. It took decades to make that point.

In a number of provinces, but particularly in Ontario, coal-fired power generators spewed damaging greenhouse gases, acid rain and heavy metal emissions across the landscape, destroying forests and ruining lakes once brimming with fish and waterfowl. Added to this disgrace, the final tally for our foray into nuclear power generation—complete with its radioactive legacy—is still a long, long way off. Some peg the date at as much as 15,000 years at half-life, according to what little we know about radioactive longevity.

There was a time when many of us characterized public power utilities and the many services they delivered as endlessly benevolent. But like the release of the closeted secrets of an embarrassed family, we now know more about their indiscretions than we want to. In some cases we have been rightly horrified at their excesses. No one would ever consider allowing them to continue with the costly, contemptuous and imperious ways of the past. But are we at risk of throwing out the good with the bad?

It is clearly a time for change. That *tsunami* is bearing down upon us. It is coming. Make no mistake. It will change the very relationship we have had for decades with all those pleasant protons and neutrons, and with the people we have entrusted to get them to us. Still, we should be sceptical about politicians, academics and Electric Surfers bearing glittering promises—just as we should be about those public-utility sages who once wrapped themselves in that patina of power and infallibility. Some have been blissfully correct on occasion. Some have been disastrously wrong. Perhaps, where future electricity is concerned, we should rely on no one's words. After all, as the old saying goes: "The believer takes his lessons from faith. The wise man takes his lessons from history."

3 / Prometheus Bound

With us begins the reign of man with severed roots.
Man multiplied who will mix with iron and nourish
himself on electricity.

— *The Futurist Manifestos*, Emilio Filippo Tommaso Marinetti, 1920

WE OWE BOTH THE GOOD and the bad of electricity to Prometheus, one of the Greeks' mythological Titans and our original rebel. As one fable has it, Prometheus (whose name means "forethought") travelled to the heavens, where he stole fire from the sun against the wishes of the gods. He brought that fire down to earth as a gift for man, the better that mortals could defend themselves and survive in a world surrounded by vicious wild beasts. Presumably, this gift of the sun's fire marked the birth of human culture.

Prometheus's thievery did not go unnoticed. An angry Zeus, the supreme deity of Greek mythology, sentenced him to be chained to a rock on the peak of Mount Caucasus, where vultures consumed his liver during the day. As if to continue making the point that crime—even well-intentioned crime—does not pay, each night his liver grew back in, only to be eaten away the next day. As American psychotherapist Rollo May once wrote of our rebel's plight: "This is a tale of the agony of the creative individual, whose nightly rest only resuscitates him so that he can endure his agonies the next day."

It also parallels, to some extent, the relationship between the contemporary consumer—with our insatiable appetite for electricity—and our perception of the power utility that provides us with electricity; like a new liver, it had better be there in the morning or we will complain quite loudly. Over the decades we have come to expect an almost absurd standard of service, even fealty, from our

Promethean providers. But if they dare raise our electricity rates too high, too quickly, we will be on them like wrathful vultures.

Electricity, like all forms of energy, is a gift from the sun. It does not exist in usable quantities in nature. It must be generated by human effort to serve our needs. Because the sun is our one energy source of any consequence, we must take its fuel products or matter —coal, oil, natural gas, neutrons, movement of the air, light or falling water—and convert them into electricity.

Along with religion and democratic government, no other human enterprise has had a greater impact on our lives than the development of electricity. To some, that might seem an astounding statement. But to argue with it would just prove another point: that we take very little else for granted like we do electricity.

Whole modern histories are written with only passing reference to it. We catalogue for posterity wars, massive human migrations, immense tragedies and monumental clashes of armies and philosophies, and yet we make little reference to electricity. Amazingly, at least one major twentieth-century almanac contains no mention of electricity's contribution to world developments. Neither "electricity" nor "hydro-electric power" is listed in the index. The only mention electricity receives is at the bottom of a list of "miscellaneous" items for the year 1965. The insertion mentions the massive power failure that took place that year in the northeastern United States and southeastern Canada and the fact that nine months afterward birth rates rose dramatically. This single mention follows, in order of importance, the notice for 1965 that The Beatles were awarded the MBE in the Queen's Birthday Honours that year.

Yet, for close to a century electricity has played a most consequential role in our lives and in the advancement of our cultures. Electrical power has been the most important stimulating force for our nation's industrial development. It has provided the foundation for the modernization and economic wealth we have enjoyed, dating back into the last century. Simply put, electricity has made our lives dramatically safer, unbelievably richer and unquestionably more comfortable.

Electricity in all its awe and magnificence has delivered to us radio and television, mass telecommunications, genetic engineering, the cyclotron and the computer. It has allowed us to leap into space, speed up the manufacture of arms, split the nucleus of an atom to produce both nuclear energy and the nuclear bomb, and it has carried us into the cyberspace kingdom of the World Wide Web.

Electricity takes substances of seeming little real economic value—a river of water put in motion by gravity, for instance—and converts them into immense prosperity. One could easily claim that in early hydro-electric power our society achieved what the alchemists of the Middle Ages could not in their quest for a Philosopher's Stone.

Early hydro-electric generation may not have turned base metals into gold and silver, but the wealth it did create, by transmuting water and wilderness and gravity into values as attractive as gold and silver, made us as rich as any alchemist could ever have hoped. It even helped, as the alchemists also sought, to prolong our lives.

"We live like fish in a sea of electricity," John Negru wrote in *The Electric Century*. "Our homes, like coral reefs, surround us with a gossamer net of power, and shelter us within their glimmering chambers. Each day we call upon this source of power, in more ways than the poets can imagine."

So much so that Canadians are the second-highest consumers per capita of electricity. We are considered "energy gluttons," consuming more than eight times the world average, according to the Royal Society of Canada. Each Canadian uses more than eighteen thousand kilowatt hours of electricity annually—a figure more than fifty percent greater than that of American electrical consumers, and *double* the consumption rate of any other Group of Seven country.

Despite our voracious energy appetite (only Norway consumes more power per capita) the price of electricity is a rare bargain for Canadians. In constant dollars, prices have been falling for years. Averaged Canadian electricity prices are second only to those of South Africa —and only marginally so. Electricity rates in Germany are almost two-and-a-half times higher than in Canada. The residential price of electricity in New York City is double that of the average Canadian city. Only one major U.S. power utility, Ohio Power, has rates substantially lower than those of Ontario Hydro.

To underline the bargains consumers enjoy and have come to expect, Toronto Hydro—one of the 306 municipal utilities that distribute electricity from Ontario Hydro—publishes a chart on how much a dollar will buy in electricity power terms, use-by-use. In downtown Toronto, one dollar will get you forty-eight pots of coffee, or 484 slices of toast (two at a time). A dollar will give you thirty hours on the home computer, fifteen showers (with a low flow showerhead), 2.5 months use of a hair dryer, forty hours of television viewing, four loads of washing and twelve hours of ironing. That buck will also provide you with two hundred hours of reading (with a 60-watt bulb), sixteen hours of microwave use, 117 hours of running a thirteen-cubic-foot refrigerator, three baths (full tub), 240 hours on the VCR, sixteen hours of window air conditioner operation, 3.5 days of keeping the waterbed heated and eight hours of vacuuming (with a centrally installed vacuum). Put another way, a Toronto consumer receives all these services for roughly sixteen dollars, give or take a quarter or two.

It is easy to list the essential uses of electricity in our lives—for lighting, heating and cooling, household conveniences, entertainment, cleaning and personal hygiene, for instance—but when you begin to list the number of products we use that exist on the periphery of our lives we begin to realize just how ubiquitous electricity is: steam irons, hot-air popcorn pumpers, food processors, hand blenders, juicers, food dehydrators, electric knives/toothbrushes/can openers, crockpots, shavers, vaporizers, electric blankets, bread makers, curling irons (including electric crimpers), humidifiers, facial saunas and plaque removers.

It is electricity that opens and closes your garage door, keeps your car's oil from freezing in Swift Current, Saskatchewan, at minus-forty-two degrees, works the traffic lights that allow you to make your way safely to and from work, gives you access to your money through the bank's automated teller machines and lets you visit and return from the farthest fringe of our cognitive universe—the Internet.

On a more prosaic note is the realization that those rambunctious little electrons, protons and other charged particles can, on many occasions, change the whole nature of how we entertain ourselves. No other show of euphony, from folk song to symphony, has been as influential in music as the electric guitar.

Without electricity, rock-and-roll would have been a gentler, less adventurous sound, the Beatles might still be playing beer halls in Liverpool and Hamburg, and there would be no need for Eric Clapton and Bob Dylan to go "unplugged." Boomers may never have witnessed the oracular riffs of Jimi Hendrix and Stevie Ray Vaughan, as they manipulated their Fender Stratocasters. For Gen-Xers, the absence of electricity would mean no Metallica, no Nirvana and, perhaps, no electric lure strong enough to take Kurt Cobain over the edge of mortality's stage.

My first understanding of the vast chasm that lay between life with and without electricity came when, as a youngster—and before the days of rural electrification on the prairies—I travelled with my mother each summer to spend my holidays with my grandmother and my uncle on their farm in the rugged and largely uninhabited Interlake district of central Manitoba.

At the beginning of July, I would leave behind a world of light bulbs, electric stoves, electric kettles and street lamps, and enter a marvellous yet dim world of kerosene lamps, wood stoves and the inky blackness of the outdoors at night. Often the only evidence other human beings existed on the planet would be a faint, distant glow, a quarter-mile away or more, another window with another lamp, where perhaps a neighbour might be reading the *Farmer's Almanac* or the *Free Press Farmer's Weekly*. When the lamps were turned down and blown out, the entire world—except for the brilliance of the stars in the heavens—would quickly fade to utter black.

Without electricity, my grandmother's world was barely more advanced than that of our Scottish ancestors in the eighteenth century. She bought "coal-oil," or kerosene, to fuel the storm lamps and the lamps in the barn she needed to see her way for milking and feeding the cows. She chopped wood to feed the stove in the kitchen. Late at night she would make her way across the farmyard in the dark, using that pale, yellow light from the coal-oil lamp in the window as her beacon, feeling her way instinctively across the hardened mud ruts in the ground.

At the time, the once-a-week bath meant heating tubs of water on the Gurney wood stove. There were no hair dryers, curling irons or electric hair crimpers for either my grandmother or my mother. There certainly were no facial sauna machines. Clothes were washed in the same tub on the floor, with a hardened-glass scrubbing board to scour difficult stains from work clothes. There were no electric steam irons (irons were simply placed on a hot stove, then pressed upon the clothes to get the wrinkles out), no blenders, no vaporizers, no electric can openers. There certainly were no electric knives or hot-air popcorn pumpers. For entertainment in the living room there was a small battery-powered radio. There was no television. There was one large storm lamp, used for reading for a few minutes before bedtime.

For my uncle, who lived with my grandmother, there was no electric milking machine, no bright yard light to help him with his nightly chores, no fancy hydraulic pumps and electric-powered machines to help him lift heavy machinery he needed to repair. Loads were moved by hand. When winter struck, his team of horses replaced the tractor for farm work. There was no "plug-in" way to keep the oil in the engine from freezing. The battered old Reo truck he used to drive back and forth to town went up on blocks to keep the tires from freezing and cracking. To escape damage from the deep freeze to come, oil had to be drained from the crankcase and water from the engine block.

Yet here we are, barely five decades from those dim, rural Manitoba moments, John Negru's modern "fish in a sea of electricity." We no longer praise Prometheus for his gift so much as demand that he be there when we want him to be.

Electricity has become so fundamental to our lives, so much a part of our life's rhythms, that we take for granted its reliability. We accept odds for and against an immense number of life's events, odds that sometimes things will be good and sometimes things will be bad. We accept that entry into the world at birth can on occasion swing tragically wrong for unforeseen reasons. Our idea of a career for life can, within a decade, change to three or four careers, if we are fortunate, and we take it as it comes. Our marriages swing on odds of fifty-fifty and we accept the risk and the discomfort of failure. But if a sudden fluctuation in voltage disrupts the transmission of an important business fax message, kicks us off someone's Home Page or trashes the blessed memory of our word processor, we are racked with despondency and the unfairness of life. (Writing this, reminded of the fragility of it all and the possible loss of the Promethean hand, I immediately punch F10 and "save" the thoughts I will need in order to be paid for this book.)

By and large, Canadians have treated the harnessing of the gift of electricity as a simple mechanical function. But when one stands back, one can see it exists as a metaphor for a convergence of immense powers; from the simplest (light to see by, heat to warm and help feed us) to the enormously complex: sustained economic growth, industrial might, exploration of space and cyberspace, the mutation and delivery of information, even the power to govern.

As Thomas Carlyle might have put it, electricity is the vehicle, not unlike faith or quantum mechanics, that propels tiny, little, susceptible Man, into the Centre of Immensities. Those little sparks that permeate and enrich our lives are power within power, wrapped with powers. If you use electricity, you make your life better. If you hold the power of electricity, you may hold secrets to the universe.

And it raises a simpler question: If all that we say electricity represents is true, then why would we risk placing it in the uncertain hands of market competition? With the historical track record we already have for relying too heavily on Adam Smith's Invisible Hand of the Marketplace, why would we be prepared, even eager, to gamble with an endowment as important as the one we receive from Prometheus?

Although American Thomas Alva Edison is often mentioned as the inventor of electricity, in fact, it was a discovery made long, long before Edison arrived on the scene. Six hundred years before the birth of Christ, the Greek philosopher and mathematician Thales noticed that rubbing pieces of amber with cloth or fur would first attract, then repel, small objects brought near it. Over the centuries the experiment was repeated many times by numerous curious investigators before English chemist Humphrey Davy demonstrated, in the early days of the nineteenth century, the first electric tri-arc lamp, made up of two carbon rods separated by a thin gap.

"When Davy applied an electric current to one of the electrodes, a glowing arc leaped across the gap and provided light," according to Richard Munson in *The Power Makers: The Inside Story of America's Biggest Business ... and Its Struggle to Control Tomorrow's Electricity*. Lamps such as those Davy invented were, by 1844, being used in gala events like that year's Paris Opera production. Two decades later, Davy's former assistant, Michael Faraday, articulated the laws affecting electromagnetic induction and built a working generator, then referred to as an electric "dynamo."

Although early equipment was crude and not entirely practical for commercial or business use, by the late 1870s, a number of inventors were introducing new applications for electricity, including one for the installation of a dozen arc lights for Cleveland streets. Outdoor lamps preceded indoor lighting because currents were dangerously high and had to be kept away from people. Also, the intense glare of the roughly four-thousand-candle-power generated made the light too bright for home use.

By the 1870s, reliable generators, driven by hydro power as well as wood- and coal-fuelled steam engines, helped electric street lighting spread throughout America. In 1881 a 1.86-kilowatt steam-driven electric generator was installed in downtown Toronto and the first skating rink was lit by arc lamps. Electric arc lamps were installed at the Canadian National Exhibition in 1882, and a year later street lighting was installed in Toronto and Montreal. In 1884 the Ottawa Parliament Buildings were lighted electrically with steam-driven generators.

By the time Thomas Edison formed the Edison Electric Light Company to work on the development of the incandescent lamp with Francis Jehl in the late 1870s, he was treading on inventive ground covered with the footprints of hundreds of other inventors. There is no straight line of inventive development between Thales and Davy or Davy and Edison. Many others worked as hard to capture light within a globe of glass.

The moment for Edison's introduction to fame took place on October 21, 1879, when, along with his collaborators, he was able to present a high-resistance incandescent lamp, using a carbonized filament in an airless globe, that glowed for forty straight hours. But like so many other "inventors" or original discoverers, it was not the fabled Edison who was first past the post with his idea for electricity or even for the first electric lamp. As Thomas P. Hughes wrote in *Networks of Power: Electrification in Western Society, 1880-1930*, "Edison did not invent the incandescent lamp; his achievement was an incandescent lamp with a high-resistance filament."

In fact, Edison's innovation of an existing concept was also not something the man achieved in the dreamy form Americans have long loved to visualize: the dedicated scientist-inventor, sitting alone, hunched over his laboratory tables cluttered with bits and pieces of his mysterious technology, working late into the night, until—"Eureka!"—it arrived.

"Edison is in reality a collective noun and means the work of many men," Edison's chief collaborator, Francis Jehl, once pointed out. The work that went into the discovery of the high-resistance filament that made the incandescent lamp an authentic breakthrough required the work of a team of talented collaborators, including Charles Batchelor, the English-born mechanical genius who also helped Edison design the stock ticker, and Francis Upton, who had been trained in mathematics and abstract science at Princeton and Berlin universities. It was Upton who brought order and systematic thinking to Menlo Park. It was Jehl who played the role of chief technician and has long been recognized as being jointly responsible for the Menlo Park breakthrough.

Americans lionized Edison, calling him their "Napoleon of Science" and their "Purveyor of Light," as well as the most common epithet for the man: "The Wizard of Menlo Park." He was not only their hero but their manifestation of a modern Prometheus. According to Richard Munson, one evening fifty thousand admirers stood for hours on San Francisco's foggy streets just to catch a glimpse of Edison passing buy. Worshippers and curiosity seekers boarded special trains from Philadelphia and New York to visit Menlo Park in New Jersey. On New Year's Eve in 1879, three thousand people gathered for a demonstration that involved nothing more than Edison turning on sixty of his incandescent lamps strung on poles. Like modern Elvis supplicants strolling the lawns of "Graceland," each year, fifty years after his death, two million Edison admirers visit his laboratory, now located in Greenfield Village, Michigan.

Where Edison truly did shine was as the driving force for the work at Menlo Park. It was his persistent will and vision that spurred his collaborators to continue experimenting, even in the face of adversity and failure, until success was won. Edison was as much promoter and entrepreneur as dedicated inventor. What made him stand out was his insistence in pushing beyond the creation of the first long-lasting incandescent bulb. He would take advantage of subsequent discoveries, turning them into a system of electricity applicable to a wide array of consumer needs.

Where others focused on either one component of an electrical system—the lamp, or a generator or distribution lines, for instance—Edison worked with his eyes fixed on a commercial system of electrical lighting. And so The Wizard, backed financially by the likes of the Vanderbilts and J. P. Morgan, expanded his 1879 "invention" of the modern light bulb by hitching it as a development project to work on parallel wiring, even higher resistance filaments, the manufacture of electric generators and construction of ten-thousand-lamp central generating stations. In the end, and despite many technical and financial ups and downs, it would make him a millionaire and an American deity.

Edison sold control of the Edison Electric Light Company and his electric light inventions for $50,000 in cash and $250,000 in stock to a group of investors that included J. P. Morgan in December 1880. He then turned around and formed the Edison Electric Illuminating Company of New York to build the first central station electric generating plant, on Pearl Street in New York's financial district. On September 4, 1882, an Edison electrician threw a switch that propelled electric current from Edison's generating station to 106 lamps in Morgan's office—to the wonderment of gathered financiers and potential investors. Just as important, the current also turned on fifty-two bulbs in the editorial offices of the *New York Times*. The next day the paper reported the soft light was "mellow to the eye" and made it seem one was "writing by daylight." That current also lit up the front page of the nation's most influential daily newspaper on Edison's behalf, referring to him as America's "provider of light."

Improvements in technology and the growing durability of the incandescent lamp sparked a consumer revolution. Demand for electric lighting began to take off. By the end of the first year of operation, Edison business had tripled. The injection of competition into the marketplace meant that by the end of the decade 1.3 million lamps lit American offices and homes.

Between December 1880 and 1883, Edison formed at least four companies to take advantage of his work on the incandescent lamp: a utility company to build and operate a central generating station in the heart of New York's financial district; a machine works for building dynamos, or generators; a tube company for underground conductors; and a lamp works to turn out his incandescent lamps in marketable quantities.

In that three-year period, Edison, a man with almost no formal schooling and someone who neither understood nor appreciated scientific theories, applied for 320 different patents. Eventually his discoveries would result in more than two thousand patents, including the stock ticker, the automatic telegraph, the phonograph, the telephone transmitter, the motion-picture camera, the electric storage battery, the mimeograph machine and the industrial research lab.

"Power systems are cultural artifacts," Thomas P. Hughes wrote in *Networks of Power*. "Electric power systems embody the physical, intellectual, and symbolic resources of the society that constructs them." Surprisingly, there is not much one can consider "universal" in the historic development of the worldwide electrical society. How it was developed, used and applied in each country—but in particular, how it was organized to serve the citizens—reflected the truism that "technology is never neutral." Its uses and impact on a society are always moulded by the culture that surrounds and uses it—sometimes prudently, sometimes creatively and sometimes chaotically, inequitably and expensively.

In a sense, in harnessing, developing and adapting to this magnificent force and the technologies it has spawned, we begin to accept how electricity comes close to being our own servomechanical invention. We did not so much invent it as it was there waiting for us. It was and is so entwined with our lives and our expectations that its history is a history of how the relationship we developed with it changed us body and soul: technologically, socially and, of late, cybernetically.

Just as the absence of electricity—and the lack of alternative power sources—governed how my grandmother and my uncle led their lives in post-war rural Manitoba, so did it dictate the way we designed cities and lived our lives within them and around them. As Richard Munson points out in *The Power Makers*, the absence of electricity meant we relied on horses and steam for transportation and each, in its way, limited the range of our daily commuting. How many stairs we could climb dictated how high most buildings were built, although steam-assisted elevators in large cities helped push buildings beyond four or five stories. Candles and burning oil, or kerosene, provided the light we needed, but in very modest—and often dangerous—ways. Factories were located close to waterways where power wheels could be used to move machinery to make goods. The leap from that limited social and economic existence to a modern society filled with services and life-options could only come about through the discovery and application of electricity.

Look at the development of Berlin in the forty years before World War I. By 1900 Berlin was a heavy-industrial city in transition to a very successful electrical one. Its political structure allowed for local autonomy, which made it easier to establish a sound electric utility with close government regulation. The job of running the utility was given to the private sector, but the city retained tight regulatory control of its operations, of how it provided service to customers and at what price.

Electricity fuelled Berlin's thriving economy, so much so that the city came to be known as "Elektropolis." Commercial and investment banks readily invested in electricity ventures. The city expanded and modernized its impressive transportation system, with Berlin's electrical utility supplying the power. Electric light and power helped shape Berlin's architecture, influenced the design of factories, buildings and apartments, determined the location of the city's transportation and, by substituting for coal-driven steam plants, lessened the curse of dirt and noise pollution.

"In short, electrification affected the way in which workers laboured, management organized and Berliners lived," Hughes wrote. "Because of this, the private company that supplied most of the electrical light and power for Berlin until 1915, and the municipal government that regulated electrical supply, shaped the history of Berlin."

Except for the Berlin experience, the early days of electric light development were conspicuous by the chaos it spawned. More than twenty different electric systems were in operation in Philadelphia, for instance. By 1894, there were more than four dozen power companies competing for business in Chicago. Some offered direct current. Some offered alternating current. (Direct current, or DC, maintained the same low voltage from generator to customer, which made it difficult to transmit over long distances. On the other hand, alternating current, or AC, could be converted to higher voltages, and that made it valuable for transmitting long distances without significant power loss.)

Dc was Thomas Edison's preferred service, but in a long conflict, dubbed "The Battle of the Currents," Westinghouse's AC current prevailed over Edison's system. Some companies offered DC in frequencies of 100, 110, 220 or 600 volts. Some AC electrical firms provided 40, 60, 66, 125 or 133 cycles. The resulting disorder and confusion in the U.S. electrical marketplace under open competition was not unlike the chaos that existed in pre–World War I London where, for political reasons, mostly to do with the strength of municipal governments, being an early electrical consumer was perplexing and costly.

"Londoners who could afford electricity," Hughes wrote, "toasted bread in the morning with one kind, lit their offices with another, visited associates in nearby office buildings using still another variety, and walked home along streets that were illuminated by yet another kind."

In early electric America, a move across the street to a new home could mean a customer's appliances were unworkable. It was as confusing and costly for the power utility suppliers as it was for customers. The new technology was risky and expensive. Electrical demand was growing but not as fast as the number of suppliers. The many new competitors in the electrical lighting field meant—even for people as well entrenched as Edison—fierce competition (for both customers and investors), shrinking margins, mergers and bankruptcies. As usual, on the level playing fields of that ever-so-prized open-competition marketplace, the guiding or "natural" instinct was not to compete, but to try to do just the opposite—merge and take control of the marketplace. As Munson points out: "To ensure order and to protect themselves from 'ruinous competition,' executives initially tried to fix prices and production levels among themselves."

These were the days when John D. Rockefeller was almost able to turn Standard Oil into the world's largest, most domineering petroleum company by eating up the competition through mergers or driving competitors out of business. J. P. Morgan tried to do the same with steel. And the early American railroad scene was a picture of unmitigated greed and private-sector arrogance. The names read like a rogues' gallery: stock manipulator Jay Gould, the notorious Jim Fisk, Cornelius Vanderbilt (the "Railroad Croesus") and stock manipulator William H. Vanderbilt—who coined the lasting epithet "The public be damned."

During an interview in October 1882 Cornelius Vanderbilt announced that "the railroads are not run for the benefit of the 'dear public.' That cry is nonsense. They are built by men who invest their money and expect to get a fair percentage on the same." When asked by the reporter what the railroaders' social or public responsibility might be in such a Manichean world, William Vanderbilt blurted out his famous declaration about the public's after-life possibilities.

But for decades there had been immense pressure put on Congress to provide protection from these criminals and swindlers for farmers, urban consumers, small businesses and labour. America was fed up, and the passing of the Sherman Antitrust Act—prohibiting any contract, conspiracy or restraint of trade—came just as the electrical power industry was beginning to expand.

The Act was a reaction to two recognized evils within American commerce. First, the "unfettered free enterprise" and "open competition" American commercial and industrial interests liked to talk about was essentially a fabric of lies and distortions that left consumers and taxpayers at a tremendous disadvantage. Second, there was a glaring need for government regulation and control of the unscrupulous private monopolies that materialized on what most Americans thought was that level playing field of commerce. "Break Up the Trusts!" was the dominant political theme just as the budding electrical power industry was hitting its development stride.

Even with growing demand for the light shed by the magic incandescent lamp, by the early 1890s the electricity business was still struggling to survive. The majority of factory owners still preferred to rely on steam-powered, belt-driven systems rather than risk depending on unreliable and expensive electrical generation. As a consequence, by the end of the century, electrical motor power was only in use in about one in thirteen factories.

Most residential and office consumers still preferred less-expensive gas lamps for lighting. Electrical lamps were largely seen as a novelty or luxury product. And the generator of choice was not the central power stations that might distribute electricity to a wide range of customers but small-scale, on-site systems of generation—at office buildings, industrial sites, even street car operations.

The next twenty-five years would change all that. The development curve for electricity distribution and utilization was beginning to move almost straight up. Technology was the stimulus. Consumer demand was the driving force. And privately or investor owned monopolies controlling the marketplace were the rule of play on that supposedly level field.

By the first years of the twentieth century, larger and more efficient generators were being developed. A new tungsten filament made incandescent bulbs preferable to the gas flame. Long-distance AC transmission lines meant that more power became available in both urban and rural areas. By the end of World War I, thirteen million Americans were receiving electricity. Electricity was no longer a luxury. It was a necessity.

"On the business front, electricity companies raised more than $8 billion from five million individual investors," Munson reports. "They also eliminated competition, formed [their own] state regulatory commissions and created monopolistic empires. By 1930, three [electrical] holding companies controlled 40 percent of the nation's electricity."

The sheer audacity of the men who controlled these monopoly utilities reached such proportions early on—buying politicians, manipulating the stock markets and propagating fraudulent public-relations campaigns—that it prompted Franklin D. Roosevelt, then governor of New York, to raise the possibility that electrical power control was so monopolized "that we may have to bring forth a new declaration of independence" with which to fight these rapacious private monopolies. The man with some of the strongest instincts for controlling the marketplace was Sam Insull.

Samuel Insull once worked for Thomas Edison. He went on to become the head of Commonwealth Edison. One of America's most powerful businessmen of the 1920s, Insull thought competition "economically wrong" and that the only way to run a profitable business was by way of a private monopoly—with as little public oversight as possible.

Insull's work laid the foundations for the modern electrical utility, certainly within the context of the United States of America. His use of promotional rates, public relations and sophisticated engineering techniques blended well with his need to capture absolute control of a market, distorting whatever regulatory mechanism might be put into place to stop him. His style was said to carry a "craving for expansion." It had two polar-opposite results. It made his companies, and himself, very rich and powerful, which put nervous politicians on notice. And it angered and frustrated consumers, engendering a lasting distrust in the public mind about the integrity of private power monopolies.

The significant difference between Sam Insull and his colleagues was that Insull was prepared to trade his grant of exclusivity in an electrical marketplace in exchange for limited regulation of his dealings. He was not demanding, as W. H. Vanderbilt did, that he be free of any public oversight. Insull wanted a public regulatory mechanism in place—to keep out competition. This would ensure him uninterrupted revenues, low costs from lack of competition and a return on his investment substantially more than "cost plus a reasonable profit."

Insull was also a master of corporate propaganda. His public-relations efforts were so effective that his fellow monopolists began emulating the messages his company sent out. He created the industry's first advertising department. His company distributed free copies of "Electric City" throughout Chicago. The tabloid recounted the wonders of electricity and why consumers should expect to spend more money on its acquisition. As head of the Illinois State Council of Defense (a World War I policing agency searching for disloyal Americans) he became so successful with his patriotic efforts to raise money for War Bonds—and influence public opinion about the war—that after the war ended, the name of the council was changed to the Commission on Public Utility Education. Insull was able to distort the organization's purpose so it began equating, in the public mind, patriotism with support for privately controlled electric utilities.

Power utilities across the country picked up on Insull's propaganda techniques, exploiting everything to get the message out. Pre-packaged editorials about the wonders of electricity and how to judge issues affecting the industry were sent regularly to local newspaper editors—who ran most of them without question or change.

The messages were not dissimilar to those circulating today. "Economies and efficiencies" justified mergers, takeovers and control of the marketplace by private or large investor-owned companies. Public utility power, although not yet prevalent as a competitor to the private sector in the days leading up to 1932, was disparagingly referred to as "political ownership" or outright "socialism."

Employees of private utilities were also encouraged to get involved with local political organizations and lobby on behalf of their utility by giving speeches and addresses about the wonders of electricity and the sense of public responsibility possessed by their friendly, neighbourhood monopoly utility. School children were an attractive target for Insull's electrical evangelicals. One device used was a colouring booklet about "The Ohm Queen" and the marvels of her electrical Queendom. Other utilities were successful in getting high school text books revised to include messages supporting the utilities' position on issues before regulatory commissions or other public oversight groups.

To further slant reality their way, the private utilities resorted to playing both softball and hardball. They continued to use slogans and advertising to influence public opinion. Some utilities hired battalions of lawyers to monitor regulatory deliberations and attempted to intimidate the regulators from enacting any legislation inhibiting the utilities' operations. Others formed thinly veiled "taxpayer leagues" to promote their campaigns.

The tougher the utility, the faster the hardball. By controlling the ebb and flow of campaign contributions, and by persistent lobbying, some private utilities became untouchable. In North Carolina, Connecticut, New Jersey and Alabama they virtually controlled their state legislatures. By the end of the 1920s, as few as ten holding companies controlled three-quarters of America's power and light business.

Despite this barrage of proselytizing about "open competition" (which was not allowed), "economic efficiencies" (dubious at best, seldom if ever in terms of social utility and equality) and "the benefits of free enterprise unfettered by government intrusion into the marketplace" (providing you either owned the company or were one of its large investors), American private power utilities inevitably became targets for the Sherman anti-trust crackdowns.

Although later in getting to the public trough than the Goulds, the Vanderbilts and the Fisks, electricity's robber barons had the misfortune to be caught in the sights of a battery of new progressive reformers and trust-busters, such as Senator George Norris of Nebraska. It was Norris who once noted that practically everything in the electricity world—prices, capital investment decisions, the rate of expansion of service and profit levels—"is controlled either directly or indirectly by some part of this gigantic trust."

The power trust (or, at least, their holding company counterparts) was also one of the larger casualties of the stock market collapse on "Black Friday," October 29, 1929. Utility stock prices had been artificially high throughout the late 1920s. Newly formed utility companies had been eagerly backed by banks flush with cash and willing to invest millions on the slightest speculation. In one of many cases, eager bankers backed at least one buy-out—the Associated Gas takeover of the General Gas and Electric Corporation—for 159 times what the utility was worth on paper.

A crash of the private, investor-owned utility power sector was inevitable. What made it worse was the discovery by the Federal Power Commission (FPC) investigation into the industry in 1928 that much of the "wealth" from the electric power industry's steadily mounting earnings was achieved fraudulently. Those powerful holding companies, according to Richard Munson, "created fictitious income by selling property to their subsidiaries at high prices and taking payment only in the subsidiaries' overvalued stock."

The economic thuggery of U.S. electrical trusts notwithstanding, Sam Insull and Senator George Norris were on side on one fundamental belief at that time: that the most effective way to generate and distribute electricity was through a monopoly structure. Like the good North American entrepreneur he was, Insull hated competition and, unlike his counterparts, said so openly. He wanted a monopoly and he wanted it to be controlled by the private sector.

Norris, on the other hand, wanted to see electrical power in "a gigantic monopoly," but a public one. To Norris and his many followers, if electricity were to be left in the hands of the private sector, the result would be "tyranny." America's power development must "be under public control, public operation and public ownership."

By the late 1920s, Norris had most of America on his side. Public anger existed over unreasonably high electricity prices. In rural areas, and in some urban peripheral areas, consumers were frustrated and furious that private utilities could disdainfully ignore their pleas for electrical service, simply because the expense of extending their power distribution might reduce profits and dividends to their investors. So there was no lack of an audience when the FPC reported that the private utilities' "public relations" campaign of the past decade had been so diabolical that they had gone beyond propaganda in massaging their message. According to the FPC, the campaign had bordered on "thought control."

Norris was able to rely on a number of sources for support in his fight against the private power monopolies, including popular New York Governor Franklin D. Roosevelt. During his 1932 run for the White House, Roosevelt denounced the advertising techniques of the monopolists as "a systematic, subtle, deliberate and unprincipled campaign of misinformation, of propaganda, and, if I may use the words, of lies and falsehoods." Norris vigorously attacked the electricity trusts for their lack of public obligation and demanded, along with FDR, that they lower their rates so all Americans could enjoy the convenience of electricity, a commodity which by now had become a necessity.

To prove his point and further the argument for public control of electricity, Norris travelled to Ontario to compare systems and rates in the United States with those under that province's public utility— the Hydro-Electric Power Commission (HEPC) of Ontario. At the time HEPC was unique among North American utilities. It was the only regional electrical system on the continent under public ownership.

To his delight, and to the surprise of few people, Norris found that a family living in a common, eight-room home in Ontario, cooking all their meals with electricity, using an electric vacuum for cleaning, ironing with an electric iron, heating water for baths and washing with electricity and with more than twice the number of electric light bulbs in the typical American home, paid only $3.55 per month—or, at best, one-sixth the price paid in a comparable American home. The same amount of electrical service cost $24 in Washington, D.C., $32 in Alabama, $40 in Nashville and $60 in Florida.

"Norris also compared the costs of lighting the Canadian and American sides of the International Bridge at Niagara Falls," according to Richard Munson. "The same number of lights, the same bridge and the same method of production; the only difference was the price: Ontario's Hydro Power charged only $8.43 per month for the Canadian half of the bridge, while the private U.S. corporation billed for $43.10."

The electric power trusts became a major issue during the 1932 presidential election campaign, contributing to Roosevelt winning fifty-seven percent of the popular vote. In April 1933, shortly after his inauguration, FDR proposed to Congress the legislative cornerstone of his administration's "New Deal": the building and operation of the famed Tennessee Valley Authority (TVA) power scheme. The TVA would bring new life and hope to the destitute Tennessee Valley in the form of cheap power, flood control, soil revitalization and industrial diversification. Within weeks of the TVA's signing, valley residents received their first big return on their vote of confidence in public power versus private monopolies: their electricity rates were cut in half.

It was a major victory for people like Norris who had long held that the only way to properly serve Americans with the wonder of electricity was through public control of their utility. It was an expensive lesson that Ontario, for one Canadian province, did not have to learn the hard way.

Thanks to Adam Beck, the father of Ontario's public power utility, the province, at a critical moment in the development of its hydro-electricity, opted for public ownership and control of power generation and transmission. The decision made electricity cheaper and more accessible for most citizens, and it allowed Ontario to use this marvellous new power source as the essential instrument for the economic development of the province. After all, in the Tennessee Valley case, it was clear that no private company on the face of the earth—monopoly or no monopoly—would have undertaken such a venture, at least not without government guarantees or cost-plus contracts.

Sam Insull? He went from being one of America's richest men to being all but flat broke less than three years after the 1929 Wall Street Crash. He was hounded across continents by charges of embezzlement and fraud. After watching his holding company empire dissolve about him, he skipped the country, fleeing extradition on charges of embezzlement and fraud from country after country until he was picked up in Istanbul in 1934. Returned to the United States, he spent one night in jail and was later acquitted of charges. He died, still broke, in 1938.

Insull's passing marked the end to the era of huge electric power trusts in the United States. On the plus side, he and his colleagues had introduced the technology that helped improve power generation and made its distribution more efficient. They had helped modernize what was, in the early days, a sputtering and staggering industry. But, as Munson points out, "they also built a financial house of cards that initially brought great wealth to a few and eventually delivered financial ruin to thousands."

"Monopolies were made, not born," wrote Christopher Armstrong and H. V. Nelles in *Monopoly's Moment: The Organization and Regulation of Canadian Utilities, 1830–1930*. It cannot be said the Canadian electrical monopoly experience after the turn of the century was any more enlightened than that of our cousins to the south. Except in Ontario, the early Canadian monopoly development experience was not significantly different. Only a slight distinction in malfeasance separated the two episodes.

By 1930, as Armstrong and Nelles show, private monopolies "dominated completely in Quebec and British Columbia, directing the pace and focus of network development along lines that were familiar in the United States. State enterprise controlled most of the market in Ontario, the largest and most prosperous province, a pattern increasingly familiar to Europeans. What seems to have been a distinctively Canadian style was the mixed public-private systems that evolved in several provinces."

What should be remembered is that it was roughly the same people who talked about the need for monopoly in providing electrical power who talked about letting the marketplace be the ultimate adjudicator and controller of price, service and choice. But when they attained the former, they quit talking about the latter. As Armstrong and Nelles put it, "At critical junctures monopoly was the product of purpose, choice, policy, influence, tactic, and human effort... In specific historical circumstances ... capitalists had to make monopolies as an act of will, overcoming fissiparous tendencies in the face of strenuous opposition." However, by the end of World War I, electricity had gone from luxury to necessity, and monopoly control of what was now perceived as "community property" led to the early sparks of consumer revolt.

When governments and municipal officials moved toward tighter regulation of these monopolies, it angered the monopolists who considered that it was their property under attack. Monopoly control of public utilities only seemed to set off the darker nature of the private-sector soul. The excesses that often resulted—usurious rates, inferior service, indifference toward any sense that electricity might have a greater social role to play through economic development—led to public outcries for stricter regulation of these monopolies, and, in the Canadian experience, outright takeover by provincial governments.

In fact, the basic Canadian organization style of electrical power development, was then, as Thomas P. Hughes pointed out, a matter of a variety of styles, or shifts in the balance between public and private enterprise over time. Ontario aside, by the 1920s, if electrical power was not in the hands of private monopolies, in some jurisdictions it was a mix of private and public. In some cases the two shared the market, and in others they competed, but always to the advantage of the private sector.

The province of Quebec held the same grand potential for industrial wealth founded on its hydro-electric power as Ontario did, yet control of the province's system was in an interlocking web of private companies, which eventually became one, privately controlled monopoly—Montreal Light, Heat and Power.

On the West Coast, the privately controlled British Columbia Electric Railway (BCER) Company, as it was originally known, eliminated its competition, as well as any serious regulation, and rang up electricity rates that were among the highest on the continent. By the middle of the 1920s, BCER was returning between eleven and thirteen percent annually on various classes of shares for its investors. At the same time, BCER exhibited an annoying reluctance to invest any capital in expanding electrical service beyond the major cities, where it controlled the electricity market.

Manitoba, New Brunswick and Nova Scotia were hybrids: part of the system private and part of the system public. Compared with Ontario, the results were—in terms of broad economic development, price and enhanced customer service—listless and undramatic. The same could be said for Alberta and Saskatchewan, two provinces that had just joined Confederation in 1905 and did not have the urban infrastructure to warrant investment in large-scale electrical power expansion. It was left to the private sector to keep the lights, such as they were, shining.

There were a number of reasons why Canadian power utilities did not immediately pass into public ownership. First, Canada was and is a nation of regional disparities. Our ability to use natural-resource development as an economic base depends on having those resources and on being able to access cheap electricity to develop them. Some provinces, such as Prince Edward Island, did not have the resource base for either private or government interests to invest the huge amounts of capital required for proper development.

Second, in some jurisdictions, like Quebec, cheap and abundant hydro-electric power was the tool used by a monopoly-protected private utility to provide power to industrial users at rates so low they stifled the normal business criticism about rates that normally might have stirred the government into making changes and moving toward public power.

Third, the British North America Act gave the provinces jurisdiction over natural resources and waterways. This caused a certain amount of uncertainty in the minds of private utilities—as did the tension between the federal and provincial governments when it came to waterways and federal control of navigation—looking to invest in hydro-electric projects.

Still, with their disparate beginnings and with their different political motivations, eventually almost all of the Canadian utility experience would be sheltered under the umbrella of public ownership. The largest would become "institutional mammoths," as Armstrong and Nelles called them. And these very Canadian publicly owned utilities would go on to set, in the interests of their citizens, capital development goals and strategies that no private-sector corporation—no matter how large—would ever have the investment or financial courage to undertake.

They helped shape public policy in a way few other entities have. They helped provincial governments achieve social goals, not just economic targets. They were also used at times as blunt, insensitive instruments of public policy.

On occasion, these electrical power mammoths were run almost as private fiefdoms, operating not with daily accountability to the legislature or cabinet, but at a comfortable distance from those democratic controls. At times these power utilities have engaged in borrowing, on the international money markets, sums large enough to shake the financial stability of the provinces. At one point in the 1920s, Ontario Hydro's debt from less than two decades of generation, construction and capital expansion represented every penny that the province of Ontario owed international money lenders.

Author Paul McKay pointed out in his book, *Electric Empire: The Inside Story of Ontario Hydro*, that capital borrowing of that magnitude not only provided the province with more electricity than it needed, it also tragically skewed provincial spending priorities. McKay called the modern Ontario Hydro "a 500-kilovolt Frankenstein whose actions threaten to tear the economic, political and social fabric of the province." Its appetite for public funds for expansion triggered a dramatic realignment of government economic priorities, he wrote in 1983, "and this has effectively traded deep cuts in social services, education and health care spending," all for the goal of amassing a fifty percent surplus of electricity, "most of it meant for U.S. markets that never materialized."

It is little exaggeration to say that most Canadian public power utilities became, at times, more powerful than the governments they were meant to serve. They grew silently to awesome proportions.

Until cracks began to appear in their decision-making in the late 1960s up to the 1990s, their political influence was unmatched by any other enterprise—public or private—in our history. Yet, they operated, by and large, in relative secrecy, skilfully avoiding detailed scrutiny by the public.

In Ontario, Quebec, British Columbia and Manitoba, if not in all provinces where public utilities reigned, these utilities have at times run "out of control" and have operated independently of their political masters, often to the eventual detriment of ratepayers and taxpayers.

In the foreword to McKay's book, U.S. consumer advocate Ralph Nader termed Ontario Hydro "a utility gone berserk." It had become "inflexible, arrogant and intransigent." It was a corporation owned by the citizens of Ontario, yet it displayed a need to act in secrecy where data and corporate operations were concerned. It was run by a nonrepresentative, insulated board of directors. It had no mechanism for either ratepayers or taxpayers to access policy or decision-making. And it "presented a growing threat to the economic and social equilibrium of the province itself."

Yet this was an institution that, for most of its first half century of existence, had held a cherished position in the hearts of most Ontarians. How in roughly the next half century did this respected public institution go from divinity status to one of the worst manifestations of corporate incompetence imaginable?

4 / Power at Cost

Communism is Soviet government plus the electrification of the whole country.

— Vladimir Ilyich Lenin, 1920

SHORTLY AFTER he was appointed chairman of the board of directors of Ontario Hydro in October 1992, Maurice Strong—international investor, financier, sustainable-development proponent and the head of the United Nations' Earth Summit conference in Rio de Janeiro— looked into the future of his latest charge and said: "I see a kaleidoscope of trouble. I see a public corporation in crisis, a crisis of public confidence."

At one time Ontario Hydro was one of the country's most revered and powerful institutions. But in 1992, Ontario Hydro was in huge trouble. After nine decades, the country's largest public utility was now one of the world's largest debtors. The bottom seemed to have finally fallen out of the utility's dream of relentless growth and expansion on behalf of all Ontarians.

Strong had inherited a financial predicament of staggering proportions. After almost three decades of what critics saw as profligate and misguided spending, most of it on nuclear power generation, Ontario Hydro was $34 billion in debt. The debt cost the utility more than $3.5 billion a year, or roughly $10 million a day in interest charges. Ontario Hydro was faced with a massive surplus in electricity—enough to last almost two decades and the exact opposite of the situation the utility had been forecasting. Board members and management had watched with a certain amount of detachment as consumer demand for electricity melted almost as quickly as the reputation of its fast-aging nuclear reactors.

The financial warning signs had been evident for years, but Strong moved quickly to stem any further hemorrhaging. By January 1993 he had initiated a number of actions. He established a task force to draft tough cost-cutting plans. He had Ontario Hydro cancel a $13 billion contract to buy 1,000 megawatts of power from Manitoba Hydro beginning in the year 2000. He went looking for provincial government help in offsetting the crippling annual interest charges. Strong also considered sending Hydro executives off to study how the Tennessee Valley Authority had successfully brought itself back from the financial brink. He did two other things as well: He began closing the door to a horrid and confusing corporate past, but he opened a new door to a controversial and just as confusing future for the utility.

With the support of the board, in late January the corporation announced it planned to pull the plug on the costliest environmental review in Canada—a three-year assessment of Ontario Hydro's plans to construct up to $100 billion worth of new generating facilities by the year 2014. The reason was simple: there no longer was any need for all that new electrical capacity. That move marked the closing of one door.

But at the same time, Maurice Strong let it be known to the province's New Democratic Party government that he supported a study on the pros and cons of privatizing a utility that had been in public hands since 1906. That opened a whole new, confusing door of perception for ratepayers and taxpayers alike—the debate over who should own Ontario Hydro.

To many Ontarians, the once-venerable Ontario Hydro had been a major focus of controversy, going back into the late 1960s. The utility had gone from being one of the most reasonable, most reliable and most efficient power generating utilities in the country to the most expensive and one of the least efficient. Besides carrying a massive debt, Ontario Hydro was also top-heavy with staff. On a per employee basis, the electricity that Ontario Hydro produced cost fifty percent more than B.C. Hydro's and twenty percent more than the cost of production for Hydro-Québec. During the 1980s, Ontario Hydro had as many as thirty-five thousand employees. The design, construction and start-up operation of the ill-fated Darlington project alone accounted for a staff increase of about four thousand employees.

Because of the enormous cost overruns for the Darlington nuclear generating station—a project which came in five years behind schedule and at a price $11.3 *billion* more than the original $2.7 billion estimate—Ontario Hydro had been forced to raise rates for electricity by thirty-four percent since 1989. In 1992 alone, rates went up about twelve percent. Yet by the time it was commissioned Darlington's generating capacity would turn out to be entirely surplus to Ontario's needs.

Strong had been personally appointed to the chair of the province's power utility by Premier Bob Rae. Like many Ontario premiers, Rae had problems with the aloof, distant—and expensive—manner in which Ontario Hydro had been run to that point. As he said in his biography, *From Protest to Power*, many senior people at Ontario Hydro had too often regarded the government of the day as an inconvenience.

"One of my favourite encounters was with the executive committee of the Hydro board," Rae wrote, "where two notables, Gordon Bell of the Bank of Nova Scotia and Alex Mackintosh of the old Toronto law firm of Blake Cassels, made it very clear they were running things and the sooner I learned that the better off everyone would be."

Regardless of who had been "running things," Ontario Hydro was a gigantic mess in late 1992. Its financial state was referred to as "a death spiral." When the New Democrats were elected in 1990, of all the financial bad news they inherited from the Peterson Liberals, "Ontario Hydro's saga stood out," recalled Rae. One very uncomfortable political reality for the new premier was the fact that the Darlington cost-overruns, when added to an already burdensome corporate long-term debt package, meant Ontario ratepayers were now faced with "a constant increase in rates way over inflation indefinitely into the future."

Strong wasted no time. By March 1993 he had cut $10 billion off Ontario Hydro's $42 billion capital expansion plans, called for a major review of the utility's existing assets and offered as many as twelve thousand employees voluntary severance packages, all in an effort to deal with the huge costs that were strangling the corporation. Strong also went in search of some relief for angry ratepayers, hoping at the very least a temporary freeze could be placed on rate increases. At the end of this tumultuous fiscal year, Ontario Hydro would take a write-down of $3.6 billion.

Together, these measures signalled clearly that the province's power utility had bottomed out—in financial terms, in terms of its management effectiveness and in terms of public respect. It also marked the end of the corporation's "Age of Arrogance." The board and management could no longer act as imperiously as they had. The decision not to pursue the environmental review was a signal that maybe the utility's board and management had been wrong about the future for too many years now.

It also capped what had been a very stormy couple of decades for Ontario Hydro. Beginning in the late 1960s, the public utility had been on the public-relations defensive, arguing with its critics and detractors before one public inquiry after another. Until the winter of 1993, the corporation seemed to have been operating in its cocky, business-as-usual style. In the minds of most critics, there was no excuse for the kind of load forecasting that helped result in embarrassing construction cost overruns, the huge debt and the surpluses of electricity. There had been intense and persistent public opposition to the corporation's decision to rely on nuclear power generation. The costly list of problems and signs of early deterioration in a number of Hydro's nuclear reactors kept the critical heat on from environmentalists.

While Ontario Hydro was defending its plans to increase capital spending on generating capacity for an unknown future, the shift to a conserver society had already taken place. The consequent drop in demand for power was a further variable that would skew the utility's spending plans. Another variable that upset Hydro planning was the damaging economic recessions the country slipped into in the early 1980s and early 1990s. However, it was not until the environmental review processes began in earnest in 1989 that even larger cracks began to show in the way Ontario Hydro was doing business.

When Ontario Hydro requested the environmental hearings be brought to an end, the process was already three-quarters finished. It had taken up two hundred days of hearings, entertained over a thousand exhibits, covered thirty-two thousand pages of testimony and cost Hydro (or their ratepayers) $57 million. The public utility was finally admitting their world, and their planned view of it, was quite incorrect.

The once predictable days of annual growth in electricity demand had long ago disappeared. For decades Ontario Hydro's board and management had remained locked in megaproject mode, persisting in the belief that demand would continue to double every decade and that their job was to build the necessary generating capacity to meet that growth.

"When you look at electricity demand growth in Ontario from the 1940s to 1967/68, this is a particular period where the electricity demand rate of change was seven percent a year," said Tom Adams, executive director of Energy Probe and a well-known utility analyst. Energy Probe is a citizen-based environmental and consumer advocacy group based in Toronto. "It was uncanny ... I am sure there were some folks around Hydro who thought this was the divine word of God coming down. The word from the heavens was seven percent. They had a thirty-year run where seven percent was the right number. It starts to get pretty hard to persuade people to change their thinking."

When the environmental hearings were announced in 1989, Ontario Hydro was intent on almost doubling its generating capacity by 2014. The utility's plans included the construction of three more large nuclear generating stations, two coal-powered generating stations and a series of other generating facilities that could cost an estimated $60 to $100 billion.

Critics argued the corporation's load forecasts were patently out of whack. Demand was actually falling, not rising. To compound the errors by building expensive new nuclear and fossil-fuel generating capacity—in the Age of Environmentalism—was folly of the maddest sort.

At first, Hydro executives warned government, regulators and ratepayers with certainty in their minds: unless Ontario Hydro received approval for the massive package of projects now on the corporation's drawing boards, the province could face future power shortages, perhaps even blackouts. As recently as 1991, Hydro had encouraged private power producers to invest in new generating capacity and to sell their electricity to Hydro, helping the utility to avoid those predicted shortages.

But on January 14, 1993, acting Ontario Hydro President Allan Kupcis announced a further startling step in the corporation's austerity march. He told about 150 private power producers that those generation plans Hydro had called for in 1991 were now on hold. These were independent power producers who had struck formal deals with Hydro to provide them with the extra electricity the utility predicted it needed. The decision put on hold sixty-six non-utility generating projects. The news shocked the independent producers. Many had invested in expanded capacity on faith and a promise from Ontario Hydro. The news also shook the international financial markets Ontario Hydro relied on for underwriting its capital projects.

Kupcis announced that Ontario Hydro was now "awash in unneeded electrical generating capacity," as the newspapers put it. The utility had thirty-six percent more capacity than it needed to meet the province's needs. The province now had a surplus capacity of electrical power that could last at least seventeen years. Once again, Ontarians were thrown into confusion about the state of their publicly owned power utility, its financial health and its management acumen.

Kupcis laid the blame for this sudden glut of electricity on an unprecedented decline in electricity consumption that had begun in 1989. To date, it had been the longest period of declining demand for Ontario Hydro since 1940. Despite the positive effect of new energy conservation in the 1970s and 1980s, demand for electricity had been growing annually through the 1980s at about four to five percent. But demand plummeted after the peak year of 1989, falling 4.5 percent. According to Hydro officials, provincial growth demand would now not reach the 1989 level until 1995, or later.

Kupcis pointed to the entrenched economic recession in Ontario as the principal culprit for the three-year drop in demand growth. Roughly one-seventh of the demand for electricity had simply disappeared as many commercial operations, resource-based industries and manufacturers shut their doors, laid off employees or faded away.

Ontario Hydro had already responded to the crisis by cancelling the $13 billion long-term supply contract with Manitoba and mothballing some of its coal-fired generating units. Hydro was also reviewing the estimated $3 billion cost of refurbishing the troublesome Bruce A nuclear generating facility. It was looking at shutting down rather than overhauling Bruce A generating units. Taking its 3,270 megawatt capacity off-line could help eliminate Hydro's surplus electricity problem.

But closing down a nuclear facility, however vexatious, that only a few short years ago was being flaunted as absolutely essential to the utility's long-range demand forecasts raised even more questions about the quality of the decision to build nuclear generating capacity in the first place.

According to Energy Probe's Tom Adams, "at one time Hydro was forecasting a need for 100–120 operating power reactors by the year 2000. There were to be reactors on almost every block, limited only by the amount of water available for cooling. You can find these statements back in the records. The corporation clearly fell victim to fanciful views of the future based on simple-minded extrapolations."

The lifetime of the Bruce A units was originally set at up to fifty years. If it were closed down now it would mean the expensive nuclear facility would never make it to its operational "half-life." The radioactivity of its spent fuel and its contaminated equipment would, however, have an estimated "half-life" of some 15,000 years.

Strong's swift dose of corporate tough-love was overdue. It would help alleviate some of the public and financial pressures, but it would not alter, for the moment at least, the increasingly negative opinions Ontarians now held of the once respected public corporation.

Ontario Hydro's debt-to-equity ratio was, even in utility terms, an embarrassment at .918, an increase from the 1992 ratio of .841. Its once unassailable promise of providing "power at cost" to even the most humble citizen was in tatters. Detractors now saw the utility as a fat, unregulated, unresponsive bureaucracy that gouged its electricity customers with unwarranted annual rate increases. Its heavy reliance on nuclear generating power was perceived by many members of the public as dangerous, and in the long term, more expensive than it was worth. Ontario Hydro nuclear generating plants seemed to be sprouting leaks, or showing the corrosive effects of old age, on a shockingly regular basis.

Those first economizing measures bought Strong and his board some time and some applause from critics. It showed that the corporation now understood the seriousness of the situation and was determined to go about cutting costs to avoid further hemorrhaging. Ontario Hydro also needed to be modernized. It needed a new organizational structure and ways of doing business if it was to survive in a quickly changing continental electricity environment. The power market south of the border was being deregulated, and competition for electricity customers—in both the United States and Canada—seemed on the horizon. Ontario Hydro might have to change from being the all-powerful monopoly, controlling the marketplace, to one of a number of utilities competing for customers. This led Strong and his board to pose the ultimate structural question: Did Ontario Hydro have to be publicly owned? Would it better survive—and still provide the citizen with inexpensive electricity—if its assets were placed in the hands of the private sector? Was it time to privatize the publicly owned Ontario Hydro?

Strong did not immediately recommend to the NDP government that Ontario Hydro be privatized. What he did was announce in January that he was gathering a group of senior executives from the private sector to study the pros and cons of privatization, how the utility might be sold to private-sector investors and what the costs and benefits for the taxpayers of Ontario might be.

As odd as it seemed, the idea of selling off Ontario Hydro had not been wholly dismissed by Bob Rae's government. As much as Liberals and Conservatives would like to characterize it, the Rae team was not a pack of raving ideologues intent on nationalizing, like nineteenth-century socialists, the means of capitalist production or preserving the sanctity of public institutions. There were members of the NDP caucus and the cabinet who pressed to have Hydro privatized. Their reasons were not profound. The public utility was in deep financial trouble. Its debt was a burden on provincial borrowing. The Hydro board had not exactly pledged its fealty to the NDP government. Its problems and the public displeasure over electricity rate hikes delivered bad public vibrations that were too easily blamed on the NDP. Some felt it was wiser to just dump the troubled corporation into private hands, take the money and put as much distance between the utility and the Rae government as possible.

"A large organization like Hydro develops its own personality, its own style, and a stubborn sense of its independence," Rae wrote. "This was true in Adam Beck's day, and it is true today. Making a Crown entity of Hydro's size responsive to any elected government is never easy."

On March 9, 1993, barely three months after assuming the reins of the troubled utility, Maurice Strong unveiled his sweeping new plan to reorganize Ontario Hydro. Although privatization of the Crown corporation was not the suggested immediate solution to its problems, Strong was clearly reorganizing Ontario Hydro "along private-sector principles," as the press put it.

To make the "new Ontario Hydro" more effective and competitive, Strong's plan called for offering more than ten thousand employees enough financial incentive to retire or leave voluntarily. Another $10 billion was slashed from the utility's capital spending budget. Plans were tabled to reduce its $34 billion debt by $13 billion over the next ten years. As Kupcis had indicated in January, purchases of now unneeded electricity from independent power producers would be severely reduced. The *pièce de résistance* for anxious ratepayers was the announcement that electricity rates would be frozen for 1994, and possibly beyond that date.

Strong's medicine also included a long-overdue admission that the nuclear component of Ontario Hydro could now be as much a liability as a profit centre. According to the new corporate plan, unless new markets could be found for its product, the Bruce heavy water plant would be closed. Also, a promise was given to phase out the Bruce A nuclear generating station. The plant could be mothballed, along with its four tired nuclear reactors, by 1997.

Just as significant, Strong announced that the process of reorganization of the venerable Hydro would include structural changes that would go a distance to making the public monopoly utility look like—and act somewhat like—a private-sector corporation. Ontario Hydro would henceforth be divided into three distinct operating units: one responsible for the generation and delivery of electricity, one to look after energy management services, and a third to act as a profit centre, including selling Hydro's technology for profit on international markets.

Many saw this last move as "the prelude to privatization" and began attaching dollar figures to those portions of Hydro which could now theoretically be sold to private interests. Strong's radical, hard-nosed approach to Hydro's dilemma, even the nudge toward privatization, won the endorsement of the premier.

"The status quo is not sustainable," Rae said, in citing Hydro's importance in the rebuilding of the province's economy. High electricity rates had dampened growth, even contributing to a worsening of the recession Ontario was suffering through. Hydro's $34 billion debt, when added to the province's own debt of some $65 billion, had international lending agencies concerned enough to place the province on a credit watch.

"We've got a situation where there's a huge excess of supply, where all those people, all those companies and individuals who are working in the province have had to make huge adjustments because of the recession," Rae said at the time. "For Ontario Hydro to continue in a sense oblivious to the very different world in which we are now living, would be the height of unreality, and would be the height of irresponsibility."

This fundamental shake-up may have publicly raised for the first time the idea that the venerable Ontario Hydro might be sold off to private interests. But what Premier Rae, or even Maurice Strong, may not have known at the time was that privatization was not as clean an option for Ontario Hydro as they might have liked to believe. The next few years would prove that the issue was both highly complex and emotionally charged. There would not be enough data, science or even a good rumour around to confirm clearly and unequivocally that a privatized Hydro would be more efficient and less expensive to operate than one publicly owned. As the various privatization studies completed their work and published their estimates of what it might cost and who would be winners and who losers, there began to appear significant gaps—sometimes in the tens of billions of dollars—between what Ontario Hydro might bring to the taxpayers' coffers as a saleable asset and what bills those same taxpayers might be stuck with.

With Rae's endorsement, Strong put into motion the forces and issues that would be debated at least until the end of the century. As more debate ensued, more attention was given to the origins and first organizing principles of the utility. The one piece of history that stuck in some craws, the one that even made critics pause in their pursuit of privatization for Ontario Hydro, was that this utility had been given birth in 1906 as a publicly owned and operated monopoly because the private sector, when given its chance early on, had failed the citizens of Ontario.

It is written that when Adam Beck died in 1925, Ontario switched off its electricity for a moment in his honour. As his funeral cortege moved through the streets of Toronto, mourners lined up eight and nine deep to pay their last respects. In 1936, more than a decade after his death, Ontario Hydro mounted a display at the Canadian National Exhibition. The centrepiece was a reverential altar built to honour Sir Adam Beck. The focus of the display was a huge cameo of the man. Beneath the cameo was a rendering of Niagara Falls. Above, the words *HYDRO* circled his head much like the large, brilliant halo depicted on a medieval portrait of a saint.

In a land too short of heroes, it would be nice to think that everything Beck did in bringing "power at cost" to Ontarians was, like the actions of Prometheus, both beneficial and an act of high virtue. In beating back the private power interests, contrary politicians and even some colleagues and associates as harshly as he did, Beck delivered a wondrous gift for the people of his province. But he was also an opportunist who took advantage of a situation others had worked for, quickly cutting them out of the power and most of the glory. His goal was to monopolize Ontario's electric power business in public hands, though letting the public actually claim ownership was often the last thing on his mind.

He was been called a "megalomaniac," "tyrannical" and the "dictator of Ontario." In building what turned out to be Canada's largest utility, one of the nation's largest business enterprises and one of the largest utilities of its kind in the world, Beck appeared to listen to little advice other than his own. Although he professed to be working in the public interest, Beck, in fact, seemed largely indifferent to the interests of the public.

The public paid the bills and were saddled with the risks, but the Hydro-Electric Power Commission that became Ontario Hydro was his company, as far as Beck was concerned. He ran it as he saw fit. As H. V. Nelles wrote: "Beck helped establish the public enterprise tradition in Canada, though his methods did little to render such enterprises more politically accountable." Beck was, as one historian wrote, "a public servant who was master of the public."

There is little argument that the important issues that would eventually lead to the formation of the Hydro-Electric Power Commission of Ontario in 1906, and Beck's abrupt ascendency to its throne, were in play before the cigar-box manufacturer, sometime mayor of London, Ontario and, for close to nineteen years, Member of the Provincial Parliament, arrived on the scene.

The events that would open the way for Beck's ascendency began in the demand for a drastically improved distribution of electric power in Ontario before 1900. Electricity came slowly to Ontario, after the late 1870s. In rural areas, people were living much like they had in 1800. Throughout the nineteenth century wood, water and steam power were the principal sources of energy. Some gas was available for street lighting in larger cities later in the century. But the decimation of forests and consequent shortage of wood as a fuel source led to the widespread use of coal-fired generation to produce electricity, despite the fact the main reserves lay in the northeast United States and had to be imported.

In the summer of 1897 a series of violent strikes by miners working in the coal fields of Pennsylvania, Ohio and West Virginia broke out with severe implications for Ontario. The strikes tripled the price of imported coal, providing Ontario utilities could even acquire it. This "coal famine" drove Ontario into serious economic depression. Factories closed and unemployment rose dramatically. These events triggered fear in the hearts of rural Ontario politicians and small enterprises, already doing battle with the private utilities holding the electrical power franchises. The private monopolists were not exactly held in high esteem. Most seemed bent on controlling any future electrical output from coal, and later, from the principal source of hydraulic power in southern Ontario—Niagara Falls.

Ontario wanted to use this marvellous new source of energy to facilitate massive industrial development. If hydro-electric power from Niagara Falls could be harnessed it might allow the province to get out from under dependence on volatile and expensive U.S. coal. Niagara Falls represented a gold mine of hydro-electric power, or "white coal" as Edison called it. But the whole question of who should control this vast resource which would determine the future course of the province's prosperity became an overriding issue and a matter of great political debate and combat.

Like characters out of a Nasty Jack cartoon, the private interests set a goal of acquiring the last franchise on Niagara Falls power, and holding it as a private, vertically integrated monopoly. Their interests were wrapped up in an enterprise called the Electric Development Company. This syndicate was formed in 1902. The principals were a group of very wealthy Toronto businessmen and investors. William Mackenzie was a well-to-do railway builder who controlled the Toronto Street Railway Company. Frederic Nicholls was the head of the Toronto Electric Light Company and, along with others, was involved in Canadian General Electric. Henry M. Pellatt was a financier less known, perhaps, for his capitalist ways than he was for his Toronto home—Casa Loma.

These three brigands were referred to as the "Electric Ring" by Beck and his supporters. In *The People's Power: The History of Ontario Hydro*, Merrill Denison labelled them "a band of robber barons intent upon placing the people of Ontario in a state of perpetual economic bondage."

The Electric Ring sought to control power distribution throughout southern Ontario and, in particular, in Toronto. As a working collective, they were loathed for the exorbitant prices they charged for electricity. They were vilified for their lofty indifference to complaints about slow and shabby service. They did little to dismiss the accusations that they and their companies were arrogant and much too powerful.

They were reviled by a public forced to use their electricity services, by the press, by other business interests—even by the Canadian Manufacturers' Association—and by numerous municipal power co-operatives that feared being cut out of attractive Niagara hydroelectric power and forced to rely on U.S. coal for future electricity needs.

Merrill Denison, writing in his 1960 history of Ontario Hydro, captured the feeling about the early electricity monopolists: "Without exception, the attitude of the private electrical interests was both arrogant and avaricious ... [They] had secured a monopoly position, and not unnaturally, like their mercantilist forebears, were determined to exploit that position to the utmost in terms of profits. Viewed in retrospect, their 'customer relations,' or, better, lack of them, are seen to have been nothing less than suicidal. So bad were they, in fact, that the first protests against them came not from the small domestic consumer but from Ontario's manufacturing industry itself."

The concerns of the Ontario municipalities—who would prove to be almost as influential as Adam Beck, if not more so, in the early development of Ontario Hydro—were real ones. The question of rural electrification was already an ominous component of a dangerous social rift developing in the United States. As constitutional historian William E. Leuchtenburg once noted, America was being divided at the time into two distinct nations, based on the availability of electricity: city dwellers, who had increasing access to it, and "country folk," who did not.

The issue of monopoly control by private interests sparked a round of civic protest action referred to as "civil populism." Civic populism had been an active force against private utility monopolies in both Britain and the United States, almost since the first private franchises were granted in the 1880s. But, as political scientist Neil Freeman pointed out in *The Politics of Power: Ontario Hydro and Its Government, 1906–1995*, civic populism in Canada was guided by a leadership made up of municipal and provincially elected officials, not just concerned citizens. Paradoxically, this anti–private-monopoly leadership also included members of the local boards of trade. Their collective fear was one which ran across class, social and economic lines—that expensive, privately controlled electricity could mean the economic decline of their communities.

The idea of a public power corporation was first raised by the Waterloo Chamber of Commerce in February 1902. Adam Beck's first appearance on the scene was at a subsequent meeting in Berlin (or Kitchener, as it was later called) in February 1903, which included representatives from nineteen very concerned municipal councils. Beck encouraged the meeting to adopt the idea of a government-run electricity transmission system. He pressed for a public corporation that would buy electricity from private power producers and distribute it to municipal co-operatives. With minor modifications, this was essentially the structure Beck would pursue until his public power goal was finally achieved three years later.

As mayor of London and an MPP, he was able to elbow his way into a leadership position in the municipal co-operative movement. By 1905 he was made head of a public inquiry that ultimately recommended creating a municipally owned, provincially financed, co-operatively based hydro-electric distribution system.

In Beck, the municipal co-operative movement finally had a charismatic leader to match its growing membership of angry citizens opposed to the establishment of a private power monopoly. Buoyed now by massive public support, Beck went on record to say that if the government was going to have to act as banker in the future development of electrical power, it might as well run the system.

At the same time, the Electric Ring went on the offensive. Facing certain bankruptcy of its Electric Development Company without a monopoly franchise, the Ring started putting heat on the provincial government. But Beck was prepared to fight even these politically influential robber barons. Only eight days after the release of his own commission's report, on April 11, 1906, Beck led fifteen hundred public power enthusiasts who marched from Toronto City Hall to the legislature. The marchers called for "cheap power," by which they meant publicly controlled power. They demanded government ownership of the electricity system in some form of crown corporation. They demanded an end to price gouging. Premier J. P. Whitney acquiesced and introduced legislation to create the Hydro-Electric Power Commission of Ontario (later Ontario Hydro). Its chairman would be Adam Beck.

In opposing the Electric Ring, Beck had taken on the financial powers of the city of Toronto and won what would turn out to be the most important electricity battle in the province's history. Even though the Ring was actively buying up editorial space in local newspapers to write about government "confiscation" of their investments, and even though Beck and his supporters had to prevail in two referenda in each municipal area before HEPC could set up shop, support for public power fanned out across southern Ontario.

Thanks in part to Beck's own shrewd use of propaganda and the press, public opinion had swung so demonstrably in his favour that by 1910 "switching on" electric lighting ceremonies were taking place across southern Ontario. On October 11, the citizens of Berlin watched in awe as Premier Whitney guided Beck's hand to throw a switch that would take electricity from Niagara Falls, and in a sudden burst of light, illuminate a sign arched across the city's main street spelling out: "For the People."

In his address to the crowd, Whitney summed up what the battle had been about: "We have been attacked, vilified and slandered ... Large sums of money have been expended in creating and fomenting prejudice and ill-feeling against us." Hostile forces had "sought to destroy our power legislation and render it impossible for the wonderful new force to be used and enjoyed by the people, except by terms laid down by private corporations and individuals." Adam Beck received a standing ovation as the band struck up a rousing march: "See the Conquering Hero Comes."

The bill to establish Ontario Hydro, known as the Power Commission Act, passed the legislature in three days with little discussion. Contrary to popular mythology, the legislation did not "nationalize" or "confiscate" private-sector holdings. Instead, it created a unique hybrid public institution: part government department in character, part crown corporation in appearance and part municipal co-operative by notion of political force and citizen support. This hybrid pattern of ownership would help defy any clear answer to the question of just who "owned" Ontario Hydro almost up until the present time—the province or the municipal utilities formed to distribute the power. But for the first two decades there was no question of who "owned" Ontario Hydro: it was Adam Beck.

"Beck ran [Ontario Hydro] like a satrap from its creation in 1906 until his death in 1925," Keith R. Fleming wrote in *Power at Cost*. "Only rarely did he trouble himself with matters of political account-ability. So long as Beck lived, Hydro was in many respects a one-man organization; every decision of consequence ... passed over his desk."

Beck promised Ontarians that public power would be reliable. It would be provided compliments of their elected government, not by capitalists seeking a guaranteed return on their investment. Most of all, it would be power provided to them "at cost."

"Power at cost" was a brilliant public-relations slogan because it was never clear what "cost" really was. But just saying it—"power at cost"—allowed Beck's Hydro to gain immense public respect and appreciation, even if scrupulous accounting and auditing rules were seldom applied. "'Power at cost' thus put a conveniently simple face on a highly complex matter," Fleming wrote. "'Power at cost' ended up meaning a lot of things—or nothing at all. But Beck never let up in its use as a principal corporate message.

The establishment of a publicly owned electrical power system in Ontario sparked controversy and denunciation in Britain and in the United States. Members of the international investment community mumbled about this dangerous experiment in "socialism" but made little rhetorical ground because the true believers and supporters of publicly owned power in Ontario turned out to be, more often than not, civic business leaders—small businessmen, the editor of the local newspaper, local and provincial politicians. It was tough making a case about "creeping communism" when one was battling fellow free enterprisers.

Once Beck had established a strategic toe-hold for public power, it seemed there were no limits to his aspirations for it or for him. He alone interpreted the gospel of public power for his followers. The liturgy became anything he said it might be. And there seemed to be no adversary that worried him in carrying out his crusade, not even the people he pledged to serve.

Beck had been able to steal Prometheus's gift and was only prepared, not to share it, but to use it as he saw fit. Consequently, his legacy is as puzzling as his megalomania was intimidating. He moulded the organization with his vision, his biases, his combativeness, his suspicions and his innate sense of mistrust. His mark on the organization was so profound that even ninety years later it still bears his stamp in many ways.

Beck had a particular manner of getting his way. What he said Ontario Hydro should do—enter into costly expansion programs using public funds or publicly backed borrowing, for instance—was what it should do. He simply refused to act "as a biddable servant of Cabinet," as Fleming wrote. "Beck's attitude towards the heads of the provincial governments ... was invariably that of an independent potentate whose powers and perquisites must be respected and whose drive for expansion must be supported without question."

Excluding himself, of course, Beck saw legislators as "meddlesome politicians." It was his stated intention to keep Ontario Hydro "out of politics" by continually muddying the waters of accountability and ownership. He was so effective that the label most frequently applied to Hydro by Beck's critics, not unlike the corporation's days up to the winter of 1993, was that Ontario Hydro "was out of control."

Beck's defence was that if Ontario Hydro was to be run as a business, and keep its promise of "power at cost," then the organization had to be free of damaging political appointments. It should also be free to pay, in the interests of attracting talented people, salaries higher than those of the average civil servant. Hydro was a highly technical, complex business, he argued, and keeping politicians out of the mix would ensure success.

Beck also knew that the pendulum he relied upon swung the other way as well. Development of electricity was hugely expensive. Investments of public funds in the tens of millions of dollars were not out of the question, even in the early 1900s. There were large risks involved for politicians if things went awry. Keeping Beck and his expensive plans at arm's length sometimes worked both ways for them. If Ontario Hydro did good things, the politicians could step forward and reap the rewards. If things went sour and proved politically costly, the politicians could distance themselves from the province's troubled electrical utility and blame it all on the management of Hydro.

The problems this concept of arm's-length stewardship could cause were often so pronounced that the political fallout splashed upon the politicians whether they denied responsibility or not. It led, after Beck's death, to the evolution of a "public" utility that continued to rely on Beck's mantra of corporate independence to the point where immense and costly mistakes in planning and operation could be carried out without scrupulous legislative or regulatory oversight. At times this "institutionalized ambivalence," as a number of historians would term it, caused Ontario ratepayers and taxpayers to be saddled with enormous bills—socially, financially and economically—for what should have been "power at cost."

Beck's power seemed to grow with each confrontation with government. At certain testy points, in 1914 for instance, he threatened to bring down the Whitney government if they did not comply with his view of the relationship between Hydro and the municipal cooperatives. He had wanted the municipalities, which he often relied upon as his straw dog of "ownership," to be restricted in responsibilities and power to nothing more than distribution in the electrical chain of generation–transmission–distribution. After acrimonious debate, Beck got his way. He was allowed to move Hydro directly and unrestricted into the field of electrical generation. The Whitney government not only conceded, it arranged for a knighthood for Beck, perhaps as a means of appeasing this often angry god.

Knowing where real power lay, Beck resigned from cabinet in 1914 following Whitney's death. He became even more disparaging of attempts at legislative control over Hydro. Beck now reached a point of perilous arrogance, making little effort to keep cabinet informed of how Hydro spent its money. By 1916, Beck's domineering and his frequent public proclamations before the province's politicians about Hydro's autonomy had so infuriated certain cabinet members that efforts were made to constrain, once and for all, this powerful renegade. An investigation ensued and the provincial auditor all but stated that Beck had been operating Hydro by his own fiduciary rules. He had charged the government for unauthorized expenditures. He had undertaken commercial responsibilities beyond his authority under the Act. He had even set electrical power rates above the cost of generation—in clear violation of the rules of "power at cost." Beck was playing fast-and-loose with rates to be able to retain surplus revenues for discretionary spending. The audit revealed the amount

Beck had burrowed away was $4 million, almost a third of its $13 million government appropriation. In post-Watergate terms, this might be referred to as an "illegal slush fund."

This was no small political matter. In the first place, there were real concerns about what Beck's indebtedness might do to the province's credit rating, even to its solvency. In the second, As Neil Freeman put it in *The Politics of Power*, "Beck had subverted the cabinet's power to control taxation and spending, central tenets of responsible government." In another time and another place, Beck's actions might have made him a candidate for a lengthy stay in the federal penitentiary.

But Adam Beck repented before no man. Beck reacted by blaming the law for placing unnecessary burdens upon him. He claimed the legislative control over Hydro, as set out in the Power Commission Act, was simply unworkable as it read. Therefore, the law was wrong, not Adam Beck. Making no attempt at denial, Beck accepted personal responsibility for all that had transpired, based on his defence that what he had done simply made good business sense. By haughtily accepting responsibility for operating beyond legislative accountability, Beck was challenging the elected politicians to counter his claim that Hydro—and therefore Beck—was autonomous and beyond their control.

By hiding conveniently behind the protective shield of municipal co-operatives—arguing one time that Hydro was a child of the municipalities and not a government department, and arguing the opposite on other occasions—Beck won his first big test with the government. He did make one small concession. He agreed he would at least get Hydro to file an annual report, disclosing current and expected assets and liabilities, income and expenses, and the state of the utility's indebtedness. But he balked at even doing that when it was insisted that the annual reports be filed through a comptroller appointed by cabinet. Beck refused to be "comptrolled" by anyone.

In the years following 1906, Ontario Hydro had grown at a phenomenal rate. In only its fourth year of operation, it provided two thousand kilowatts of power to Ontario's municipalities. Four years later, it provided fifty thousand kilowatts to a system that included almost one hundred municipal co-operatives. At the end of its first decade, the load was a quarter-million kilowatts.

"Nothing is too big for us," Adam Beck liked to preach, as he took

Hydro from one massive capital development project to another. "Nothing is too expensive to imagine," he would say with roguish abandon. "Nothing is visionary."

The provincial government's decision in 1914 to allow Beck to move Ontario Hydro into power generation as well as transmission triggered a growth spurt that became the foundation for one of the most successful industrial expansions in Canadian history. When Beck began buying out private power producers, and wrenching up investment in new hydro generation power, he began the process of making modern Ontario.

By 1923, Ontario Hydro was the largest hydro-electric utility in the world. Given the pace at which Beck was pushing construction of new generating capacity, it was also beginning to generate huge electrical surpluses, something which had begun to show up as early as 1912. At this time, Hydro was also singularly responsible for about one-half of the debt of the entire province. Still, Beck was eluding public scrutiny. But noises were being made, particularly in cabinet, about how Hydro was being run, about its debt and about how Beck was padding his personal power base with public funds.

Beck always seemed to be one step ahead of his detractors. Never one to miss a public-relations opportunity, he had secretly organized, and financed out of Hydro funds, his very own lobby groups. Beck was clearly a public-relations genius of Machiavellian proportions. Earlier on, he had sponsored the "Hydro Circus"— a caravan that travelled the province extolling the virtues of cheap, public power and parading all the new electrical appliances available to make life easier, especially in rural Ontario.

At the same time, he began to realize that recurring power surpluses could be a major political weak spot for him. Consequently, Beck came close to convincing the government to underwrite one of his more risky pet projects: an all-electric "radial" railway system that would branch out from Toronto in all directions, like spokes in a wheel. The radial system would be the perfect vehicle to use up Hydro's surplus electricity.

Although Beck estimated the radial system's cost at a mere $30 million, a provincial royal commission pegged the price at closer to $45 million—a grand price for any project in its day. Beck's plan was largely derailed by World War I and the need to restrain spending in support of the war effort. During the same period, the province's system of roadways improved, making the introduction of an inter-city electric railway system less feasible, given the mass introduction of automobiles and trucks. But the fact that such a grand plan could be seriously considered by the government testified to the depth and reach of Beck's powers.

Beck was diagnosed with pernicious anaemia in March 1925. He was given only six months to live. It is reported he took the doctor's diagnosis with "outraged indignation." Being the caesar that he was, Beck only seemed capable of perceiving death as another obstacle to be overcome. He had wrestled away the gift of Prometheus from the political gods and had used it to light and heat Ontario. He had subverted the democratic process with impunity. Why then could he not stare down the Pale Horse, wave it away, and just keep moving toward his destiny? But it was not to be. According to his friends gathered at his death bed, Beck's only regret at the end was that he "had hoped to forge a band of iron around the Hydro to prevent its destruction by the politicians."

Beck had been a harsh deity with huge defects in character, sparked no doubt by his need to see power—real potency, not just electricity —in his hands. To Merrill Denison in *The People's Power*, looking back at Beck from the less critical time of 1960, he "was the most formidable egoist in an entire roster of Canada's great men: opinionated, intolerant and violently irascible. Ruthless to his enemies, he treated even his best friends as expendable, when necessary to further public ownership's greater good."

Beck reviled the democratic process because it was not businesslike enough for him. In an act that would perhaps make J. Edgar Hoover smile, he once hired private detectives to sleuth for him in his propaganda war with politicians, part of what he called his "eternal vigilance" program. He loathed politicians, yet he was one for most of his life, and he never hesitated to use the political system to achieve the ends he sought. He could never see the paradox: His defence of public power was a constant battle with the public's democratically elected representatives.

But in the end, if one strips away the arguments over the theology of power and the dangers we suffer when it rests in the wrong hands, Adam Beck may have been right more times than we would like to admit. He was right in claiming electricity was too valuable to be left solely in the hands of private interests. He was right in assuming those private hands would never reach out into the intimidating ether of the financial risk and take giant gambles that would help build a province.

He was right in building a publicly owned monopoly to generate and dispense electricity at the lowest possible cost. He was right in thinking public power would make Ontario rich beyond nineteenth-century expectations—a province to lead a nation, both rich in natural and human resources. He was right in saying that a great province had to take great risks in the public interest, if its people were all to benefit and succeed. Perhaps he was even right in playing the game he did in the manner that he did—arrogant, sometimes cruel, unyielding, but always in defence of public power.

As biographer William R. Plewman wrote in *Adam Beck and the Ontario Hydro*: "He was a hard man and sometimes brutal. He was anything but pleasant in a number of his personal contacts. But let this be said to his everlasting credit that a man of greater refinement and tenderness could not have mastered the alliance between predatory interests and pliant politicians and given Ontario the cheapest hydro-electric power in the world and the greatest publicly owned power system."

"When Sir Adam Beck died in 1925, he bequeathed an institution of incredible size, power and technical mastery," Paul McKay wrote in *Electric Empire*. "Its construction projects were having a major impact on the provincial economy. It was expanding at breakneck speed, with no end in sight. Electricity already served about two-thirds of Ontario's citizens and was rapidly transforming the social, cultural and economic life of the province."

Beck's legacy continued to frustrate politicians who tried to get a handle on Ontario Hydro, even after his death. It had a maddening quality of keeping them at bay. Surpluses of electricity were the politician's headache during the 1920s. By the end of the decade the utility was warning the government that the surpluses could turn into shortages. Then during the Great Depression, with Hydro faithfully forecasting the seven percent annual growth formula, the utility was caught again with surplus electricity.

The period between Beck's passing and the election of the Progressive Conservatives led by George Drew in 1943 was a troublesome time at Hydro. Yet, little of the fighting with politicians or the pompous performance of the commissioners and management did anything to mar the corporation's status with most ratepayers. The tone of that relationship seemed to be one of unending gratitude from the ratepayers. What served to lessen the acrimony and combat between Hydro and the legislature by the mid-1940s was the recognition by the politicians that, the odd dust-up aside, there were more political benefits to be had by being closely identified with this revered public utility than there were costs. "Hydro was the embodiment of the public good," Neil Freeman wrote in *The Politics of Power*, "bringing electricity to the people, bringing it to them cheaply so they could use it and make life easier ... and the government was doing good by facilitating [this]."

Ontario Hydro began riding an even larger wave of public appreciation in the 1950s. Now moving in lock-step with the expansive plans of the Drew government, the corporation began building massive new generating stations throughout the province, bringing the marvels of inexpensive electricity to the furthest reaches of its rural empire. Its presence, in the form of new power lines, a new dam, perhaps a newly arrived service vehicle, seemed to promise comfort and modernization. Hydro and its services became the embodiment of progress. Nothing seemed beyond Ontario Hydro's mastery or capability. The people's power machine spurred massive economic growth and stayed comfortably ahead of growing demand.

The 1950s was a time of huge capital expansion in hydro-electric power—on the Ottawa River, the St. Lawrence River, even the re-development of Niagara Falls, with construction of Sir Adam Beck–Niagara #1 and #2 generating stations. Peak electricity capacity reached 3.3 million kilowatts in 1952—an increase of seventy-three percent from 1945. But by the late 1950s, Hydro was beginning to run out of accessible, southern rivers to harness. The nature of the demand for electricity began to change as well.

Non-residential demand began to shift from the industrial sector to the commercial sector (businesses, offices, schools, hospitals, universities and government offices), putting more pressure on planners' forecasts. But more importantly, as Ontario Hydro's prestige was arching toward a new apogee of public appreciation, a number of forces began to converge that would turn the next forty years into a series of graphic spikes—from apogee to perigee—in public appreciation.

"It was in 1958 that a couple of important events happened at the same time," says Energy Probe's Tom Adams. "One was the completion of the Robert H. Saunders dam on the St. Lawrence near Cornwall. It was the last of the very large-scale hydro-electric facilities in southern Ontario. It represented the end to what economists call the declining marginal cost curve. So economies of scale for the power system at large were reached in 1958, and incremental sources of supply were now going to have higher costs."

Coincidental with the completion of the Saunders generating facility was the completion of the Trans-Canada Pipeline and the arrival of seemingly infinite quantities of cheap Alberta natural gas in southern Ontario. That cheaper gas replaced oil as the new, robust competitor for hydro-electric power. "Hydro panicked in 1958," says Adams, "and their response was to try to protect their market share. That turned out to be a crucial mistake because they failed to understand they had hit the bottom of the declining marginal cost curve and were now facing increasing marginal costs with coal and nuclear in the future."

Ontario Hydro made the fateful decision to fight for market share by encouraging consumers to use more electricity than ever. They would ignore the real cost of electrical power by discounting price and driving up demand for electricity in an expensive and almost surreal spin they later could not control. It was a strange decision, indeed. It would eventually prove to be one of the most damaging decisions, in the long term, the public utility ever made.

The utility would turn back the threat of competition from natural gas with an aggressive new marketing program that would be called—quite ironically—"Live Better Electrically." This ill-advised strategic decision would eventually cost billions of dollars for the extra generating capacity it triggered, and it would add massive amounts of debt to the utility's books. It would also distort for decades real consumer demand for electricity—as well as its true costs and benefits.

"Many Ontarians still remember the Live Better Electrically slogan as an extravagant but harmless promotional campaign that overplayed the lifestyle themes of convenience and conspicuous consumption," Paul McKay wrote, "In fact ... the campaign had almost nothing to do with meeting public needs ... it was the visible part of a bitter civil war over energy." The battle between electricity and gas took place not just in Ontario, but in a number of other provinces, too. It would turn out to be terribly wasteful. Electricity consumption would triple in Ontario by the mid-1970s. The ratio of electrically heated homes in the province would rise to one in four. It was a wholly artificial manipulation of consumer demand that, as McKay put it, "catapulted Ontario Hydro into the most precipitous, expensive and technologically speculative construction in its history."

In many respects, natural gas was a substantially cheaper source of power than electricity. This was especially true where water heating was concerned. Electricity for heating water in the home was the largest single source of revenue for the municipal utilities which bought the electricity from Ontario Hydro and re-sold it to the consumer. But physicist Amory Hovins would later compare heating water with electricity to "cutting butter with a chain saw." Electric ranges were another weak spot for the utilities. Cooking with a gas range was cheaper than cooking with electricity. With the possibility that a large part of its electric empire might be in imminent danger, Hydro fought back tenaciously and recklessly.

It took full advantage of its monopoly position to reach, by direct mail, nearly every household in the province. Hydro never hesitated to use public funds for "marketing" reasons. This extravagant promotional campaign received support from the province's many municipal utilities, who would see their revenues climb with increased demand, and from electrical manufacturing firms like Canadian General Electric and Westinghouse, who would realize substantial profits from the increased market for appliances and electric conveniences.

Hydro was gambling that increasing demand for electricity would not only guarantee jackpot revenues but would also tie the consumer more tightly to electricity use, thus blocking natural gas competitors from making inroads into their market. Hydro encouraged contractors to build thousands of electrically heated homes that used up to five times the power of standard homes. It held endless sales promotions and drives to sell more refrigerators, dryers, freezers and other electrical appliances.

These were the days of Betty Furness—the Lady from Westinghouse. The former ingenue, with three dozen B movies to her credit and a career going nowhere, was suddenly thrust into the commercial spotlight by the Live Better Electrically euphoria. She became a North American TV icon, peddling refrigerators, freezers, stoves and any form of electrical appliance Westinghouse could attach to its logo.

By 1960 the average electricity-consuming home owner had access to a surprising array of appliances—even by today's standards. And still the advertising blitz continued. Appliances were given away free of charge to schools for home economics classrooms. Cut-rate appliance sales appeared in local furniture and appliance outlets. News releases were churned out by the tens of thousands, championing the benefits of electricity. Appliance and furniture stores were plastered with "Live Better Electrically" slogans and symbols. There were even Live Better Electrically bumper stickers, badges, pens and plastic measuring spoons.

For years, the campaign took on a momentum that exceeded even the marketing department's growth projections. Not just Ontario but most of the country came to believe that, first, electricity would always be an unbelievable bargain for consumers and, second, maximizing the use of electricity was "a modern thing to do."

However, as consumer demand seemed to shoot straight up and off the sales and marketing graphs, Ontario Hydro would be forced—by its own hand—to build new, more expensive generating capacity, transmission lines, facilities and distribution systems to try to keep up. The provincial utility now faced a major problem. As high as revenues climbed, they could not cover their costs of constructing new generating capacity to meet the very demand growth the utility had triggered.

For a time, Ontario Hydro began to defy the economic laws of supply and demand, if not gravity. New generating capacity came on stream as fast as Hydro could build the plants, usually powered by more expensive coal. Strangely enough, Ontario Hydro did not raise rates appreciably between 1954 and 1967. In 1961 the utility actually reduced them as further incentive to Live Better Electrically. In fact, throughout this period of concocted demand the price of electricity was actually declining, in consumer price index terms. Ontario Hydro's decision to not increase the price of electricity was either a magnificent example of management incompetence or public malfeasance, or, as McKay put it, "a clear decision to postpone reality."

Ontario Hydro was caught within its own web of competitive aspirations. The spiral of market share competition with natural gas kept driving demand higher and higher, while revenues fell further and further behind. This bizarre game of encouraging maximum consumption seemed to be driven by two grotesque corporate motivations. First, that never-ending, exponential consumer demand for electricity (and the extra revenues that might come with it) would guarantee that the generation or supply of electricity would parallel economic growth. Second, should that assumption be incorrect and should things get dicey on the supply side (blackouts began appearing on Ontario Hydro's system during peak winter hours in the mid-1960s), there was always the option to burn more coal to make more electricity, or to start making use of that miraculous nuclear option lurking ominously just beyond the horizon.

As early as 1952 discussions were held between Ontario Hydro, the Conservative government of Leslie Frost and the federal Atomic Energy Control Board about the possibility of working together to develop nuclear power on a commercial basis by 1962. The board and management of Ontario Hydro had, at first, been reluctant to get into the nuclear power generating business. It was still a new and untried technology in the 1950s. There were many fanciful thoughts about its future uses—from nuclear power "pills" that could be used to fly airplanes or power ships endlessly, to the somewhat credulous belief that power from the atom was not only "free as the air," it would also probably be "too cheap to meter."

"In hindsight, the fifties and sixties were a period of incredible hysteria," according to Energy Probe's Tom Adams. "This is the era of 'the atomic cafe.' Fanciful, absurd things were being written about 'nuclear nirvana'—nuclear cars, nuclear airplanes, nuclear toasters. Having nuclear reactors was just part of the dream."

At the time, coal-fired generation was still the number one alternative after hydro power. But nuclear did appear to promise those important long-term power characteristics—high initial capital cost but low operating cost. In addition, the federal government had been pressing through its new nuclear agency—Atomic Energy of Canada Ltd. (AECL)—for Ontario to become the development site for CANDU technology. If nuclear energy could be successfully introduced into Ontario, it would greatly aid AECL in marketing its nuclear power technology internationally.

The pressure to build commercially viable nuclear reactors was intense. So much so that, according to Adams, Ontario Hydro would end up being "dragged more or less kicking and screaming into the nuclear era." Canadian research into nuclear reactors had begun at Chalk River, Ontario, during World War II. When the war ended, Canada had some nuclear technology but no place to apply it. It was not in the arms business, like the United States, Britain and the USSR. So it was decided that commercial and industrial uses were the most logical alternative. The federal government established AECL in 1952 with the express purpose of building a nuclear reactor that could heat water, create steam and thus drive a turbine to generate electricity. In effect, a CANDU reactor, as we now know, is little more than an expensive way—and, to many, an extremely dangerous way as well—to boil water.

The CANDU reactor (CANDU is short for Canadian Deuterium-Uranium) differed from other nuclear technology in that it was powered by natural uranium rather than enriched uranium. CANDU technology used heavy water to moderate the atomic reaction and act as a coolant. Unlike other forms of nuclear technology, it allowed for refuelling without having to shut down the reactors. Still, it was a raw, unproven technology. Even though the intention was to eventually market it to Third World countries, there were, at least initially, no buyers lining up to take advantage of Canada's offer to take home its heavily subsidized CANDU reactors.

Federal politicians at the highest level applied a full-court press on the province of Ontario to help them use Ontario as a showcase for CANDU technology. In 1954, Ontario Hydro joined with AECL to plan and build a twenty-megawatt nuclear demonstration project at Rolphton on the Ottawa River. Rolphton was not meant to be a commercial reactor. It was a prototype that tested the drawing board theories about CANDU technology. But before Rolphton was up and running, the decision was made in 1959 that, given steady increases in demand for electricity, it made sense to build a 200-megawatt nuclear facility at Douglas Point, on Lake Huron. The decision was made despite the troubles AECL was having with the untested Rolphton prototype.

"At the time, no one of importance wondered what sense it made to undertake a four-year project," Walter Stewart wrote in *Uneasy Lies the Head: The Truth About Canada's Crown Corporations,* "to check out the process and, while it was still in the early stages of construction, start building another project, ten times the size, on the assumption that the first one would pass muster."

Douglas Point "was a real headache," according to Energy Probe's Tom Adams. "Ontario Hydro could see it and they were very nervous about proceeding to the next step—building Pickering. From a business point of view, they thought coal plants were a much better deal." Essentially, the federal and provincial governments had to bribe Hydro by promising to pay two-thirds of the cost of construction of the Pickering units as an inducement to build. After those early years of caution and hesitation, Ontario Hydro would quickly and comfortably swing into nuclear step with the two levels of governments.

For a series of Ontario Conservative governments, the shift to nuclear-generated electricity would appear, for the moment, as an industrial and economic godsend. It meant Ontario could continue its robust post–World War II economic growth on the back of a glowing new technology. Nuclear energy held a terrific capacity for rekindling Ontario's now-lagging industrial development. These developments, both in research and in the construction of power generating facilities, would provide more jobs. The technical complexity of nuclear energy would also mean a need for higher skills and a better-educated workforce. Added to this was the whole new possibility of boosting generating capacity in quantum terms to meet the still booming demand.

There seemed no downside to the opportunities. At that time, in many quarters, nuclear energy was considered to be as safe and clean as hydro-electric power. Ontario would be able to keep providing "power at cost" and, at the same time, stimulate substantial hi-tech capital spending on reactors and heavy water.

This thirst for a new and larger nuclear motor to drive the provincial economy would certainly fill the demand gap, but it would be a costly venture in the long term. It would change the very nature of government spending and priorities, as well as the size, structure and indebtedness of Ontario Hydro. By the mid-1980s, Hydro's assets would make it the province's largest commercial institution after the country's five chartered banks. The electric utility would come to dominate government expenditures, representing three-quarters of all capital spending, and account for one hundred percent of the province's debt.

"Through its adoption of nuclear power on a large scale [Ontario Hydro] no longer acted as merely a passive agent of economic growth," Neil Freeman wrote in *The Politics of Power*, "but assumed a lead role in promoting the Canadian nuclear industry and Ontario uranium over technology and resources from other jurisdictions." By 1964, Ontario Hydro had set off on one of the largest capital expansion programs in Ontario's history. Pickering was now on the drawing boards, and by 1968 the belief within Ontario Hydro was that large-scale nuclear plants could provide power cheaper than fossil-fuelled generation, perhaps even cheaper than hydro-electric power from more remote areas of the province. Ontario Hydro's initial nervousness about nuclear energy had been overcome and, as chairman George Gathercole put it in the corporation's 1968 annual report, nuclear power represented the "advancement of a new industry in Canada with broad implications for the whole national economy."

What was good for Ontario Hydro was good for Ontario. And what was good for Ontario was good for the country. But the questionable burden of nuclear leadership had not been lifted as easily as it might appear. The foundations for the application of this magnificent new energy source were far from being fail-safe.

Even before Douglas Point was completed in 1964, Ontario Hydro announced it would use what had been learned to date to build the grand Pickering nuclear-generating station. This was a major step forward. Pickering would provide over four thousand megawatts of badly needed electrical power. It was a massive leap of both faith and technology.

To this point, Canada had yet to produce a single commercial kilowatt of electricity from nuclear power. Billions of dollars would be committed to Pickering, partly on the science available at the time and partly on the hope that it would work as the plans on the drawing board indicated.

But this kind of "technical leapfrogging," as McKay put it in *Electric Empire*, was not based on established scientific practice or proven engineering experience. Instead, it proved to be a highly risky way—a sort of nuclear fast-tracking—of getting into the expensive and hazardous world of nuclear-generated power. Leapfrogging the technology also contributed to the huge cost over-runs and rapid deterioration of Ontario Hydro's plans for the long-term nuclear future. Douglas Point was intended to cost $13.5 million. It cost $81.5 million and was mothballed after seventeen years of spotty performance. Pickering would be taken out of service in 1983 after problems with pressure tubes, causing a spill of one thousand litres of heavy water containing lethal tritium. This would lead to a three-year shutdown and almost one billion dollars in repairs.

Ontario Hydro's reluctance to wait for completion at Rolphton or Douglas Point to ensure that the technology was reliable and safe was understandable for the time. They were "motivated more by a sense of panic," as McKay writes. This sense of urgency, driven by the need to dramatically increase electricity output as well as continuing the province's dream of ratchetting up the economy through massive nuclear-development projects, would result in basic design flaws in the reactors that "would come back to haunt Hydro within the decade."

As late as 1969, Hydro executive management was still saying that there was no reason to suppose that demand would fall short of the long-term trend of the past fifty years. It was still believed that demand would continue to double each decade. And nuclear power could be depended upon to keep costs down and provide the needed excess electrical capacity for the future.

The mammoth utility seemed to have been infected by a capital version of Mad Cow Disease. There was no limit to the billions of dollars it was now prepared to spend on nuclear development and generation. It was not long before management and planners were projecting Ontario Hydro would need at least one hundred nuclear reactors by the turn of the century. Chairman George Gathercole predicted in 1969 that the number of reactors needed by Ontario Hydro might reach 160 at the millennium.

Yet, by the early 1970s, Ontario had all but reached appliance saturation. One in four homes was now heated electrically. Two decades of appliance shopping had left consumers sated with electric hair dryers, kettles, toaster ovens, can openers and curling irons. The OPEC embargo, along with its impending oil price shock, was just around the corner. And still Ontario Hydro board and management could not erase the idea from their minds that the rolling consumer demand of the last twenty-five years would just continue forever. Opposing this assumption was like arguing that there was no law of gravity.

In 1974, Hydro's board of directors drafted a plan calling for nine new provincial "energy centres." Sprinkled along Ontario's side of the Great Lakes, these centres would each house up to two dozen nuclear generating units the size of the Pickering plant. This output would be in addition to the new capacity already on the drawing board, meant to carry Ontario to the year 2000. There was also talk of adding a new coal-fired or nuclear plant every three to four *months* just to keep up with anticipated demand for electricity. Nowhere in all these forecasts was there much discussion about conservation—or the fact that the market for electricity could turn down instead of ever upward.

But even before the OPEC cartel turned the world's energy expectations upside down in 1973, chickens were starting to come home to roost. Electricity rates had been edging up ever so slightly since the late-1960s, quite logically, to begin paying for capital expansion. In 1969, rates increased 4.5 percent for the average home owner, but they were pegged higher for municipal utilities and large industrial and commercial users. When rates jumped another six percent in 1970, it set off a public backlash. Ontario Hydro responded that, given the huge bills for nuclear plant construction, all ratepayers could expect "large annual rate increases" for some time to come.

Even then, with evidence indicating consumer demand growth was falling, Ontario Hydro was still predicting that load growth might go to about 88,000 megawatts by the end of the century. The difference between what was estimated and the demand for electricity that eventually transpired in 1997—less than 30,000 megawatts—would have necessitated, it was once estimated, construction of sixteen more plants the size of Darlington. Had Ontario Hydro been allowed to act on those predictions, the bill for the sixteen Darlingtons could have rounded off at about $100 billion.

A substantial part of the impetus for dramatically expanding capacity came from Ontario's large industrial users. Many large industries were concerned that the cheap and reliable power they were receiving might someday run out. They were hearing the same forecasts about the future need for expensive new generating facilities to be built, and they helped keep the pressure on. They encouraged Ontario Hydro and the provincial government to keep aiming for those expensive supply-side stars.

Even today, many of the province's major industrial users will admit they were a part of the forecasting problem. "I absolutely agree that we, the government, hydro, the economists all had the projections wrong," says Arthur Dickinson, executive director of the Association of Major Power Consumers of Ontario. "That's a fair criticism. At the time there was great concern that we wouldn't have enough supply, and if you haven't got enough supply you can't run your plants, you can't expand. We were wrong. I think a lot of people were wrong."

Ironically, now that Ontario Hydro is saddled with surplus electricity and heavy long-term debt, the refrain from the industrial-user side is that they need cheaper electricity prices to remain competitive in the continental marketplace. It is argued that while Ontario Hydro rates have remained relatively flat the past few years, rates for their U.S. competitors have dropped twenty to thirty percent. But one of the major reasons for Ontario Hydro's current rates being uncompetitive is, of course, that all those bills for constructing too much generating capacity still have to be paid.

Although the William Davis government—and other Progressive Conservative governments before it—had sanctioned Ontario Hydro's ambitious plans, the issues had by 1975 become serious enough to appoint a royal commission on electric power planning to be chaired by Dr. Arthur Porter. At almost the same time, Ontario Hydro proposed that its electricity rates for 1976 be increased by thirty percent. The proposed rate increase was pared down to twenty-two percent by a legislative committee. But the committee raised some serious questions about how Ontario Hydro was arriving at its growth projections.

Again, Ontario Hydro seemed out of control. It was now a major political problem for the government. In January 1976 the Davis government did something no other government had ever done to the giant utility. It threatened to withhold its debt guarantees if the utility did not start using a different growth measuring stick and trim its expansion plans from seven to at least five percent a year. An interim report of the Porter Commission claimed it would be more accurate to use four percent as an annual growth figure. The commission also claimed the provincial utility was making a huge mistake by relying on large-scale nuclear plants for adding new capacity.

Nevertheless, in July 1977 the Davis cabinet approved the proposal to build the Darlington nuclear generating plant. A different set of reasoning tools was now being used. The Darlington decision was only partly a decision about future electricity capacity. At this point, it was estimated that Ontario Hydro was priming the province's economic pump to the tune of $1.5 billion in direct annual spending. Despite the controversial evidence about future demand growth, the government was not willing to bring that kind of economic stimulus to a halt.

Ontario Hydro was no longer just a very large electrical utility. It was *the* major instrument of economic development. It was like a giant construction company. Its financial movements sent shock waves through the economy. On occasion, its spending clout was strong enough to stem the tide of recession or spur the province's growth. It was a throttle for wealth. A long parade of provincial politicians understood this and had been more than willing to provide the utility with new objectives and terms of reference. The big decisions were no longer electricity decisions. They were now economic, social and political decisions. And they were now most often made, as political scientist Neil Freeman put it, "in the Premier's office."

Ontario's rush to nuclear power expansion also compelled the utility—with the support of the Progressive Conservative government—to enter contracts for fuel that were so costly and scandalous that by 1990, Ontario Hydro would be paying seven times the going price for uranium.

Driven by the nuclear imperative it had helped set in motion, Ontario Hydro began to search in the early 1970s for contracts to provide the utility with long-term supplies of uranium to feed its investment in nuclear reactors. At roughly the same time, the price and supply of uranium around the world were being manipulated by a cartel of suppliers that included Canada's Denison and Rio Algom Mines, located in Elliot Lake, Ontario. Ontario Hydro was looking to buy as much as two hundred million pounds over a thirty-year period, meaning a contract signed while cartel pricing was in effect could cost over $15 billion. Hydro was caught in an expensive bind. In 1973 the utility had already committed to moving ahead with another $10 billion in nuclear facilities and heavy-water plants. This was not the time to be shopping for fuel.

The per-pound price of uranium at this point was so high that Ontario Hydro planners proposed the utility simply buy the Elliot Lake mines, in particular the Denison Mine, owned by Stephen Roman. The plan might have saved Ontario taxpayers as much as $5 billion, but the government turned the idea down. Roman, in particular, played hardball, driving up his price and demanding massive concessions.

Premier Davis's personal intervention, and his decision to overrule the recommendations of an all-party select committee of the Ontario legislature looking into the proposed uranium contracts, "led Ontario Hydro into the most disastrous deal in its history," according to Paul McKay in *The Roman Empire: The Unauthorized Life and Times of Stephen Roman*. In the end, Denison and Rio Algom would realize windfall contracts "unprecedented" in the history of the world uranium industry.

According to McKay, "[o]nly weeks before the price of uranium began a decade-long descent, Ontario premier Bill Davis ... authorized Hydro to sign a thirty-year contract to buy 126 million pounds of uranium from Denison, and a second 72-million-pound deal with Rio Algom. The contracts were valued at $7.4 billion in 1978, and promised the two companies a minimum profit of $2.2 billion." By 1985 Ontario Hydro would be paying $90 a pound for uranium from Elliot Lake, while the rest of the world would be paying roughly $20 a pound on average. By 1990, Ontario Hydro's price would be $70 a pound and the world price about $10 a pound.

But Davis and his government had no way of knowing that the price of uranium was being manipulated by the cartel. And none of the cartel conspirators, including Stephen Roman, as McKay put it, "were about to tell Davis otherwise." The cartel's price fixing would not be discovered until after the contracts were signed in February 1978. The cartel was so effective that at one point it looked like the frantic activity on the world market might drive the price of uranium as high as $100 a pound.

The Porter Commission's recommendation that Ontario Hydro should be looking at more flexibility in power production, and quit relying on expensive nuclear generating facilities, received a boost in March 1979 when a serious nuclear accident occurred at Three Mile Island near Harrisburg, Pennsylvania. Design faults, coupled with human error, produced the threat of a meltdown. A catastrophe was averted, but the incident sparked public fears about nuclear safety and cast serious doubts on the future of nuclear-powered electricity generation.

But the expansion drug was a hard one to kick for Ontario Hydro. Even the now-menacing "nuclear question" did not seem to have that much of an effect on the planning process. As late as 1981, Ontario Hydro still called for the construction of two more Darlington-sized nuclear generating plants. By the time serious deliberations began, the nation was in the midst of a serious recession. Electricity demand plummeted. And the onset of a troubling series of accidents and reactor problems began to cool what ardour Ontarians might have left for nuclear-power expansion.

In 1983, two Pickering reactors began having nasty radioactive problems. Shortly afterwards, Douglas Point sprouted a leak of 2,700 litres of heavy water. In October, the Bruce station started leaking, forcing a shutdown. A second Bruce unit shut down because of an electrical fire shortly after that. In February 1984, a third Bruce unit was forced to shut down because of the failure of a $7 switch. In May, Hydro was forced to shut down a fourth reactor at Pickering, which had only been back in service for a few months.

The days of Ontario Hydro's nuclear program seemed decidedly numbered, but there remained a strange, dogmatic stubbornness to the utility's sense of purpose. The board and management seemed still to believe in numbers that other people had already dismissed. When environmental hearings were announced in 1989, the utility was still intent on pursuing the construction of three more nuclear generating stations, as well as two coal-powered facilities.

But the January 1993 announcement that Ontario Hydro had asked that the hearings be cancelled, because it no longer needed the new generating stations it proposed building, signalled that the three-decade megaproject binge was over. It would turn out that by 1997, when Canada would be awash in electricity surpluses, only twenty-two commercial reactors would be in place across the country— twenty in Ontario, and one each in Quebec and New Brunswick. In hindsight, Ontario Hydro's past projection that as many as 160 reactors might be needed for Ontario by the turn of the century seemed to have been off by a degree or two.

Beyond their costly technical problems, the reactors' expected lifetimes would dwindle to half that of the original estimates. Ontario's nuclear program would end up costing more than $30 billion, not taking into account the future cost of disposing of nuclear waste and the cost of plant decommissioning. According to reports, Hydro's nuclear-power generating program would, in the end, produce only about $18 billion worth of power. The cost to the taxpayer if these assets were eventually to be "stranded" was estimated to be $16 billion.

By the end of 1996 Ontario Hydro announced it was taking a special one-time charge of $2.5 billion to write off surplus assets, mainly related to its poorly performing nuclear division. Included in the write-off was a $250 million charge for the early closing of the Bruce A unit 1 reactor, the second one to be mothballed. The unit originally had a designed life of forty years but was being shut down after twenty-three years of operation because it was not worth the money to retube the reactor. The 1996 write-down of nuclear-related assets resulted in a net loss of $1.9 billion for Ontario Hydro's current fiscal year.

It goes without saying that this is not what Adam Beck had in mind a hundred years ago when he began pledging that Ontario would be provided with "power at cost."

5 / Maîtres Chez Nous

How come you want to dam our river? Don't you have enough electricity? When you go south you see glamorous lights every-where. Even at night it's like daytime.

— elderly Cree woman speaking during a meeting on the
Great Whale project with Hydro-Québec representatives,
in the National Film Board documentary, *Power*

ON NOVEMBER 18, 1994, Quebec Premier Jacques Parizeau put the $13 billion Great Whale hydro-electric development on hold indefinitely. Quebec, he said, no longer needed the costly megaproject. Great Whale was going to be the second of three phases of construction in completing the province's James Bay power development project.

Great Whale would have added an extra ten percent to Hydro-Québec's generating capacity, or roughly 3,200 megawatts. Construction of Great Whale's three generating stations was to have begun in 1996. It would have been completed in 2005. The project also would have flooded nearly 2,400 square kilometres of land and shoreline in northwestern Quebec.

Hydro-Québec's feasibility study indicated the roughly 500 Cree and 450 Inuit who inhabited the area planned for Great Whale would have had to adjust their fish-eating habits to avoid developing mercury poisoning. The report downplayed the problem of methylmercury poisoning somewhat, pointing out that it was a temporary phenomenon manageable over twenty to thirty years if the native people were careful of what they ate.

Parizeau's announcement marked the first serious pause in the march of Quebec's power juggernaut. It came at a time when the entire continent was beginning to re-evaluate the role of, effectiveness of and wonderment over electrical-power megaprojects. And it said that those dreams about tens of thousands of jobs, renewed economic might and the people of Quebec finally achieving the goal of being masters in their own house, thanks to the heft and might of Hydro-Québec, would be put on ice for a time.

Jacques Parizeau claimed he shelved Great Whale because a federal-provincial report had found serious flaws in Hydro-Québec's environmental-impact study of the second stage of the James Bay Project. But the real reasons for Parizeau calling a halt to almost a quarter-century of billion-dollar spending and grand dreams of building Hydro-Québec into a continental power giant were more complex than that.

Export sales of electricity to the northeastern United States had been dropping dramatically. In large part, this was due to the public-relations efforts of Cree and Inuit activists. They had worked hard to convince American buyers that the cost of Great Whale—to their lifestyles, to their economy and to an environment they had inhabited for centuries—was just too high. A number of state governments and their power authorities had been moved by the plight of the Cree and Inuit.

In 1992, New York had cancelled a contract worth as much as $17 billion it signed with Quebec in 1989 to supply the state with 1,000 megawatts of power between 1995 and 2015. In the spring of 1994, the New York Power Authority cancelled a $5 billion contract with the Quebec power utility. Also in 1994, Consolidated Edison Co. of New York had cancelled a $2 billion substitute contract for the delivery of Quebec power.

The decisions to cancel contracts were made partly because of the negative impact Great Whale would have on native peoples and partly because the price of electricity was falling and many states did not want to be locked into expensive, long-term contracts.

Other factors were coming into play as well. Energy demand was falling in New York and the New England states, thanks largely to conservation efforts and the lingering effects of an economic recession. Alternative fuels, such as gas-fired generation, were becoming cheaper to use, partly due to intense competition for electrical consumers. But just as readily, many people, Quebecers among them, were beginning to question the economic wisdom of what the province and its public power utility had been doing to the wilderness of northern Quebec. Some people were beginning to think that the effort to equate cultural and economic sovereignty with the growth of James Bay power had started to look like a monumental waste of money.

When Premier Robert Bourassa unveiled his plans for the James Bay Power Project in 1971, it was considered by the premier and his government to be the "construction project of the century." It was to be "the key to the political stability" of the province. It was a political and development opportunity just too golden to pass up. In Bourassa's eyes, all that water and wilderness was just sitting there doing nothing. In his 1985 book, *Power From the North*, he declared northern Quebec as simply a vast hydro-electric project-in-the-bud, where every day millions of potential kilowatt hours flowed downhill and out to the seas. He considered this a tremendous lost opportunity.

The plan Bourassa would begin sketching shortly after the Liberals' 1970 election victory seemed to have no restraints, no definable limits. The more it was talked about, the larger it grew. It became a scheme so immense in scope and impact that it probably rivalled Mao's 1958 Great Leap Forward as an industrial strategy. Some might say it contained, at least in the formative stage, about the same degree of attention to detail.

Bourassa wanted to harness the waters of this vast wilderness and boost Hydro-Québec's electrical generating capacity eight times over. The chief target for this massive increase in capacity was the province's export market, primarily the northeastern United States. Bourassa wanted to expand electricity exports, as a percentage of total capacity, from 1.5 to as much as fifteen percent. The magnificent electricity excess provided by this "project of the century" would also offer a safe margin for future use within Quebec. Bourassa expected domestic demand to rise by as much as forty percent by 2006, calling for at least eight thousand more megawatts by that time. In that sense, the James Bay Power Project would also act as a major lever for industrial development within Quebec. It would provide inexpensive electricity for a variety of aluminum and magnesium smelters planned for sites along the St. Lawrence River. Bourassa hoped the end result would be at least fifteen thousand new jobs in Quebec.

By 1994, Hydro-Québec had spent close to $25 billion on the James Bay Project. Estimates for its three-stage completion were now as high as $60 billion. The initial La Grande portion of the project was a mind-numbing litany of statistics. It took thirteen years to complete. It cost more than $16 billion when all related costs were factored in. Enough rock and soil fill was used to build the dams and dikes to equal eighty versions of the Great Pyramid of Cheops. The reservoirs the dams produced cover an area equivalent to half of Lake Ontario. The sixteen turbines of the mighty La Grande 2 dam, buried 150 metres below the water's surface, would be capable of generating enough power to boost fifty Boeing 747s into the air at takeoff.

The La Grande dam structure is almost three kilometres long and is a kilometre thick at the base. It stands higher than a fifty-storey building. The project took 150 million man-hours to build. Sixty-eight workers died in construction accidents. When completed, the three main dams—La Grande 2, 3 and 4—would provide enough electricity to power a city of four million inhabitants. And this was all only the start of Bourassa's vast electric dream.

His vision for a completed James Bay Power Project was not a timid one. Breathtaking might be a more appropriate term. When finished, it was expected that the James Bay Power Project would provide Quebec with 27,000 new megawatts of electricity—only about 3,000 megawatts short of Ontario Hydro's total capacity. La Grande's "baby sister," La Grande 2-A, would eventually generate 2,000 megawatts, more than equalling the electricity generated by all Quebec's fossil-fuelled generators, and its lone nuclear facility, combined. That one facility alone would be able to provide enough electricity to power seven hundred shopping malls of one hundred stores each.

As many as thirty dams and five hundred secondary dikes would plug all but one of the twenty mightiest rivers flowing into James Bay, draining a tract of land two-thirds the size of France and creating a mass of water equal in size to the state of Montana. The spillway for La Grande 2-A, blasted out of sheer granite, would eventually carry a flow of water equal to the flow of all the rivers in Europe. Hydro-Québec engineers would begin changing the very nature of how water had flowed in northern Quebec since creation. The flow of one powerful river, the Caniapiscau, would be reversed from northeast into Ungava Bay to the west into James Bay.

"The James Bay project is one of the largest energy projects ever," wrote geophysicist Sean McCutcheon in *Electric Rivers: The Story of the James Bay Project*. "It is no mere megaproject. 'Mega' denotes only a million, but the magnitude of this project is measured in billions of watts and dollars. 'Giga' denotes a billion. This is a gigaproject."

The development and construction activity in the James Bay region would create at least five new towns—complete with airports and recreation facilities—out of the wilderness. More than seven thousand kilometres of transmission lines would be needed to deliver the power to southern Quebec. More than 1.6 million tons of fuel would be consumed during the construction phase. The total cost for powerhouses, dikes, transmission lines, roads, towns and airports would rough out on the drawing boards at $60 billion.

This was a far cry from the original cost estimates. In 1970–71, the La Grande portion of the project was supposed to cost less than $6 billion. Ultimately, it would be triple that. But cost seemed no object for Bourassa, the Grand Helmsman. Six billion or $60 billion; it all seemed a pittance. Bourassa was so entranced with the mystical economic and cultural possibilities of power development that the process was begun without a precise feasibility, environmental or social impact study. It was said that planning began without even a detailed map of the region in which the project was to be undertaken.

Bourassa's vision seemed so unchecked by reality that he also advocated a project—called his "Grand Vision"—that would have eventually seen Quebec construct a 160-kilometre dam across the northern end of James Bay. It would presumably turn the lower portion of Hudson Bay into a mammoth freshwater reservoir. It was acknowledged that this grand scheme might take decades to complete. Its cost was guessed at a $100 billion. But the contents of this enormous artificial lake of freshwater—approximating the size of Lake Superior—could then be sold, Bourassa reckoned, to eager customers in the arid U.S. Southwest and Great Plains regions.

When the planning wheels for the James Bay Power Project began to turn in 1971, few native inhabitants of the James Bay region would express concern. A few of the roughly five thousand Cree and thirty-five hundred Inuit would read about Bourassa's scheme in three-day-old newspapers. Some heard it over the radio. Neither the Bourassa government nor Hydro-Québec would make any serious prior effort to consult with the native people living, as they had for centuries, in northwestern Quebec.

It would take native leaders about a year to properly digest the news and begin taking legal action to try to stop the project. By then it was too late. The fire-that-shakes-the-land, or *nimischiiuskutaau*, as the Cree call electricity, was coming. The beauty of Bourassa's vision was that there appeared to be no political downside; all that power, all those jobs, all those contented American electricity customers. Who was the James Bay Project going to hurt? A bunch of Indians? "The project," McCutcheon wrote, "was going ahead no matter what the Indians wanted."

Flooding would drive the Cree from the land and destroy their traditional hunting, fishing and trapping economy. In less than twenty years they would make the transition from a contented aboriginal lifestyle into a branch of modern, twentieth-century society with all its questionable benefits and afflictions: electric lights, TVs, VCRs, high rates of alcoholism and drug abuse, family violence, suicide and juvenile crime. It even took away their appetite for fresh fish.

After James Bay I was complete, high levels of methylmercury, a neurotoxin, were discovered in pike and lake trout. Concentrations were as high as five to six times normal levels, making it dangerous for the Cree to continue consuming one of the protein staples of their traditional diet.

Mercury, in an insoluble form, is commonly found in rocks throughout the Canadian Shield. But bacteria associated with decomposing organic matter, caused by the flooding of the reservoirs, converts mercury into methylmercury. It enters the food chain and reaches high concentrations in fish, like pike and trout, that prey on other fish. A 1984 survey of Cree living at the river's mouth found that more than sixty percent of the villagers had hazardous levels of mercury in their bodies.

But within a generation of the announcement heralding the start of the James Bay Project, Bourassa's majestic plan had deteriorated enormously, not unlike Chairman Mao's 1958 Great Leap Forward for the Chinese economy. Just as the Chinese never came anywhere close to their overstated goal of an industrial growth rate of twenty-five percent a year, Quebec's power utility was never able to live up to the overstated extremes of Bourassa's aspirations. It was a cultural disaster for native people. It was an environmental debacle, perhaps unmatched in Canadian history. And by the early 1990s it was also becoming, against all the grand plans and dreams Bourassa and his beloved Hydro-Québec could muster, a simmering debt disaster as well.

On October 27, 1979, Quebec taxpayers were allowed to pick up a $750,000 bill just for the ceremonies associated with the first-stage completion of a James Bay dam. The Parti Québécois (PQ) was now in power, but the enthusiasm for mega-spending had not dissipated with Bourassa's exit. Close to four hundred guests—Canadian and foreign—took part. There was a live television show, beamed via satellite to a number of francophone countries and featuring popular Quebec entertainers. Cost was no object for such a splendid occasion.

Although somewhat less fanatical in their quest for massive power development, the PQ had accepted that continuing Bourassa's quest was a worthwhile economic enterprise. To a party committed to independence, the James Bay Power Project could also be a valuable instrument for sovereignty. It could be visible evidence that an independent Quebec was quite capable of standing on its own, self-sufficient in capital, technical skills and hydro-electric power. As René Lévesque said during the ceremonies, with James Bay nearing completion and a referendum on independence only seven months away, "Quebec can now choose, in all serenity, its energy future as well as its political future."

During the intoxicating days of the mid-and late-1970s, Hydro-Québec was, not unlike its sister utility in Ontario, quite capable of ignoring evidence that rapid and continuous industrial growth was beginning to taper off, and with it, consumer demand for electricity. Throughout the decade Hydro-Québec planners inexplicably touted eight percent annual growth rates as the motivation for their capital expansion targets. As writer Peter Hadekel put it in a 1984 article in *Saturday Night* magazine: "Hydro-Québec was driving a Cadillac with the accelerator to the floor while the rest of the world had switched to compact cars."

In 1980 Hydro officials tempered their wildly inflated growth projections, but only a bit. Even with the minor adjustment, their best projections would still turn into a colossal planning mistake. That year, Hydro officials put together an ambitious ten-year development plan for stage two of the James Bay Power Project. They based their plan on annual growth rates for future electricity demand of six percent. But by 1982 energy consumption had actually contracted by one percent, and prospects for future years looked just as glum.

Hydro-Québec was suddenly stuck with enough surplus electricity to light a couple of cities the size of Montreal. But politically, it seemed impossible to put the brakes on their blueprint for new generating capacity. Given the dependence on James Bay as Quebec's economic panacea, any thought of cancelling the ambitious capital expansion plan could severely cripple the province's economy, bankrupting contractors and suppliers and throwing thousands of people out of work.

Hydro-Québec and its admiring political masters were stuck in a Hobson's Choice. Either stop the make-believe ferris wheel of James Bay's full-scale development, admit mistakes had been made, and watch the provincial economy go into the tank; or brave out this period of suppressed demand, let the debt pile up and pray for a return in consumer demand in the future.

And so, without a ready market for the surplus James Bay electricity now coming on stream, Hydro-Québec had little choice but to give the order to allow water from those massively rearranged northern rivers to spill uselessly over the edge of those very expensive dams.

By 1994, after one more attempt to move on to Phase Two of the James Bay Power Project, Great Whale was throttled by Premier Jacques Parizeau. Hydro-Québec was in sorry state of financial affairs. Had it not been for the hundreds of millions it received in annual revenue from the Churchill Falls agreement with Newfoundland, Hydro-Québec would be running in the red. Under the agreement, Quebec buys electricity from Churchill Falls at a quarter of a cent a kilowatt hour from the Labrador project and then resells the power for as much as six cents a kilowatt hour. It is estimated by Newfoundland that annual profits for Quebec from Churchill Falls generally exceed $600 million. In 1996 Hydro-Québec reported overall net income of $520 million. In 1995 it was $390 million.

If many Ontarians gaze with temporal pride at Ontario Hydro's historic accomplishments, with awe at the magnitude of its growth and the services it provided over the decades, and with some consternation over its inability to properly prepare for the future, Quebecers are decidedly more spiritual when their thoughts turn to their provincial power utility. After all, Hydro-Québec is not just an engine of economic growth. It is a power edifice that both represents and radiates the institutional authority many Quebecers feel they need to eventually realize a true and lasting sense of independence. In that respect, the foundations of Hydro-Québec's important social and cultural role go much deeper than those of any other provincial power utility.

The history of Hydro-Québec is entwined with the modern history of the province's move toward the status of a distinct, perhaps independent, society. It aided immeasurably in freeing Quebec from the tyranny of Maurice Duplessis and his Union Nationale governments. It helped Quebecers loosen the infuriating yoke of having to live with a domestic economy dominated by the English. It helped free them from many of the antediluvian restrictions of the Roman Catholic Church. It helped make them masters of their own destiny.

"Power has always been the chief manifestation of divinity," Sean McCutcheon wrote in *Electric Rivers:* "The engineers who turn the awesome power of waterfalls into electricity were seen as priest-like mediators between the ordinary and the Omnipotent; the transformation they effected was, like that the priests bring about at Mass, magical; and respect for Hydro-Québec's mastery and authority provided some of the social cohesion once provided by respect for the Church. In building dams that 'subjugated,' 'vanquished,' or 'conquered' rivers, the utility showed the world that Quebecois were as good as anyone else, including the English who had conquered, colonized and humiliated them."

By the mid-1960s, Quebecers were growing justifiably proud of their utility: *Nous sommes tous Hydro-Québécois* ("We are all Hydro-Québecers"), many proclaimed lustily. In some circles, even to question their provincial utility was considered unpatriotic. For years it was immune from public scrutiny and criticism. Liberal and Parti Québécois politicians basked in its inspiring light. The Montreal offices of the premier of the province were on the seventeenth floor of 75 boulevard René Lévesque ouest, the head office of Hydro-Québec. As McCutcheon put it, Hydro-Québec had grown "into a state within a state."

"Find me another business capable of inspiring a song on the hit parade!" René Lévesque wrote rhetorically in his 1986 biography, of a popular tune written about the massive Manicouagan-Outardes generating complex built by Hydro-Québec in the early 1960s. There was even a brand of cigarette named after the same generating station on the north shore of the St. Lawrence: "Manic." By 1997, and despite decades of financial troubles and disputed directions, Hydro-Québec had become the subject of a six-part television series produced by Radio-Canada. The series, entitled *Les Batisseurs d'eau (The Water Builders)*, told the story of the founding of Hydro-Québec and the early political battles that brought it to life.

Hydro-Québec, or Commission hydro-électrique de Québec, was created as a public utility on April 14, 1944. The utility's birth pains are familiar. Private utility owners were realizing extraordinary profits from their electrical monopolies. They paid out huge dividends to their investors yet charged customers intolerable rates. Demands for extension of electrical service to areas such as the Gaspé and Abitibi were generally ignored, or offered grudgingly—at usurious rates.

By the Great Depression of the 1930s, ratepayers, politicians, the business community, even the Roman Catholic Church were angry with the private electric monopolies. A public call for government intervention, led by Quebec City dentist Philippe Hamel, resulted in a 1934 commission of inquiry that led to a limited version of regulation over the private utilities. In the 1943 provincial election, Liberal leader Adelard Godbout promised to place the world's largest privately owned utility at the time—Montreal Light, Heat & Power Consolidated (MLHP)—under public ownership.

Godbout followed through on his election promise. He expropriated MLHP for $135 million. MLHP was the financial centrepiece of the empire of Irish-born magnate Sir Herbert Holt. Holt was considered a financial genius. He had become one of North America's richest men, manipulating his banks, hotels, railroads and shipyards in such a way as to drive up the value of his power company's stock, and with it, the electricity rates he charged.

Large Montreal businesses and newspapers were quick to support Holt. *The Gazette* responded to the nationalization with a headline that stated: "Russia pays for Property Seized! Will Quebec do likewise ... and when?" But throughout the debate over private control, not many supporters of publicly owned power missed the fact that the province's private utilities were controlled by *les anglais*.

Maurice Duplessis's Union Nationale government replaced the Godbout government but did little to further the aspirations of public-power supporters. The Duplessis government refused to make any further moves on private utilities. But throughout the late 1940s and 1950s, demand for electricity began escalating, as it did in all provinces after World War II. In Quebec's case demand growth was quite spectacular—easily doubling every ten years but some years hitting as high as ten percent.

This dramatic surge in demand helped make Hydro-Québec the major player in the field of electrical generation. New plants were built along the St. Lawrence River as well as on its tributaries. An important twist in this rapid capital expansion of public dams, power stations and transmission lines was that, toward the end of the decade, these initiatives were now being designed, built and operated by French Canadians.

It was perhaps the first modern evidence that Quebec possessed the necessary technical and managerial skills to begin thinking about a public utility that could eventually become that crucial lever needed to achieve the goal of more jobs, more power and more cultural independence for francophones.

In 1960, Jean Lesage led the Liberal Party to victory in the provincial election. The election launched Quebec's "Quiet Revolution." Compared to the reactionary and conservative days of the Duplessis government, the Liberals were an incredibly activist government. They immediately embarked on a sweeping program of public expansion, building new schools, colleges, hospitals, new highways and roads, and generally helping to ignite a renewed sense of pride and self-confidence among Quebecers.

Lesage made René Lévesque, a well-known former television journalist, his minister of public works. Lévesque was also given ambiguous responsibility for something termed "hydraulic resources." After inquiring into how Hydro-Québec operated, Lévesque discovered that his little ministerial "afterthought" responsibility would hide, as he put it in his biography, "the goose that laid the golden egg." In 1961, Lévesque's responsibilities were grouped under the title of minister of natural resources and he immediately began drawing up plans, in his words, "to decolonize the hydroelectric sector." But cabinet support for his radical initiative into public ownership of power was shaky. Many colleagues were nervous about his intentions. However, with Lesage's backing, Lévesque pressed ahead.

On February 12, 1962, speaking to a group of Montreal business leaders at a luncheon, Lévesque drew their attention to the now extremely important field of electrical power generation. Almost quietly he let slip that "the future in this sector is [now] state business." The Liberals would proceed to nationalize the eleven power companies that represented what remained of the private electric-utility sector in Quebec.

All hell broke loose among "this bunch of feudal barons," as Lévesque referred to the private utility owners. A Quebec City newspaper called the move "a crime against society." A Quebec member of Parliament rose in the House of Commons and claimed Lévesque was "another Castro." An American businessman with investments in one of affected companies suggested Quebec should muzzle Lévesque, a politician he characterized as one "who talks like his name is Robespierre and acts as if aristocrats are to be lined up for the guillotine."

At the time, Lévesque and his fellow cultural philosophers—Pierre Trudeau, André Laurendeau, Jean Marchand, and Gérard Pelletier—would gather frequently to debate and discuss political issues among themselves. Trudeau, for one, balked when he heard that the nationalization plan would cost about $600 million. The move would virtually double Quebec's debt just to "take over a business that already exists." Trudeau reminded Lévesque of the economic and social progress a sum like that would generate if put into health care, education and business development. Trudeau called Lévesque's move "nationalist suspender-snapping."

But the benefits far outweighed the costs, as far as Lévesque was concerned. In public hands, Hydro-Québec would a very valuable provincial asset with attractive cash flow. ("We could ... pay the whole goddarn [$600 million] off in fourteen years," he claimed.) Besides, a publicly owned Hydro-Québec would be a "security" that would stand almost in perpetuity. It would give Quebec control of a vast sector of the economy that would produce many jobs. It would also be "a veritable school for skills, a training ground for the builders and administrators we so urgently needed."

The anti-nationalization dust had not settled by late summer. Many of Lévesque's cabinet opponents refused to sit idly by and see a Liberal government leap head-long into nationalization, no matter what the economic and social benefits might be. During a bitter debate in a cabinet meeting in September 1962, Lévesque prevailed over what appeared to be a party split down the middle on the issue. A decision was made to put the issue to the people: call a provincial election on the issue of nationalizing the remaining private power utilities.

It was a bold and risky stroke. The Lesage Liberals were, in a sense, rolling dice even more dramatically than Brian Mulroney did in his later constitutional efforts. It was The Revolutionists against the paternalistic barons of the English "electricity trust." The Liberals either were going to be able to press on and complete The Quiet Revolution in lofty fashion, or they would be turfed out of office.

Later, at a portentous meeting between Lévesque and a number of campaign workers, efforts were being made to "hunt for the magic words" the Liberals might use to ignite widespread support for them. *The* issue was nationalization of the private utilities. Some way, some words, had to be found to link this bold political initiative toward public power for Quebec with the gut aspirations of modern, confident Quebecers. Someone suggested *"maîtres chez nous"*—"masters in our own house!" The rest is history.

Still, deep down, Lévesque could not help thinking the phrase was a little too strong. "Masters of a huge new sector, okay. But masters of everything else?" he wrote almost hesitantly in 1986. "[T]his exaggerated slogan gave me a feeling of uneasiness, which has, for that matter, never entirely left me. But as slogans go, *"Maîtres chez nous"* was a fine one, and seeing as it was getting late ..."

The mandate the Liberals asked the Quebec electorate for was simply put: The unification of Quebec's hydro networks was the key to industrialization of every region of the province. It was essential as "the first condition for economic liberation" and "full employment," as Lévesque put it. This important stride toward the future necessitated, as the Liberals' manifesto made clear, "the nationalization of eleven companies that produce and distribute electricity." The question put then was much more simple than those that would follow on the issue of sovereignty or separation; to nationalize or not to nationalize. It was simply, "Yes?" or "No?"

On November 24, 1962, the Liberals won a decisive victory, claiming sixty-three seats to the Union Nationale's thirty-one. The publicly owned Hydro-Québec would go on to become, for Lévesque, "the flagship of our development." On May 1, 1963, the Liberal government paid $604 million—then, the largest commercial transaction in the province's history—and took ownership of its new utility. The trip toward *maîtres chez nous* had formally begun. The event signalled to Lévesque that the people of Quebec had finally set their clocks to the twentieth century.

René Lévesque jumped the Liberal ship in 1968 to form the Parti Québécois. Its declared goal was now the separation of Quebec from the rest of Canada. But in the winter of 1969, Robert Bourassa—a man who wanted to be premier of Quebec even when he was a teenager but was then the Liberals' opposition finance critic—was toying with the idea of running for the leadership of the Liberal Party. He was searching for a platform that would carry him to the party leadership and then to the premier's office.

Bourassa went after Hydro-Québec officials, quizzing them about when they intended to capitalize on the massive hydraulic power rushing into James Bay from the rivers of northern Quebec. Since the early 1960s, Hydro-Québec officials had been studying the hydro-electric potential of the southern rivers of the region. But at the time of Bourassa's questioning, there was little collective appetite within Hydro-Québec for embarking on projects twelve hundred kilometres from Montreal or Quebec City.

In the late 1960s, Hydro-Québec officials were reluctant to venture into costly construction projects in the far north. The enormous power and dollar windfall Quebec would receive from the Churchill Falls hydro-electric project was close to realization. It was suspected that Churchill Falls could provide enough electricity to cover both domestic needs and a suitable supply of power for export to U.S. markets for a long time to come.

The agreement with Newfoundland was signed in 1969, before world energy costs skyrocketed with the OPEC oil crisis, triggering rampant inflation and affecting the price of any form of energy. The development of Churchill Falls was spearheaded by former New-foundland premier Joey Smallwood. In typical hydro-megaproject thinking, Labrador electricity was to be the salvation of a province down on its economic luck. It would attract investment, create jobs and, over the sixty-five-year length of the agreement, pour billions of dollars into Newfoundland's public coffers.

The Smallwood government almost had to bribe Hydro-Québec into signing the agreement. Churchill Falls was only of passing interest to Hydro-Québec. It was at the time a financially risky concept. Capital costs were high and the price of electricity was low. The utility also had any number of hydro-electric project possibilities within Quebec that could be developed more cheaply. One of the inducements to get Quebec to invest in the project (Hydro-Québec still holds roughly three million of the project's outstanding 8.7 million shares) was the length of the contract, and the steady stream of revenues that it represented. The other was the price. The amount Newfoundland charged for electricity would decline over the length of the contract.

Unfortunately for Premier Smallwood and his dreams of provincial greatness, by the time construction was completed and the deal went into affect in 1976, the OPEC shock was almost three years old and Newfoundland was stuck with a very bad deal. One estimate states that between 1976 and 1995, Quebec made $14 billion reselling Churchill Falls power, compared with $2 billion for Newfoundland.

For Hydro-Québec, the 4,300 extra megawatts from Churchill Falls was like manna from heaven. It made Hydro-Québec officials naturally reluctant to begin spending more money on more hydro projects. In fact, some of them were less interested in generating more hydraulic power for the province than they were intent on jumping on the nuclear-generation bandwagon. The Parti Québécois supported the move toward nuclear-generated electricity. Nuclear energy was considered by Hydro-Québec engineers and officials to be cheap, abundant and reliable. It also represented the technological wave of the future. And they wanted to ride that wave.

In January 1970, Bourassa won the Liberal leadership and, in the April election that followed, steered his party back into power. He did it on a platform that opposed separation and promised the create of one hundred thousand jobs. Not surprisingly, given this huge employment objective, the possibilities of developing hydro-electric power in the James Bay region became a major campaign issue.

It is difficult to conclude whether Robert Bourassa's fixation with northern hydro development was motivated by a strongly held sense of public service or by opportunism. He had spotted the vehicle that could carry him to the premier's chair, and keep him there. As Sean McCutcheon put it: "In advocating unbridled hydroelectric development he could sound like a nationalist, for Hydro-Québec and its monumental dams had come to symbolize the emancipation of Québécois, but he did not have to make the politically risky commitment to independence."

Three days after becoming premier, Bourassa ordered Hydro-

Québec officials to begin working on the James Bay dossier. On October 5, 1970, members of the Front de libération du Québec (FLQ) kidnapped British trade commissioner James Cross. On October 10, Pierre Laporte, Quebec's minister of labour, was kidnapped by a second FLQ cell. Laporte was later found strangled. On October 16, Bourassa requested Prime Minister Pierre Trudeau to invoke the War Measures Act, giving the federal government sweeping powers of search and seizure.

By relying so heavily on federal intervention during the crisis, Bourassa came across to much of the Quebec public, not as a strong and decisive leader, but, as Lévesque called him, "a puppet of the federal rulers." Given the fierce criticism he received over his role in events, Bourassa had to find a political mechanism with which to resurrect himself politically. He had to do something big and something bold. On April 30, 1971, in a Quebec City hockey arena packed with five thousand Liberals, Bourassa announced the launching of the James Bay Power Project. The premier trotted out what was really a vaguely defined scheme to harness twenty rivers flowing into James Bay.

To create the kind of statement he wanted (and to try to justify his promise of creating a hundred thousand new jobs), Bourassa had to draft out a hydro-electric project of enormous proportions. The concept had to surpass anything anyone had done before. In effect, he, the officials of Hydro-Québec and its engineers would put in place a plan to increase Quebec's supply of power to gargantuan dimensions without, unfortunately, "any clear idea as to where the power would be sold," as McCutcheon put it.

Bourassa wanted to do what the OPEC nations did: turn an immense flow of energy into a constant flow of money. James Bay would be the initial step in turning Quebec into one of the world's wealthiest principalities. Yet, when he launched his magnificent obsession, preliminary feasibility studies had not been completed. When early consultation plans were being drawn up in 1968–69, there were no detailed maps of the James Bay region available to make proper calculations and the numbers of native people living there—and where, exactly, they lived—were established largely through hunches.

Few scientific studies had ever been conducted on the region's habitat or environment. The decision to begin the project with a construction complex at La Grande was not even made until May 1972, more than a year after Bourassa's showy announcement. The "project of the century" was, to put the most positive spin on it, *noblesse oblige* gone haywire.

Tracing Robert Bourassa's passionate and grand prance into the wilderness of northern Quebec reminds one less of Adam Beck than of Charles Townsend. Townsend was the British Chancellor of the Exchequer who bequeathed to the Empire the infamous Townsend Acts—the 1767 set of five categories of taxes on such items as stamps and tea, the latter resulting in the "Boston Tea Party" of 1773. It was once written by Sir Robert Walpole that Townsend "studied nothing with accuracy or with attention, had parts that embraced all knowledge with such quickness that he seemed to create knowledge instead of searching for it … in him it seemed a loss of time to think."

Initially, Hydro-Québec was reluctant to become involved. But the utility's forecasters were predicting that demand for electricity could more than double in the next decade—growing at an average annual rate of 7.9 percent. With ten-year construction lead times, there was now little question in anyone's mind that the James Bay Power Project should be built. Hydro-Québec would soon need, so it was thought, more electricity to meet Quebec's growing domestic demand, not to mention what amounts might be sold to hungry customers south of the U.S.–Canada border.

Hydro-Québec's engineering group was now quite excited about future prospects. Along with the James Bay Development Corporation, they would be allowed to design the massive La Grande complex. The geographic scope of their work would cover an area larger than most U.S. states. It was not rocketry, either. They would decide where to find the amount of dirt and rock they required and move it to the site in big dump trucks, like kids in a sandbox, and then pour lots of concrete into gigantic containment structures.

Quebecers were all but addicted to electricity. Per capita use in the province was higher than in almost any place on earth. Almost two-thirds of Quebec homes were heated by electricity and, later, eight of every ten new homes constructed would be electrically heated. Boosted by the offer of cheaper and cheaper electricity from James Bay, the number of electrically heated homes in the province would double between 1979 and 1989.

There seemed only passing reference at this time about serving export markets. It would not be until about 1981, as Hydro-Québec geared up for construction of Great Whale, that the invocation would shift somewhat to exports as a rationale for the huge developments in northwestern Quebec.

The supporting dogma that prevailed was that this was "the greatest construction project in the world" and its completion would make Quebec one of the wealthiest societies in the world. Little was said of the fact that eventually, it would take export sales, not domestic demand, to make most of it happen. When stuck for further justification, most proponents would fall back on Bourassa's simple, "we must conquer the North," anthem.

Even though roughly nine thousand native people lived in the territory, it appeared the James Bay region was considered by the Bourassa government and many Hydro-Québec officials to be all but deserted. The Cree had lived on the land for centuries, yet the first time many of them came face to face with French-speaking whites was in the 1960s when survey crews were conducting cursory hydrological studies. Astoundingly, the matter of native rights to the land and waterways was never a major consideration in the project's formative stages.

In October 1971, Bourassa's grand audiovisual show was replayed for some Cree tribal members. They began to giggle when the video showed bison grazing, supposedly, along the James Bay coastal area. The highly amused natives had to explain to the video presenter that there were no bison in the subarctic region of James Bay.

Still, the threat to their lifestyle and economy was not taken seriously in the early development stages, by both sides. As constructions crews began bulldozing roads north into the taiga, Cree elders laughed in disbelief when they were told by younger tribal members how electricity would be made. They were told rivers would be made to run backward. Huge dams would cause great lakes to form. At first the stories seemed implausible, then insane. But the prospect that the land upon which they hunted, fished and trapped might soon be flooded, and its inhabitants forced to move to new and strange areas, finally galvanized the Cree and the Inuit into taking action.

Bourassa made a major mistake when he took for granted that the native peoples living in the James Bay area had no prior rights to the land and waterways. Their opposition would cost him dearly. The James Bay Power Project would become a *cause célèbre* for what had to this point been a rather unsophisticated and unorganized Quebec environmental movement. But as events progressed and the horror of what might happen became magnified, environmentalists merged with native leaders in a number of communities and formed the genesis of citizen activities that would eventually bring Bourassa and his dreams for the land surrounding James Bay crashing back to earth.

Although the coalition was initially prepared to oppose the hydroelectric project (as one native spokesperson put it: "Only the beavers had the right to build dams in our territory"), a consensus developed early on, particularly among the Cree. It was widely agreed that it would make more sense to accept the inevitable and negotiate the best terms possible. The native people may have been largely resigned to the loss of their rights to the land, but they were determined to drive the hardest bargain possible. But Bourassa and James Bay Development Corporation officials refused to modify their plans or to make major concessions. They would advise the native peoples of what they planned to do, but the James Bay steamroller was proceeding regardless of their opposition to it.

Bourassa could afford to be so indifferent about the demands of the native peoples. Few non-native Québécois opposed his northern hydro-electric project. The exploitation of natural resources had always been a basic and accepted premise of Quebec's economy. "Chopping down trees, digging up rocks and damming rivers" had always been what the Quebec economy was about, McCutcheon wrote. "Its territory was so immense and so rich in natural resources that most felt that *quand il n'y en aura plus, il y en aura encore* ('when we run out, there's always more'). Wilderness was a hostile force, not to be conserved tenderly but mastered forcefully."

In April 1972, the Cree and the Inuit began court action to stop the James Bay project. Hearings began in December, before Judge Albert Malouf of the Quebec Superior Court, on the native peoples' plea for an injunction against the James Bay project. One hundred and fifty witnesses were heard and the hearings lasted seventy-one days. In November 1973, Judge Malouf ordered work on the La Grande complex stopped. He held that the developers were trespassing, and since their work would have devastating and far-reaching effects, he ordered work to cease while the Cree and Inuit case for a permanent injunction could be heard.

Within a week, the Quebec Appeals Court overturned the Malouf decision. The court reasoned simply that the people of Quebec, in whose interest the project was being built, were more numerous than the native peoples, who wanted it stopped. But Malouf's ruling meant Bourassa had lost for the first time on his vision-trip. His government would be forced to settle with the natives or feel increasing political and financial pressure a legal standoff might generate among foreign bond holders and investors. His first offer to settle for $100 million was rejected. Intense negotiations continued between the Grand Council of the Cree and the Northern Quebec Inuit Association on one side of the table, and the federal and provincial governments, Hydro-Québec, the James Bay Development Corporation and the James Bay Energy Corporation on the other.

Finally, in November 1975, the Cree and the Inuit signed the James Bay and Northern Quebec Agreement. In return for waiving their aboriginal rights, and acquiescing to the project and the over 166,000 hectares of land it covered, the native peoples of northern Quebec received a sizable sum of money, land and a novel form of self-government. The compensation came to $135 million (to be paid over twenty years) for the Cree and $90 million for the Inuit. But with various ancillary agreements, the settlement added up to grand total of over $500 million.

The self-government component in the agreement gave the native peoples control of school boards, health and social service boards and municipal services, with the cost shared between the federal and provincial governments. The Cree and Inuit would also now be part of any committee structure formed to protect the environment. This allowed them to be able to review environmental impact studies and to have a say in any remedial action recommended. But the ultimate power remained in Quebec City.

That would not matter a decade later. By then, the native peoples of James Bay would develop a sense of political sophistication so simple yet effective that they would be able—just by being who they were and doing what they had done for centuries—to help drive the final wooden spike into the heart of Bourassa's costly and grandiose vision for James Bay.

Two years into construction, the projected costs for the first phase of the James Bay Power Project had almost doubled, from the original rough estimate of $6 billion to $11.9 billion. The planners had chosen the most expensive rivers to develop. Technical alterations, environmental changes and inflation all helped drive up the cost of the project. The soaring cost figures only fuelled the conviction of opposition Parti Québécois members that this multi-billion-dollar project had been kicked off much too hastily, that it suffered from questionable planning and had been allowed to proceed without proper study.

In March 1974, a fight over labour union turf at the La Grande site turned violent. Hot-headed workers ran amok with heavy-duty equipment, wrecking the camp, cutting its water supplies, toppling the diesel generators and punching holes in the diesel fuel tanks. Fire broke out in the workers' trailers. Construction came to a stop for seven weeks. The bill for the rampage topped $35 million and left 1,400 workers shivering in the dark.

An inquiry into construction labour violence, not just at La Grande but across the province, was called. It was headed by Judge Robert Cliche. The Cliche Inquiry made a number of major recommendations in the hope of bringing an end to the labour tyranny that existed throughout Quebec. But just as significant, the Cliche Inquiry revealed that one of Bourassa's principal advisers had been actively dispensing jobs as patronage.

The Cliche Inquiry findings did not do Bourassa's image and political standing any favours. The insinuation that, given the James Bay project was essentially his baby, Bourassa must have been part of the corruption, stuck to him. In the November 1976 provincial election Bourassa's Liberal government was defeated by René Lévesque and the Parti Québécois.

Even before the election, many Quebecers were beginning to question Bourassa's original assertion that all the expense and trouble that James Bay represented were justified because Quebec needed the electricity. There had been too many trips to New York's Wall Street and too many rumours about long-term export deals being planned. So, when Lévesque stepped into the premier's office in the Hydro-Québec building, it was not surprising that U.S. investors began getting nervous. Who knew what this Northern Castro might now do?

Only a few months before Bourassa's defeat, Hydro-Québec had pulled off an unprecedented $1 billion loan from several U.S.

insurance companies. It was the second-largest private placement ever carried out in the U.S. markets. The key to levering that much money was the growing interest American investors now had in Quebec's hydro-electric potential, in particular the gigantic James Bay project.

This was barely three years after the OPEC cartel had driven up the price of petroleum. Supplies were still tighter and prices higher than anyone had ever seen them. The price of energy in the U.S. market—oil, gas and electricity—was climbing to troubling heights. Quebec was prepared to sell power at eighty percent of the price of the electricity generated at oil- or coal-fired U.S. plants. Consequently, in American eyes, having a large generator of cheap electricity right next door had become an attractive option to American utility heads and their investors.

In that sense, Bourassa's decision to build James Bay, no matter what the price, seemed to be turning out as the "best bad decision ever made," as Guy Joron, the PQ's first energy minister put it. Based on the way energy markets were going before 1973, the James Bay Power Project did not make much sense. It was too big and it was being built when demand for that much electricity was not present. But the OPEC cartel drove up energy prices around the globe during the mid- and late-1970s and helped create a ready market for Quebec's new power, at least in the short term.

By 1976, Hydro-Québec was back in the hands of the man who had given it life—René Lévesque. With the support of Lévesque's PQ, Hydro-Québec began its march into the electricity export market in 1978 when it built an interconnection with the New York Power Authority to enable it to deliver electricity to the New York Power Pool. The timing could not have been better. Surplus electricity would increase dramatically when La Grande 2 came on stream in October 1979. But Quebec no longer had to worry about where it was going to sell its surplus. Lévesque used the occasion to inform voters that Hydro-Québec would now be used as a valuable pawn in the independence referendum.

As he had said in 1962, a rich and powerful public power utility would be the key to seeking a new political future. In 1962, it was there to be used as a means of realizing who really was the master of the house of Quebec. In 1979, it was the instrument that might be used to free Quebec from the shackles of Confederation. But oddly enough, when Lévesque pulled a switch to begin the flow of this new pulse of energy to the south, he would also help restart Robert Bourassa's political career.

Both Lévesque and Bourassa used the stature and potential of Hydro-Québec in their respective arguments during the 1980 referendum campaign. Lévesque blended the issue of independence with the 1962 campaign to nationalize Hydro-Québec, citing it as the manifest moment when Quebecers began to realize their full cultural and economic potential. Now they had a chance to do it again. With the power of James Bay behind it, Hydro-Québec was their glowing symbol of wealth, autonomy and independence.

On the other hand, Bourassa campaigned on the notion that projects like James Bay were just the first step on the way to making Quebec one of the wealthiest societies in North America, one that could declare "independence" based, not on political separation, but on its new-found power.

Bourassa raised the electricity ante by calling for a doubling of James Bay power output and a new aggressive sales strategy. Whatever the price of this massive capital expansion, energy-hungry Americans would pay it. There was no down-side to Quebec's potential from here on in, Bourassa seemed to be saying. His export strategy already had its adherents. But to make the export of surplus electricity a principal objective was a major departure from Hydro-Québec's traditional mandate: to provide Quebecers with the lowest-cost electricity possible while acting as an instrument for the province's industrial development. One problem was getting Hydro-Québec's senior management on side for a major shift in the corporation's objectives.

It did not matter if political leaders like Lévesque were constantly thinking of Hydro-Québec as the perfect engine to drive Quebec society into a full-scale renaissance. Even with the immense prestige and economic importance the utility had accumulated since 1963, it still functioned as that "state within a state." It was still largely independent from the legislature in its decision-making powers. It had no tight regulatory regime to follow. At times the public utility was run so secretively by its five commissioners—each appointed for a term of ten years—that their actions only served to frustrate elected politicians. Hydro-Québec was perceived by many to be an unassailable ivory tower, whose commissioners, once they were appointed, "just sat on top of the world and didn't give a shit what the government thought," as PQ energy minister, Guy Joron, was once quoted as saying.

Although the PQ government lost the independence referendum, it did not lose its enthusiasm for finally straightening out who was in charge—the commissioners and senior management, or the public's elected officials. The government wanted the utility to concentrate its service, and its planning, on Quebec's needs, so it could truly become that lever for continuing industrial development. The PQ also needed money for its impressive list of new social programs. As the largest commercial enterprise and largest debtor in the province, Hydro-Québec had a very real and, more often than not, disturbing influence on the flow of capital into the province. Huge, multi-billion-dollar sums borrowed to build dams and transmission lines often meant fewer schools, fewer hospitals and less funding for other important social programs.

In 1981 the PQ altered the corporation's capital structure to ensure that the government began receiving a share of Hydro's profits each year. They also changed the corporate structure from five commissioners to a government-appointed board of directors. By exercising tighter control over Hydro-Québec, the PQ government was also able to put a damper on the corporation's enthusiastic forecasts of annual growth in demand.

There was also evidence that in this post-referendum time the economy was heading into serious recession. Consumer spending was in a stall, population growth was falling and the over-heated provincial construction sector was going into free-fall after a decade of megaproject work on everything from James Bay I to the 1976 Montreal Olympics. Yet, Hydro-Québec was determined to go ahead with its expansionist ten-year development plan. The only concession made was to alter its annual growth prediction for the 1980s from eight percent to six percent. Two years later growth actually shrank, just as Phase One of the La Grande was about to come on stream.

Even as the world of electricity was doing a flip-flop on Hydro-Québec's projections, the corporation still persisted in pursuing its long-range objectives of completing the entire James Bay project—the second stage of the La Grande complex, followed by the Great Whale complex and, then, stage three: the development of the Nottaway–Broadback–Rupert complex, all by the turn of the century.

In 1982, Lévesque appointed Guy Coulombe as Hydro-Québec's president and chief executive officer. Coulombe was a highly respected civil service administrator. For the first time in its history, someone who was not an engineer would be running Hydro-Québec. Coulombe saw the continuation of the construction program as "ridiculously ambitious." Hydro-Québec had, to that point, been run by engineers whose primary goal seemed to simply be to build more dams. If they did not stop, Coulombe figured, the province's giant utility was heading for bankruptcy.

The first stage of La Grande had to be completed because it was now cheaper to finish it than postpone it. But Coulombe forced postponement of the rest of the James Bay project. He also got the utility to revise its ridiculous long-range growth forecast down to less than three percent per year, and implemented sweeping cost-cutting measures. Still, by 1983, Hydro-Québec was stuck with thirty billion kilowatt hours it could not sell, representing a loss of $600 million in potential revenue.

It was fire-sale time at Hydro-Québec. The utility's sales and marketing people began making deals to sell the surplus electricity, often at prices below the cost of production. Some of this power was offered to aluminum refineries, ravenous consumers of electricity. An aluminum smelter can use as much electricity as a small city. Later, it would be discovered that Hydro-Québec was selling electricity to aluminum and magnesium smelters at half the cost of producing it.

Prospects for the utility brightened when the PQ government began to allow Hydro-Québec to enter into long-term export contracts. In 1982, the utility was given permission to increase the amount of seasonal surpluses it sold to New York Power Authority. In 1983, Hydro-Québec signed the first phase of a series of agreements with the New England Power Pool. The next year it signed its first year-round power-export deal with Vermont. Following that, it concluded the second phase of the New England agreement, which meant Hydro-Québec would be supplying roughly ten percent of New England's electricity in the 1990s.

Even so, by 1985, Quebec was still wallowing in surplus electricity. It was producing more than 5,700 megawatts of unneeded electricity at peak periods while frantically trying to find more U.S. customers willing to buy its surplus power. Only slightly more embarrassing was the matter of domestic electricity rates. Given the increased costs of borrowing and costly errors in demand forecasting, Quebecers were now being asked to pay for this decade of Hydro profligacy with higher electricity rates, the exact opposite of what the Bourassa government had promised.

Despite a restructuring program that axed five hundred managers, cuts of more than fifty percent in operating costs and a severe cutback in their romantic ten-year capital expansion plan from $65 billion to $18 billion, with some large projects rescheduled to the early twenty-first century, by the mid-1980s the aspirations of Quebec's hydro sorcerers and their apprentices seemed to have come, finally, to an embarrassing end.

After all that work, planning, fantasizing and expense, Quebec, thanks to its James Bay Power Project, was now being referred to as "a North American version of a banana republic." It was saddled with large financial debts. It was stuck one-third of the way through a $60 billion energy-expansion plan. Operating expenses were growing at twenty-four percent a year. It faced new competition from natural gas and oil-fired generation. And it was forced to sell surplus electricity on the market well below cost.

The dreams that Bourassa and Lévesque had for Hydro-Québec, of a string of huge generating facilities dotted across the vast wilderness of northern Quebec, lighting up the continent and filling provincial coffers with cash, seemed to have crumbled to dust. Those shiny new power stations now looked like a chain of "white elephants that will devour the capital of the province for another twenty years," as Peter Hadekel put it. They would divert "capital from investments that could have created permanent jobs" for eager Quebecers. That pinnacle of job creation—hundreds of thousands of hours of new employment—would also disappear.

Nevertheless, in December 1985, just as the final generating station of the La Grande complex was coming on stream, the Liberals, led once again by Robert Bourassa, defeated the Parti Québécois in a provincial election. Bourassa had campaigned on the promise to expand the James Bay project. Back in the premier's office, he made no apologies for saying that he wanted more dams built as soon as more export sales to the United States could be secured. Perhaps alone with his personal vision, Bourassa could now see the Americans needing as much as twelve thousand megawatts of new power, sometime in the future.

His rationale for expansion at this time was simple. With their heavy dependence on oil-fired generation, Americans were still being held captive to Middle East petroleum interests. Oil made for expensive power. It was dirty power. It was unreliable power. "We will need those dams to generate [replacement] power someday, anyway," said the man whose entire political career seemed wrapped up in one issue—the generation of electricity. Once again, Bourassa was marching to his own drummer. Hydro-Québec, under Coulombe, had done a commendable job of cutting costs, paring back and unloading surpluses. Still, the utility was heavily in debt and carried huge interest payments. Any profit it made was tempered by the realization it would have to write off interest on loans used to build all those dams against revenue from electricity that was getting harder and harder to sell. The utility did not share Bourassa's enthusiasm for quickly getting back into the pyramid-building business.

Hydro-Québec officials did not disagree that, someday, Quebec might need the electricity the utility was capable of producing. But corporate officials were inclined to move more slowly than Bourassa in getting back into the gigaproject business. Planners felt the province might still need another nineteen thousand megawatts of power and had set fairly prudent performance timelines for increasing generating capacity over a two-and-a-half-decade period. But this planning pace was not fast enough for the newly returned premier.

Bourassa kept pushing. The economy had not rebounded from the severe recession of the early 1980s. Quebec needed jobs. To generate electricity for export, Quebec needed to build more generating stations. It was simple, to Bourassa. Quebec would need the generating capacity down the road anyway. Why not build the dams now, when costs were lower? The more electricity the province sold at export, the sooner the utility would have to build even more capacity. All that construction would create more jobs. Quebec would be rich beyond its wildest expectations ...

Before Bourassa's return, Hydro-Québec had already moved into the second phase of its export plan—to provide firm electricity for U.S. utility customers that would save those very customers from having to build more nuclear or coal-fired generating power. By early 1988, the utility had signed contracts for firm power with Maine, Vermont (Hydro-Québec would supply half Vermont's power needs in the 1990s) and the New York Power Authority—the largest export contract ever. It was expected that by 1999 Quebec would be providing New York state with about six percent of its electricity. The return from these future deals was estimated by Bourassa to be worth $40 billion.

If all contracts were carried out to the letter, Quebec could be exporting 2,400 megawatts of firm power by the end of the century. It was an impressive number, but substantially less than the 10,000 megawatts of power Bourassa had predicted in *Power From the North*. So Quebec would just have to push ahead with James Bay II.

The investment needed to make it happen was sobering. At one point it was estimated that the amount needed to be borrowed to pay for construction in the 1990s would make Hydro-Québec the largest commercial debtor in the country. Nevertheless, with the promise of at least forty thousand job-years ringing in everyone's ears, in March 1988 Bourassa announced that Hydro-Québec would be moving ahead to complete the second phase of the La Grande complex and the construction of three new generating plants capable of producing 2,500 megawatts.

As if taking a page from Ontario's "Live Better Electrically" pamphlet, Hydro-Québec tried to keep pace with the premier's escalating dream by encouraging increased consumption of electricity within Quebec. After all, there were surpluses forecast past the end of the decade and well into the 1990s. The principal focus was on residential users, but in an unprecedented way, Hydro-Québec began to go after industrial customers to use more and more electricity by offering heavily discounted prices.

Hydro-Québec began to offer heavy industrial users "shared-risk" contracts. Under these contracts, the price they would have to pay for their electricity would vary with what they received for their products. The utility was playing its role of economic stimulus—and at the same time trying to unload its power surpluses—but it was now doing it to subsidize industry.

Hydro-Québec was trying to keep its perpetual loop moving. It had to pay for construction of increased generating capacity with increased exports and escalating domestic consumption, which would increase the demand for more generating construction, which would increase debt, which would mean more pressure on consumption, and so on. In March 1989, Hydro-Québec announced it had advanced the timing for construction of both Great Whale and the Nottaway–

Broadback–Rupert (NBR) complexes. It would finally proceed to complete the James Bay II project.

The cost of Great Whale, including transmission lines, was estimated at $12.6 billion. It was expected that Great Whale's three generating stations would produce 3,168 megawatts of power. NBR would add another eleven generating stations with a capacity of 8,400 megawatts. It was hoped NBR would be on stream by 2001. At this point, Hydro-Québec expected to spend something in the vicinity of $44 billion to complete James Bay II.

The indebtedness these ventures carried with them (Hydro-Québec was already carrying $26 billion in debt at the end of 1990 and it was estimated total long-term debt could eventually climb to $65 billion by the end of the century), although immense, was offset in many minds by Bourassa's patriotic fervour about the tens of thousands of jobs that would be created. Hydro-Québec alone now had close to twenty-three thousand employees. It was just further evidence of the utility's essential role in stoking the fires of the province's economy.

Any anxiety over Hydro-Québec's burgeoning debt figures seemed shrouded by numerical hype. The public utility was pumping about $2 billion into the Quebec economy every year. It was the province's largest spender, disbursing one dollar for every twenty that went into the economy. In a good year, its dollar contribution went up to five out of twenty. The corporation also held $36 billion in assets. In 1990, it was the third-largest company in Canada. It was one of the largest power utilities in North America. It had revenues of $6 billion a year—although its net profit figures were largely made up of the profits it gained from the Churchill Falls contract.

Still, at the time the decision was made to proceed with James Bay II, Quebec had one of the highest levels of public debt in the world. Hydro-Québec's borrowing represented fully twenty percent of the provincial debt total. If the total estimated project debt to the end of the decade ($65 billion) was broken down on a per capita basis, it meant each Quebecer was in hock for about $8,500. These were pure, on-the-table kinds of dollars. No one really knew what the future social, cultural and environmental costs might be when Bourassa's dream was fulfilled.

"The problem with Bourassa's dream is that it is fast becoming an environmental and economic nightmare," Grand Chief of the Cree, Matthew Coon-Come, said at the time. "Why spend billions of dollars to destroy the environment and to destroy my people just to export electricity to the United States? Does this make any sense?"

No one really knew the full impact Hydro-Québec's plans would have on the environment in 1989. Some critics claimed the environmental impact now went beyond the question of provincial or even continental repercussions. Completion of James Bay II could conceivably have serious global implications. Scientists pointed out that not only would the flooding of forest areas result in increased global warming, by reducing the number of trees extracting carbon dioxide from the atmosphere; it would actually increase emissions of greenhouse gases. When drowned trees rot, they give off carbon dioxide and methane.

The damming of the Nottaway, Broadback and Rupert Rivers that was still to come would flood an area twice the size of the Great Whale flood. The potential of doing damage to land, forests, animals, waterfowl and fish-spawning areas was almost secondary now to what this hydraulic displacement meant in planetary proportions. Mercury poisoning would inevitably result from the mammoth earth-moving activity and make its way into the food chain of fish, animals and humans.

The New York–based National Audubon Society likened Hydro-Québec and its passion for building James Bay II to a drunken teenager driving at eighty miles per hour. Even though he had not killed anyone yet, he still should be stopped. In terms of wildlife and habitat, Audubon Society representatives claimed that "James Bay is the northern equivalent of the destruction of the tropical rain forest."

The Bourassa government and Hydro-Québec largely ignored these warnings. They papered over the dislocation of thousands of native people. They treated their complaints as so much whining. The Cree and Inuit had signed the James Bay and Northern Quebec Agreement in 1975—been paid all that wampum for rights to their land—so what was the beef now? Look at what all the dam construction and the export sales of electricity were doing for the Quebec economy: all those jobs; all those millions of dollars jingling in Cree and Inuit pockets.

But even then, cracks began to appear in the Bourassa's wealth-and-abundance argument. One revealing study by economist Hélène Lajambe raised serious questions about the arithmetic the Bourassa government was using to promote the job-making category of its northern industrial strategy. The study showed that thousands of construction jobs ended up being temporary. Some were heavily subsidized.

Lajambe, an economist who had closely followed developments surrounding the James Bay Power Project, and who had written her master's and doctoral thesis on the issue, argued that Bourassa's Grand Vision had actually damaged, not helped to improve, the province's economy. She contended that building the James Bay project had effectively starved the province's manufacturing sector of badly needed capital.

Rather than make Quebecers into the wealthiest nation on the earth, "the arabs of electricity" had, according to Lajambe, been turned into "an economically dependent Third World nation." In response to her conclusions, a Hydro-Québec sales executive sent Lajambe a candle, insinuating that her reasoning would only "send Quebec back to the pre-electricity dark ages."

As in the story of David and Goliath, it often seems to be the little things that stir the momentum needed to put a halt to the damage caused by radical and poorly thought out change. In the case of James Bay, it was a series of relatively small public irritations, capped by a modest but heartfelt gesture that almost bordered on futility. Given the immense scope and relentless nature of Hydro-Québec's plans for power development in northern Quebec, it is strange that it would be these little things that would finally force Premier Parizeau's decision, on November 18, 1994, to shelve the Great Whale project.

Electricity on its own is invisible. Only the infrastructure that manufactures it, transports it and distributes it is readily discernible. One of the most obvious, and visually annoying, manifestations of Bourassa's strategy for economic growth through perpetual hydro-electric development was the transmission lines needed to carry electricity to market. Travelling through large North American cities like New York, Los Angeles, Toronto and Montreal, some of the most noticeable blemishes dotting the urban landscape today are the massive steel pylons that hold the heavily sagging cords of power.

Hydro-Québec had no recourse but to step up the building of transmission lines and towers to deliver its increasing load of both domestic and exported electricity. This construction was accompanied by increasing public annoyance and resentment. The more electricity Hydro-Québec produced, the more it had to sell. The more it sold, the more transmission lines it required. The more often these unwieldy manifestations of power appeared on the horizon, the more they frightened and alienated people.

The breeding of those unsightly towers of steel with their humming wires sparked a public reaction on both sides of the international boundary. Urban home owners grew angry at the visual blight. Rural property owners complained about the poor compensation received for allowing these corridors of power to pass through their property. Both groups grew increasingly sensitive to the dangers reportedly emanating from electromagnetic fields generated by these throbbing lines. There was also concern over the potential health hazards caused by herbicide sprays used to retard foliage growth beneath the power lines.

This growing public concern about the aesthetics and safety of electricity transmission grew in stride with the continuing protest by scores of public-interest organizations on both sides of the border over the utility's disdainful attitude toward the massive environmental damage the James Bay Power Project was causing. Despite mounting evidence against the project and the vocal opposition to its construction plans, Hydro-Québec remained insensitive and unresponsive. Critics on both sides of the border were becoming outraged over what the utility was doing to the environment. The public anger was so pronounced—carried every day in newspapers and television news—that one could only conclude the province's power utility, and its government, lived on another planet.

With all the scientific evidence mounting against it even as late as September 1993, Hydro-Québec had the temerity to table a five-thousand-page, $400 million feasibility study of the Great Whale drainage basin, essentially saying that any damage to the environment from Hydro-Québec's presence would be "manageable, temporary and restricted to relatively small areas." Evidently, in the collective minds of those within the utility, "relatively small areas" would include an expanse of northern Quebec equivalent to two-thirds the size of France.

Finally, running in parallel with this growing sense of public distress over the James Bay II project and Hydro-Québec's mulish attitude toward protection of the environment was the legal and political action being taken by the Cree and the Inuit. Together, these groups—the native people of northern Quebec, scientists, environmentalists and concerned citizens on both sides of the U.S.–Canada border—represented a broadly based and formidable opposition to Great Whale.

Although they had signed the James Bay and Northern Quebec Agreement with the provincial and federal governments and with Hydro-Québec, native leaders like Matthew Coon-Come and Charlie Watt were now locked in a bitter battle with Hydro-Québec. They claimed the utility had abrogated much of the original agreement. Native people in the region were now facing new and unexpected versions of social, cultural and environmental damage with James Bay II. The agreement, in their minds, was null and void. The Great Whale project had to be stopped.

By 1990, the Cree and Inuit leaders had designed a legal and public-relations strategy they felt might focus enough public attention to put an end to Great Whale. The tactics were simple. They would try to apply enough media and public-relations pressure to get utilities in the United States to rethink contracts they had signed for electricity with Quebec. At the same time they would work to tie up the provincial government and Hydro-Québec in court battles. But their big hope was that they could apply enough public pressure on the power utilities, particularly in the northeastern United States, to cancel those lucrative export contracts.

In April, the native leaders stepped up their legal campaign by seeking a permanent injunction against the Great Whale project. That same month, they introduced what turned out to be one of their most effective tactics.

The voyage of the *Odeyak* was a modest but straightforward effort to raise public awareness about the many grave issues native people living in the James Bay region faced with the Great Whale Project. It was an uncomplicated, although arduous, journey of sixty Cree and Inuit representatives travelling to New York in a large canoe. But as a public-relations enterprise, it galvanized opposition to Great Whale in a way a hundred days in court never could have. The voyage also signalled that the marvellous tapestry that was Robert Bourassa's Grand Vision for the North was finally about to unravel.

Odeyak was built in the village of Great Whale. It was a vessel with a bow like an Indian canoe and a stern-piece shaped like an Inuit Kayak. In it, the paddlers travelled south through Montreal, then down the Hudson River to New York. They reached Times Square on Earth Day.

Along the voyage south, the paddlers stopped in various towns and cities to tell their stories about what was happening in the James Bay region at the hands of Hydro-Québec and its government. Vermont and New York were two important states targeted for their lobbying efforts to get electricity contracts cancelled. It was the billions of dollars those states were prepared to pay for Quebec electricity that would essentially cause Great Whale to be completed.

The voyage of the *Odeyak* was a strategic and a spiritual success for the Cree and the Inuit. It generated massive support for their position and, ultimately, led to contracts being cancelled. In October 1990, the state of Vermont made it a condition of contract that any of the 340 megawatts of firm power it might commit to buying could not come from dams in the James Bay area. In September 1991, the New York Power Authority (NYPA) announced it was extending the deadline for ratifying a contract with Hydro-Québec for 1,000 megawatts of firm power. In March 1992, with the support of New York Governor Mario Cuomo, the NYPA cancelled the contract.

In November 1994, the Canadian Bond Rating Service Ltd. put the province of Quebec and its provincial power utility on "credit watch." A check in May indicated that the province was saddled with $133.8 billion in debt and that Hydro-Québec's prospects of holding on to long-term export contracts for firm power were beginning to dim. In the spring of 1994, the NYPA tore up a contract with Hydro-Québec for 800 megawatts, worth US$5 billion. A power glut had now developed in the northeastern states. New York no longer needed Quebec's extra power. The price was too high. Environmental and native concerns now loomed as large as the price of electricity.

When Premier Jacques Parizeau announced on November 18 that Great Whale was being "put on ice for quite a long time," a spokesman for the NYPA responded that "this was very good news." Parizeau's decision put to rest, for the foreseeable future, Robert Bourassa's Grand Vision. As the *Globe and Mail* commented editorially at the time: "The biggest reason to beach Great Whale was that it no longer made economic sense, if it ever did …"

6 / Nothing More Free than Free

Electricity remains the most politicized fuel.

— Richard Munson, *The Power Makers*

THURSDAY, FEBRUARY 22, 1996 was supposed to be a day of celebration for New Democratic Party leader Glen Clark. That was the day he was to be sworn in as premier of British Columbia. But instead of revelling in the pomp and circumstance that would normally accompany this ascendency, Clark was blindsided by a wicked barrage of revelations and accusations about the province's publicly owned electric utility—B.C. Hydro.

The opposition Liberal Party charged the day before Clark's swearing in that B.C. Hydro executives and "NDP insiders" were part of a group of investors who, along with a subsidiary company of B.C. Hydro, had been given preferential access to shares in a corporation —IPC International Power Corp.—developing a $168 million generating station in Raiwind, Pakistan. The Liberals' accusation was that these insiders got first dibs at buying shares, which could see a return on investment as high as twenty-five percent, while non-NDP investors and members of the general public were left out of the moneymaking loop.

The story had everything a right-wing newspaper like the Vancouver *Sun* could ask for: strong hints of another NDP "scandal," a rogues' gallery series of photos of NDP insiders and their spouses (along with names of prominent local business people and investors with no connection to the NDP), graphics of a sinister-looking "tangled web" of companies involved in the Raiwind Power Project, multi-million-dollar sums, even the insinuation that something *very* fishy was going on because the joint venture company was based in the Cayman Islands—one of those "offshore tax havens."

The *Sun* splashed page-after-page of these revelations—provided to them by the provincial Liberal Party—as if they had suddenly discovered the identity and the home address of the anti-Christ. Liberal politicos whined, kvetched and generally tried to knock the struts out from under both the NDP government and B.C. Hydro, with its board full of "NDP hacks" and "political appointments."

As befits the rock-'em-sock-'em world of B.C. politics, Clark had hardly handed over his swearing-in rose boutonniere to an aide when he announced that B.C. Hydro's top two executives—the chairman of the board of directors, John Laxton, a well-known Vancouver lawyer and NDP supporter, and the utility's president, John Sheehan —had been fired because of the revelations.

Despite the insinuations about political favouritism, tax havens and huge investor profits reserved only for NDPers, the crux of the issue was that Laxton and Sheehan, along with some members of their families, either held shares in IPC International Power Corp., held share options in companies holding shares in IPC or had encouraged members of their families to invest in IPC. More importantly for Clark, who had been the minister responsible for B.C. Hydro when these dealings apparently took place, Laxton and Sheehan were perceived to have contradicted the spirit of his ministerial instructions regarding the IPC joint venture.

When the IPC scandal hit the front pages, Premier Clark, who had been the minister in charge of B.C. Hydro when he was a member of the Harcourt cabinet, claimed that he had verbally denied permission for Hydro executives to invest in IPC and that "the utmost probity and the highest ethical, social and environmental standards should be used in this project." His point about family members investing in IPC was covered by simple reasoning: "If you're not allowed to invest, you can't have your wife invest," he was later quoted as saying.

Ipc had evolved out of entangled effort to sell B.C. Hydro's technical and managerial expertise to overseas governments and their power utilities. For a number of years the major Canadian power utilities, in particular Ontario Hydro, Hydro-Québec and B.C. Hydro, had been trying to gain a toe-hold in the increasingly attractive international power skills market. For a number of reasons—some political, some competitive, some by virtue of mandate—these efforts to sell their experience overseas had largely been hesitant, and the return on investment, when compared with the money made from selling electricity at home, marginal by comparison.

Still, with countries like China, India, Pakistan and parts of Latin America actively shopping for North American power know-how, as well as investors, it made sense for any respectable power utility to try to increase revenue flow by signing contracts to build or manage international power projects. There were numerous problems confronting public utilities testing this market. Very often these ventures were outside their legislated terms of reference. Some critics saw foreign excursions by publicly owned utilities as being high-risk, low-return. Taxpayers could be left holding the bag if a joint-venture partnership went sour. And things could get messy with foreign or private-sector partners, especially when the marketing of expertise was replaced with a preference to invest in foreign power projects. "What did this have to do with supplying 'power at cost?'" went the critics' refrain.

In 1993, Ontario Hydro's new off-shoot company—Ontario Hydro International Inc. (OHII)—formed a consortium with Hydro-Québec International Inc. and a subsidiary of the private-sector conglomerate, Power Corp. of Canada. The consortium was called Asia Power Group Inc. Its purpose was to invest in utility projects throughout Asia.

Heads turned in May 1994, when OHII announced it was bidding for two Peruvian power-distribution systems. It was also planning to buy a rain forest in Costa Rica. In July, OHII announced it was prepared to spend $74 million for shares in a co-venture in Aruba—a well-known Caribbean tax haven—with a Chilean company, Chilquinta S.A., as a means of bidding for the two Peruvian companies.

The plan to invest in a Costa Rican rain forest could perhaps be defended as a small, but highly questionable, step toward reducing carbon dioxide emissions. But it drew as much heat from angry and puzzled Ontario ratepayers as the Peruvian and Chilean escapades did. The loud public objection centred on an almost self-evident criticism: What was debt-laden Ontario Hydro doing spending millions of the taxpayers' dollars in places like Peru? Or buying rain forests when its hydro, coal-fired and nuclear-power projects had already degraded the environment back home?

As Elaine Dewar put it in an April 1995 *Report on Business Magazine* article, why would anyone want to invest in Peru, "the centre of coca production for the Columbian drug cartels, plagued by a Maoist insurgency and [with] national politics like a soap opera"? To many Ontario critics, these escapades were light years beyond Ontario Hydro's mandate. If there had not been so much of the ratepayers' and taxpayers' money placed at risk, the ventures might have been laughable as well.

In British Columbia's case, IPC's complicated joint-venture reflected a universal truth about the relationship between new provincial governments and a province's power utility; they do not trust each other. New provincial governments are inevitably wary of provincial utilities because of the potential power they hold in political terms. They do not trust them to do their bidding. After all, their boards usually come stacked with friends of the opposition party.

Also, new governments are often reluctant to get too close to the utility in case some injudicious move by it triggers a backlash from an angry electorate. As a consequence, the two tend to circle one another in the early stages of their political relationship like a mongoose and a cobra, waiting for the right moment to strike new policy directions.

Another factor to consider is that when a change of government takes place, the implementation period for new policy directions for the utility can cover an inordinate amount of time. Often it can take years, even outlasting the mandate of a one-term government. Hydros are large bureaucracies, unable to change corporate direction swiftly, especially after long periods of being guided by a political party with a different philosophy and ideas for them.

But little of this give-and-take history applied to B.C. Hydro when the NDP under Mike Harcourt came to office in the fall of 1991. After an early assessment period, the Harcourt government issued B.C. Hydro clear, new marching orders that significantly changed the direction in which the utility had been heading. In addition to its base mandate of providing British Columbians with inexpensive and reliable electricity, and to act as an economic pump-primer, it was directed to become more socially responsible and improve its shabby environmental track record. The Harcourt government also demanded that B.C. Hydro begin paying more of its way as a "public" utility by making it pay larger annual financial dividends to the province. Finally, in keeping with the government's eagerness to look toward the Pacific Rim for future business opportunities, it gave B.C. Hydro the signal to get more entrepreneurial. Offshore joint venturing in the field of electricity generation became a desirable enterprise to pursue—so long as the public's financial interests were not put at risk.

Despite a hope chest full of insinuations by the *Sun*, the IPC issue boiled down to less a scandal surrounding B.C. Hydro—in the sense that someone had done something horribly indiscreet or illegal, and should be headed for the slammer—than the editors would have wished. The fury generated by the *Sun* and its sister tabloid, the *Province*, was about an issue of judgement. Laxton and Sheehan would continue to dispute the clarity of the instructions they received from Clark about investing in the joint venture. Sheehan would later sue for wrongful dismissal, claiming Laxton encouraged him to get his wife and daughters involved as shareholders in the venture.

The other accusation put forward by the media was that IPC was a shaky joint-venture deal, the implication being that social democrats do not make good business decision-makers, and should never be caught playing with the Big Boys of World Finance. Taxpayers presumably could be on the hook for millions of dollars if Raiwind ever went sour.

But that was conjecture. Virtually within moments after the first revelations, B.C. Hydro was flooded with telephone calls—three hundred inquiries within two days, by the newspaper's own count—made by eager investors hoping to buy into IPC International Power Corp. and get a piece of that twenty-five percent return on investment. So much for a bad investment. So much for social democrats not knowing how to do business deals.

On the home front, B.C. Hydro ratepayers and taxpayers were scratching their heads. In most cases, they were less concerned about the news media's rabid sensationalism than about what was happening to their venerable public power utility. Was "The Hydro Scandal" an indication of bad management at the top? Did that mean that B.C. Hydro was losing money? Did it mean power rates might go up? Why was their number one crown corporation playing around with Cayman Island tax havens? What was their power utility—the builder of the province's dams and transmission system, the mover of mountains, the proud legatee of W. A. C. Bennett's dream of building a wealthy, modern British Columbia—doing in *Pakistan?* And what did this playing around in international power deals say about the future of their home-grown electrical utility?

Despite the immense pressure from the two Conrad Black–controlled newspapers, and the notoriously anti-NDP furor set up by right-wing broadcast station, BCTV, Clark's moves to control the political damage proved successful. He quickly appointed a former Social Credit attorney general, Brian Smith, to the vacant chairman's position at B.C. Hydro and gave Smith the job of conducting a public inquiry into IPC International Power Corp.

A quick review of the front-page stories and supper-hour television news highlights and one could only conclude, given the uproar over IPC, that B.C. Hydro, not unlike Ontario Hydro and Hydro-Québec, was a utility basket case.

In fact, the opposite was true. In relative terms, B.C. Hydro was, and still is, one of the healthiest public utilities in the world. In 1996, B.C. Hydro reported a net income of $150 million on $2.2 billion in revenues. It held $12.9 billion in assets and reported net long-term debt of $7.6 billion, giving the publicly owned power corporation the most favourable debt-to-equity ratio (79:21) among Canadian power utilities. Even the editors of the *Globe and Mail* were known to hold up B.C. Hydro as a paragon of utility virtue and probity.

The Harcourt government had at one point inquired into what the costs and benefits of privatizing B.C. Hydro might be. The conclusion of that examination was that the province's principal electrical utility was much more valuable to the province in public hands than in private hands. It provided a valuable service to its customers. It acted as that essential implement of economic development. It helped produce jobs. It paid its bills. And it paid the province a healthy annual dividend.

B.C. Hydro electricity rates were also some of the lowest in the developed world. They were forty-three percent lower than those of Ontario Hydro. Over the past decade, electricity prices had been declining in real terms for B.C. customers. Only Manitoba Hydro and Hydro-Québec had rates lower than British Columbia's, and then only marginally. However, Manitoba Hydro carried one of the highest debt-to-equity ratios in the country (91:09 in 1996) and its overall financial health and future potential were considered nowhere near that of British Columbia's. And the only thing keeping Hydro-Québec rates from leaping skyward was that bizarre windfall it enjoyed from the Churchill Falls agreement with Newfoundland.

Not only did B.C. Hydro not have to carry the onerous long-term debt burden of an organization like Hydro-Québec, it also did not have to wrestle, like Ontario Hydro, with the fiscal, moral and ethical hardship of being stuck producing electricity primarily with nuclear power. Roughly ninety percent of B.C. Hydro's power is generated hydraulically.

Thanks in large part to the leadership shown by the Harcourt administration, B.C. Hydro was also now widely known for its efforts to protect the environment, after too many decades of doing the opposite. In fact, while other power utilities were still considering traditional and environmentally damaging power-generation investments—in coal, natural gas, hydro, even nuclear—B.C. Hydro had already started in the opposite direction. Through the introduction of a series of demand-side power management programs, B.C. Hydro quickly became a leader in sustainable power development through energy conservation.

The province's and B.C. Hydro's fortunes were also given a boost when, toward the end of 1996, while Brian Smith was still conducting his inquiry into the IPC affair, the provincial government and the Washington-based Bonneville Power Administration (BPA) reached an agreement on the return of the province's downstream entitlement from the fabled Columbia River Treaty.

The BPA agreed to provide British Columbia with 1,400 megawatts of electricity, starting in 1998 and running until 2024. Those 1,400 megawatts were enough to light and heat five hundred thousand homes. It represented between ten and fifteen percent more power to be added to B.C. Hydro's current capacity—and it was all free. It was estimated that over the length of the agreement, the 1,400 megawatts could be worth anywhere from $2 billion to $5 billion. That huge amount of extra power would also mean that B.C. Hydro would not have to contemplate undertaking any major capital expansions of its generating power until well into the next millennium—if at all.

When Brian Smith tabled his inquiry report on March 19, 1997, the B.C. Hydro–IPC affair was revealed to be little more than a political headache for the NDP government. It was hardly a "scandal" in the legal or criminal sense of the word.

Lawyer John Laxton, the utility's former chairman, was heavily criticized for personally investing his and his family's money in IPC International Power Corp. Smith's findings tied the can of responsibility for the brouhaha quite securely to Laxton's tail, criticizing him for essentially running a one-man show during his chairmanship of B.C. Hydro. As an experienced lawyer, Smith wrote, Laxton "was remarkably insensitive to conflict-of-interest issues and to a director's duty of disclosure."

Smith also cited Premier Glen Clark for making "several fundamental mistakes" while minister in charge of the crown corporation. One was not understanding the amount of latitude Laxton had in making decisions affecting the IPC–Raiwind project. Smith concluded that Clark had "enabled, but did not cause" the problems associated with the IPC–Raiwind incident.

According to Smith, John Laxton had operated much too independently. His actions escaped the scrutiny of the utility's board of directors primarily because the majority of the board were not sophisticated enough in international finance or energy matters to supervise properly the events surrounding the IPC joint venture.

Smith characterized Laxton as an "unsuitable person to be the chair of B.C. Hydro" because he failed to recognize the important differences between operating in the public sector versus the private sector. Smith went on to paint a picture of chairman Laxton as a man who essentially ran B.C. Hydro on his own whim: the government did not understand the extent to which Hydro was under Laxton's "dominating influence," he had effectively run rough-shod over a weak board of directors and so on.

But there may have been another side to the coin. John Laxton had been motivated to buy the IPC shares because the private share offering he personally had been organizing was not going well. There was some risk the necessary capital might not be assembled. The joint venture could be in danger of collapsing. It could be embarrassing to both B.C. Hydro and the NDP government if it failed. Someone had to make sure the offer was fully subscribed.

In the report, much was made of this one-man-captured-the-corporation supposition. But this was the reality of how Canada's public power utilities had been run, for good or for bad, since their origination. Power utilities end up largely being run by the strength of purpose of a chairman, a small clique of board members, a cabinet minister, even a premier. The aura of power that these massive organizations represent manufactures its own vacuum, one most often filled by the force of the strongest personality: Beck, Lévesque, Strong, Bourassa, W. A. C. Bennett, Gordon Shrum, to name a few. The report was identifying symptoms. It missed the disease.

The IPC incident also reflected another endemic problem with public monopolies. These giant utilities are serious public property. Who else but the citizens' elected representatives should be responsible for setting clear policy objectives for the utility, and then ensuring through proper regulatory oversight, monitoring and government assessment that it performs as expected?

Public corporations worth tens of billions of dollars, with billions in annual cash flow and as important to the state of the province as power utilities are, cannot be simply left in the hands of a covey of dedicated and dutiful board members. These are not appointments to a liquor board or the gaming commission we are talking about. Nor can these utilities be allowed to be captured by the inconsistent hand of even the most well-meaning politicians, as Ontario Hydro's post-1960s experience reveals. To avoid both evils, these powerful institutions must be subject to strong, third-party public regulation, a commodity sadly missing in the history of almost all power utilities.

In Quebec, Hydro-Québec did what the premier told it to do. Ontario Hydro has no regulatory control, follows no guiding light except that which shines through the premier's door. British Columbia's regulatory regime has been mandated to the British Columbia Utilities Commission, but its oversight responsibilities are restricted to ruling on electricity rates. And that is where the weakness and the source of failure lies in the structure and history of Canadian public power utilities. Electricity is too important not to be properly policed.

Leaving a lay board of directors in sole charge of a $12 billion corporation, with a couple of mission statements and very little monitoring guidance, is a little like asking them to guide a supertanker full of crude oil through ice-filled and treacherous Arctic waters after a couple of weekends practising steering a speedboat at the summer cottage. The IPC matter was less a story about a utility going off track than it was about ordinary people, with the best of intentions, but with vague directional advice from their government, wading into water more than slightly over their heads.

The fundamental issue that had plagued the relationships between politicians and these powerful public utilities since Adam Beck got his way in 1906 was: How close or how far away is the guiding hand of government supposed to be when it comes to running these giant utilities? The sheer seduction of power, and the heft and feel it must give one when placed in hand, has always been stronger than any ideological vision or purity of business action for a province's power utility. The decision for Ontario Hydro to go nuclear was not a utility decision. It was part of a broader political and economic strategy.

When Robert Bourassa decided that Hydro-Québec and his personal visions were inseparable—in effect, a modern version of *L'état c'est moi*—the utility and the province were piled high with debt and social responsibilities out of all proportion for a company that was supposed to keep the lights on and the water hot. Hydro-Québec went where Bourassa instructed it go. When Adam Beck decided that his personal power was synonymous with Ontario's electric-power potential, the fact that he was extremely effective allowed provincial governments to bathe in the glow of Beck's achievements without having to give the utility much political direction.

The relationship between political master and electrical servant has never been static or depersonalized. It has never been free of the propelling force of strong, visionary personalities. Some politicians have simply stood in awe of its power or influence—or got out of the way. In that sense, public power knows no ideology. At times, free-enterpriser Beck's performance was communistic, perhaps even Stalinist. Lévesque and Bourassa flipped Hydro-Québec like a two-headed cultural coin. Both sides carried the same symbol—greatness for Quebec. Bob Rae's NDP government talked quietly about selling Ontario Hydro—an entity that should be the cornerstone of any social democrat's institutional portfolio. And the NDP government in British Columbia tried to act like entrepreneurs on the international power stage. All of this would have made W. A. C. Bennett smile his famous Cheshire-cat smile and nod his head knowingly.

On September 16, 1964, the Canadian prime minister, Lester Bowles Pearson, and the president of the United States of America, Lyndon Baines Johnson, joined a large public gathering at the Peace Arch border crossing at Blaine, Washington. The event was the ceremonial ratification of the signing of the Columbia River Treaty. As mighty as the heads of the Canadian and American nations might have appeared on the face of it, both would be upstaged by a Kelowna hardware merchant cum premier of British Columbia—William Andrew Cecil Bennett.

In international political terms, Bennett was certainly the third man down the power pole that day. In hydro-electric power terms, W. A. C. Bennett was about to be crowned King for a Day, and would be king for many days to come.

It had been Bennett who pressured the two national governments and the International Joint Commission to get serious about finally signing the Columbia River Treaty. Discussions about the project had been going on between the governments of Canada and the United States, one way or another, since 1944. It was Bennett who forced the two governments to accept his conditions, not their conditions, which eventually made up the details of the agreement. It was Bennett who steered the negotiations in the direction of his own Two River power development dream. As a consequence of his relentless political pressure (some might say, impertinence as well), the treaty would help his province harness the power of both the Columbia and Peace Rivers. The treaty would provide British Columbia with a low-cost way to begin serious economic development of the province's hinterland.

It had been Bennett, the political sorcerer, who conjured a final agreement that had the United States purchase Canada's share of the first thirty years of downstream benefits for roughly $274 million. At the same time, Bennett's negotiating skill guaranteed that, thirty years later, British Columbia would realize further downstream benefits valued at up to $5 billion. And it was primarily Bennett who President Johnson was thinking of when he handed over a cheque that September day in 1964, in the amount of $273,291,661.25. "The Canadians even went for the last twenty-five cents," the Texan reportedly muttered jokingly as he handed over the cheque.

Johnson and Pearson "seemed like stagehands compared to the obvious star of the show," David J. Mitchell wrote in his outstanding biography, *W. A. C. Bennett and the Rise of British Columbia.* Pearson would later write that, while he was head of the Canadian government and President Johnson was head of the powerful American government, that day "in British Columbia, Mr. Bennett was head of all he surveyed."

Bennett considered it his greatest achievement in a political life notable for many achievements. "We were able to make the best deal internationally on water power ever made in the world," Bennett told Mitchell. "There's no place else that I know of where one country [Canada] gets downstream benefits from another country, keeps all their own power and gets one-half of the new power generated in a foreign country—no place else."

He had long held a dream that some day B.C. rivers would power a massive electrical-industrial surge, generating the wealth needed to develop the rugged, resource-based interior and modernize the province's economy. Despite a dramatic, post–World War II economic boom fuelled by natural resource development, by 1956 provincial growth had peaked and British Columbia was feeling the first pangs of recession.

Hydro-electric power would be the stimulus to spur a new round of resource development. Two things stood in the way of his dream: the intimidating cost of developing the hydro-electric potential of two of the province's largest rivers—the Columbia and the Peace— and the refusal of the province's privately owned monopoly power utility to buy into his dream.

Bennett was a man who religiously advocated an economic system based upon free enterprise and private initiative. But in 1961, he would rid himself of both his ideological predisposition and the final barricade standing in the way of his dream for a stronger British Columbia. He would nationalize the B.C. Electric Company, the privately owned, federally chartered monopoly utility providing ninety percent of the province's electricity. He had been eyeing hydro-electric expansion as the impetus for economic growth since he came to office in 1952. His pursuit of electricity took on "a kind of mystic importance," as Mitchell wrote, and he was clearly prepared to go to extreme political lengths to make that happen.

Bennett was a living political paradox. He believed in free enterprise and was often highly critical about ineffectual government intervention in the marketplace. But he was also a pragmatic politician who knew the second part of his grand dream—full employment, needed improvements in transportation, new schools, hospitals and other services that would provide a higher standard of living for British Columbians—was impossible if left solely to free enterprise and the invisible hand of the marketplace. In fact, that was Bennett's basic problem.

On other matters, his Social Credit governments were the epitome of free enterprise. Most backbenchers were small-town businessmen who talked of frugality, hard work and being unshackled from the chains of government. They applauded Bennett when he went on the attack against the "socialist hordes" of the Co-operative Commonwealth Federation (CCF) and later, the NDP.

Bennett did not stand on ideological protocol and he did not shrink from introducing direct government involvement in the economy when the private sector was too timid to act. His operating philosophy said government was there to ensure its broad, important social goals were met. But if the marketplace did not provide the leadership the province needed, Social Credit would. As Bennett cabinet minister the Rev. Phil Gaglardi once stated: "We really believe in free enterprise, but we don't let anyone stand in our way."

Contradictions seemed to be what Bennett lived for. His government won a renewed mandate in the provincial election of 1960 by running *against* the CCF's platform of nationalization of the B.C. Electric Company. Historian David Mitchell summed up Bennett's pragmatism: "Intervention if necessary, but not necessarily intervention."

In 1958, after a strike by Black Ball Line ferry workers had disrupted passenger service up and down B.C.'s west coast, Bennett made a cash offer to buy the line for $7.8 million. He considered the ferries an important part of the province's coastal highway system and was upset at how the two privately run ferry companies (the other was Canadian Pacific Railway) refused to modernize their fleets and expand service for the increasing number of passengers. Bennett bought the Black Ball Line (later referred to as "Bennett's Navy") and drove the CPR out of the ferry business.

Part of the secret to Bennett's mastery of these philosophical switchbacks was his ability to concentrate immense governing power in his own hands. As well as being premier, Bennett was minister of finance. He knew where every public penny was going. He was one of the first premiers to make liberal use of crown corporations as state instruments for economic development, principally because he had little fear of their wandering from his own tight fiscal grasp. Bennett could speed up or slow down the province's pace of spending and development with a flick of his pen.

Bennett's control over government departments and crown corporations reflected his thinking on the uses of power. Power, in a political context, is not an abstract concept with a multitude of meanings. It is the ability to cause or prevent change. Its application, to Bennett, was not just an expression of the life process, but the gathering of forces to make change—his change, the change that he defined for British Columbia—happen.

"In everything he did, Bennett was always 'engaged'," Mitchell wrote. "He was eternally manipulating, manoeuvring, always with his fingers in the many pies he coveted. He was not happy unless he was involved in some form of human exchange or collision of ambitions. He was not content just to savour his power; he had to exercise it and continually extend its base ... As Bennett grew into office in Victoria he came to resemble something very close to a head of state in his own right—a kind of provincial warlord ..."

Bennett's biggest battlefield was hydro-electric power. He would defy the master military tacticians by choosing to fight on two fronts at the same time, and win handily on both. It was not just electrical power he was after, but power from two of the mightiest rivers running through British Columbia. His Two River Policy was criticized by opponents as too much, too expensive and too difficult. It was felt that the energy from these mighty rivers would be surplus to the needs of British Columbians. But Bennett's vision of the future inevitably exceeded the limited view of his critics.

The Columbia River is the fourth-largest river in North America. It begins its journey to the sea in the southeast corner of British Columbia. It has long been seen as one of the most powerful rivers on the continent. Its headwaters begin at around one thousand metres above sea level. It then twists its way through the Canadian Rockies and into Washington state, where it is joined by a number of tributaries before pouring into the Pacific Ocean. The flow of the untamed Columbia had always been dangerous and troublesome for both countries, in particular during the winter and spring. Devastating floods were not uncommon, even though the Americans had constructed dams for both flood control and electrical power generation on their side of the border. Their work included the famous Grand Coulee, a concrete dam that rises over 180 metres.

During World War II the International Joint Commission (IJC) was instructed to study the costs and benefits of further joint development of the river. In particular, it was asked to assess both the flood-control possibilities and the hydro-electric potential of building large storage reservoirs to regulate water flow on the Canadian section of the Columbia. It would take a decade and a half of study by the IJC before direct negotiations began between Canada and the United States over how the Columbia would ultimately be harnessed.

From the time of his election as premier of British Columbia's first Social Credit government in 1952, Bennett kept a vigil over events as Canada and the United States weighed the pros and cons of proceeding with joint development of the Columbia River. Bennett was irked by the slow pace of international deliberations, but he could see that a judicious agreement between the two nations could only deliver massive energy benefits to British Columbia, particularly in the southern and lower mainland portions of the province. But the Columbia was not his first priority. His first love was the Peace River.

The Peace River is one of the principal tributaries of the Mackenzie River. Tucked far into the thinly populated northeast portion of the province, it begins its life at the junction of the Finlay and Parsnip Rivers and then winds its way east through the town of Fort St. John, crosses the boundary between British Columbia and Alberta, flows through the town of Peace River, then veers north and east again into the Slave River, which joins the Mackenzie in its journey to the Arctic Ocean. The valley of the Peace is fertile and abundant. It is the northernmost commercially viable agricultural region on the continent.

Although not as splendid or as powerful as the Columbia, the Peace River held a curious, personal fascination for Bennett, one centred in a difficult relationship he had with his itinerant father, Andrew Bennett. After returning from World War I in 1919, Andrew Bennett had been incapable of settling down comfortably with his wife, Mary Emma. He packed up and headed to the Peace River country. Cecil, as W. A. C. Bennett was known then, was eighteen years old. He decided to follow his father. The frontier alliance between father and son did not last. The younger Bennett eventually picked up stakes and left his father.

"For Cecil, the Peace River country would always serve as a reminder of his father," David Mitchell wrote. "The two became intertwined in his mind. The great unfulfilled promise of the territory seemed to represent the potential but never realized love between father and son."

There is a revealing story of Bennett in *Conversations with W. A. C. Bennett*, a book of interviews conducted by Roger Keene.

In the early days of his premiership, Bennett was travelling through his beloved Peace River Valley and stopped along the highway outside Fort St. John. From a small hilltop he was able to view the sweeping but desolate valley below. As Bennett stood there, an old trapper appeared. Bennett asked him what vista he saw.

"I see a muddy little river that has been running on for centuries and centuries. I come through here all the time because I have a small trap line ... But what do *you* see?"

"Well, I said," Bennett mused, "I see cities, prosperous cities, beautiful schools and hospitals, universities. I see women doing their baking in ovens that use electricity. I see thousands of jobs all resulting from what you and I are looking at right now.

"He asked me one or two more questions and then he said, 'You know, up in this north country, we get a lot of crazy people coming here. But you are the most craziest person that ever came into the north as far as I am concerned.'

"I said, 'Thank you very much.' And away he went."

In his haste to harness hydro-electric power to help spur the province's economic growth, Bennett agreed in principle in 1954 to allow the American Kaiser Corporation to build a large storage dam on the upper reaches of the Columbia River. It would be built at no cost to the province in return for a fifty-year water licence. Like a small precursor to the eventual Columbia River Treaty, twenty percent of the power generated downstream in the United States would be returned to British Columbia.

The federal Liberals opposed the deal on the basis that the project affected international relations. More importantly, it could do serious damage to the proposed joint development of the Columbia River that was still under negotiation. The Liberal government passed legislation quashing the Kaiser–B.C. agreement. The decision angered Bennett, but it also gave him a clearer idea of how weighty hydro issues might be negotiated later, issues such as downstream benefits. This reversal worked to the province's advantage. Bennett vowed that he would never again allow Ottawa to rule over provincial development issues.

Bennett's first move after this setback took him to the Peace River. A firm owned by Swedish millionaire Axel Wenner-Gren showed interest in developing mineral resources in the north-central Rocky Mountain Trench area of the province. The firm had conducted preliminary studies on both the area's resources and its hydro-electric potential. One Wenner-Gren survey showed that a large hydro-electric dam could be built on the Peace River and that its power output (estimated at four million horsepower) could exceed that of the proposed Columbia system. This survey of the massive potential of the Peace was the hole card that Bennett would use so shrewdly to set the pace, tone and direction of the development of the power of both the Columbia and Peace Rivers. It would be the second-last turn of the cards for his Two River Policy.

The entry of the Peace as a major generating option also seemed to hurry along the Columbia negotiations. The Wenner-Gren studies resulted in a new company being formed, the Peace River Power Development Company. The fact that it was a serious business venture, and that its board contained a number of imposing international and Canadian financiers, no doubt exhibited to the federal government how serious Bennett and his friends were. Soon, draft treaties were being discussed between Canada and the United States. Some were incredulous when Bennett began talking about developing both massive projects at the same time. Critics pointed out that the two projects would produce more electricity than the province required, provided they could even be constructed. But Bennett persisted. His critics were looking at present electricity demand. Bennett was looking over the horizon at future mineral, coal, gas and oil development which would require large amounts of hydro-electric power. As usual, his vision penetrated the future further than that of his critics.

Bennett was also aware that his Two River Policy required some very nifty political footwork. To avoid being stuck with huge, expensive surpluses of electrical energy, he would have to doctor any future international agreement to ensure that the power from the Columbia was sold, in the first instance, to the Americans. With the surplus problem out of the way, electricity from the Peace River could fuel the early fires of industrial and economic development in north-central and northeastern British Columbia. If he could pull it off, it would be a brilliant strategy. Beyond the pressing need for an international agreement to be signed, there was one other major obstacle holding back Bennett's bold dream: the B.C. Electric Company.

The B.C. Electric Company (BCE) was a privately owned power utility producing ninety percent of the province's electricity. BCE had been formed in 1928 and was controlled by the B.C. Power Corporation Limited, a holding company owned and operated by the eastern-based Power Corporation. By 1961, BCE was the province's largest private-sector company. Although it was a highly profitable monopoly for its investors, it was known more widely by the public for its high rates and indifferent service.

Bennett's Two River Policy required a provincial power utility that would join him in generating the electricity his grand plans for resource development of the Peace region required. B.C. Electric would not play ball. It steadfastly refused to commit to buying the necessary power from the planned Peace project.

The board of BCE saw the pursuit of power projects on both the Peace and the Columbia Rivers as dangerous and expensive folly. Perhaps they were trapped too tightly in their competitive marketplace philosophy, but the heads of BCE saw the two power projects as eventually competing for the same limited provincial market. In 1959, BCE estimated that the province already had sufficient power for another decade, once the Burrard Thermal Generating plant came on stream. If something had to be built, BCE favoured the Columbia project because of its lower construction cost.

BCE also thought Bennett's Peace River power project too expensive. In their opinion, the electricity would be surplus to domestic needs and only good for export purposes. The federal government, not the provincial government, controlled export of power. BCE saw the ongoing federal-provincial wrangling over the Columbia as evidence that easy access to export markets was unlikely for the time being. For all these reasons, the board of BCE was not prepared to join Bennett in his dream of super-abundant power from the Peace.

In an interview with David Mitchell, Bennett told the story of a meeting in London with Sir Andrew McTaggart, the former Chancellor of the Exchequer and then chairman of the board of the Peace River Power Development Company (PRPDC), Dal Grauer, president of BCE and Bennett. He had brought them together to let Grauer hear directly from Sir Andrew how BCE's refusal to take electricity generated on the Peace River meant the PRPDC could not get the investment it needed from the international bond market. McTaggart outlined his company's dilemma for Grauer, but Grauer adamantly refused to budge. He said BCE had no intention of buying future power from the Peace.

"Never forget one thing in this world," Bennett said to Grauer at that moment. "In nature, what you don't use, you lose. We are not going to stand idly by in British Columbia and not have that Peace River power development go ahead!"

It was no idle threat. Bennett was telling Grauer straight-up that one way or another he, Bennett, was going to prevail. If he filled that vacuum, the implication was there would be no room for Grauer and BCE.

"This was one of the most important meetings I had while I was premier," Bennett told Mitchell. "Perhaps this was *the* most important."

But BCE was misreading both Bennett and the province's potential. Bennett had already warned the board of the utility that they "didn't have the vision for the kind of growth our province needed." More significantly, he made sure he left no doubt in their minds "that the Peace would be developed, with or without private enterprise."

Further south, the IJC deliberations over the Columbia River Treaty dragged on. It was not until late in 1960 that a draft treaty was finally agreed to. But Ottawa—which at that time meant the Progressive Conservative government of John Diefenbaker—differed with Bennett over how the project might be financed and how the downstream benefits were to be dispersed. Bennett floated the idea of selling the downstream benefits for cash, which then might be used to pay the cost of building the storage dams on the Columbia. Diefenbaker's point man on the Columbia negotiations, British Columbian Davie Fulton, was opposed to the idea, calling it a "sell-out" to the Americans.

This was no small family squabble. Bennett was concerned about Ottawa's efforts to take control of the Columbia River project. Bennett saw this as a blatant intrusion into a province's control of its hydro-electric resources. He was so resolute that he would not even consider the idea of a joint federal-provincial entity to build and operate the Columbia project. It was going to be a B.C.-driven project, or nothing at all.

On the other hand, the federal Liberals saw control, or at the least a joint venture, as the natural culmination of the federal government's effort at negotiating an international agreement. Bennett went public. He issued a statement to the press that he would unequivocally refuse to allow Ottawa to control the Columbia project. Fulton was furious. He opposed the idea of selling the downstream benefits for cash. Fulton wanted to make sure the money did not end up in British Columbia's coffers.

The Americans were watching with renewed interest, playing an international game of wait-and-see. U.S. negotiators interpreted Bennett's eagerness to get the Columbia River project underway as a sign that the Canadians would inevitably have to develop their portion of the Columbia some day, in any case. Bennett's Two River Policy was a red herring as far as they were concerned. Why give away downstream benefits to the Columbia if the Canadians were going to be forced to develop the southern river sooner or later anyway?

But a successfully negotiated Columbia River Treaty was still the key to Bennett's Two River Policy. He would make the Americans get serious about concluding the long, dragged-out negotiations over the Columbia by baiting them with a hint about the beginning of development on the Peace River. By the autumn of 1960, the B.C. Energy Board had completed its favourable engineering study of the Peace River, although there was still no willingness on BCE's part to commit to taking power generated from the Peace project in the future. "I knew very well the way to get the Columbia was to get the Peace," Bennett told Mitchell, "then they'd know that British Columbia had lots of power and wouldn't have to develop the Columbia."

The first player to blink in this three-handed brand of international poker was the Canadian government. Despite being aware that Bennett was vehemently opposed to any federal control over a provincial resource, and despite not having concluded any agreement with British Columbia over financial arrangements, the Diefenbaker government agreed to sign the treaty with the Americans. It seemed the politically prudent thing to do. The popularity of the Diefenbaker government was falling steadily. A major international agreement, which might translate into jobs and economic development, could help stem its fall from grace with the Canadian electorate.

The second player to blink was the United States of America. After so many years of cross-border negotiations, the Americans were now eager to sign the treaty and get on with development of the American portion of the Columbia. But by formally signing the international agreement on January 17, 1961, without W. A. C.

Bennett on side, both the Americans and the Canadians had effectively given the resolute Bennett, and the province of British Columbia, last right of approval over this very important treaty.

The cunning Bennett had one more ace left in his hand. While vowing to make ratification of the treaty as difficult as possible, and still adamant that Ottawa would not get the upper hand in developing and controlling a provincial resource, he called a special session of the B.C. legislature in August 1961. Ostensibly, the session was to allow debate on the treaty's financial arrangements with Ottawa. Instead, Bennett dropped a political bombshell. He and his free-enterprise Social Credit Party were about to nationalize the province's privately owned power utility, the B.C. Electric Company.

Bennett was going to do the opposite of what he had told the electors Social Credit would do in the last provincial election. His government would practise "state socialism." Less than a year before, he had mocked the provincial CCF party, led by Robert Strachan, for moving a resolution in the legislature calling for all private utilities to be placed under public ownership. It would be a tremendous testament to the power Bennett held that he could "provincialize" the largest privately owned electrical power company in Canada with the consensus of a caucus and cabinet as anti-socialist as ever walked this country's political soil. But to Bennett, the tenets of ideology or political philosophy had nothing to do with his decision. Always the politician who lived for the moment of decision, he needed the control publicly owned power would give him to exercise the management of development throughout British Columbia. It was, to him, as simple as that.

As Hugh L. Keenleyside wrote in the second volume of his autobiography, *On the Bridge of Time*, Bennett's commitment to free enterprise "was not so total as to blind him to the political advantages of an occasional deviation from the true faith." Bennett was a prime example of Aristotle's political animal: "When he saw particularly luscious peaches beginning to ripen on [a CCF/NDP] tree, he was not above a little surreptitious thievery."

Bennett defended his move, rather thinly, by stating that the nationalization of BCE was triggered by the failure of the federal government to provide British Columbia with a fair return on the taxes paid by federally chartered power utilities. The legislation making B.C. Electric a crown corporation called for $180 million in compensation to BCE's parent company, the B.C. Power Corporation,

$104 million for replacement of preferred shares and the assumption of $400 million in outstanding debt. At the same time, to ensure that the march to eventual development of the Peace River would begin in earnest, his government acquired the assets of the PRPDC.

Bennett was playing The Hammer card. As William Tieleman wrote in his University of British Columbia political science master's thesis, *The Political Economy of Nationalism: Social Credit and the Takeover of the British Columbia Electric Company:* "By taking over B.C. Electric the province instantly gained a near monopoly position in the distribution of electricity in B.C., ensuring that it could develop the Peace to supply B.C. energy needs without fear of facing competition from cheaper energy sources ... Its control over the domestic market, plus the necessary provincial approval of the Columbia River Treaty, meant it could force the federal government into agreeing to sell cheap Columbia power to the U.S. on a long-term contract basis and reap the financial benefits to help pay for infrastructural development needed in the Peace region."

The move had substantial political benefits for Bennett as well. For years, the CCF had been calling for nationalization of the utility. Bennett's unanticipated move stole the CCF's thunder. It also countered criticism from the left that Social Credit was "in the pocket of B.C. Electric." It reinforced Bennett's populist image for Social Credit as the party always working for "the little guy." And, to rub salt in Ottawa's wound, it meant that British Columbia would no longer have to pay the federal taxes on revenues earned that the privately owned BCE had to remit.

When the takeover of BCE was finally achieved, it was marked by one event, as Hugh L. Keenleyside wrote, that might have been taken from a Greek tragedy: "On the day the provincial flag was raised over what had been B.C. Electric's head office at the corner of Nelson and Burrard streets in Vancouver, the funeral cortège of Dal Grauer moved slowly up the hill past the building in which he had until a few days before been the centre of power."

The national and international press reacted with predictable hostility. *Barron's*, the leading New York financial paper of the time, called Bennett's move "confiscation" that was "tantamount to theft." Bennett's "high-handed" government had not only struck "a bargain with socialism." It had also exhibited "a striking contempt for due process of law," the influential business weekly declared.

"Seldom, if ever, in Canadian economic history has one government been attacked by national and international capital with such unanimous scorn," William Tieleman wrote, "particularly a government which boasted of its free enterprise ideology."

Bennett was, like Lévesque would be later, compared with Fidel Castro. The Investment Dealers Association of Canada called the takeover an "unjust" expropriation. The *Financial Post* referred to Bennett's action as a "stick 'em up" proposal. Bankers in Geneva and London issued shadowy warnings about possible investment retribution (although, throughout this time, Moody's credit-rating service maintained an "A" level designation for both the province's and its new crown corporation's debt). The press criticisms read as if the good ship *Free Enterprise* had suddenly and unexpectedly been dive-bombed by a squadron of communist aircraft.

But it should have been obvious to observers at the time that the swashbuckling hardware merchant from Kelowna was going to take over B.C. Electric. In the first place, Bennett had always displayed a partiality to public power, ever since he became active in B.C. politics in the 1940s. It largely stemmed from his service on the Post-War Rehabilitation Council, which had recommended, in 1943, the establishment of publicly owned hydro-electric power to provide cheap electricity for British Columbia. His support for a more active role for the publicly owned B.C. Power Commission (BCPC) was well known, as were the frequent run-ins Bennett had with the supercilious heads of the B.C. Electric Company.

Bennett had dropped enough hints since the Canadians and Americans reached an agreement-in-principle in January for there to be little surprise at his expropriation of BCE. On February 27, 1961, he had stated publicly that he was giving notice to the federal government "and everybody else that unless we get fair treatment we will have to take over the B.C. Electric."

Taking control of almost all hydro-electric power in British Columbia would ensure Bennett's position as chief actor in the politics of power. Mitchell wrote: "The takeover of B.C. Electric earned him more prominence, both nationally and internationally, than any other active Canadian politician enjoyed. He secretly revelled in his sudden notoriety abroad, for it did him no political harm at home. "No one seems to like us but the people," he said.

It was fair public knowledge that the executives of BCE lived pretty well off those high electricity rates. In the early 1960s, Grauer's annual salary was close to $100,000. Extra perquisites included a home, a car, money for domestic staff and generous stock options. In addition, extra benefits paid to senior staff "resulted in their receiving total remuneration that even a decade later would have been considered inordinately high," Keenleyside wrote in his memoirs. "More than one senior official emerged from a comparatively short period of service with B.C. Electric in the millionaire category."

But there was still no progress between British Columbia and Ottawa over resolution of Canada's position on the Columbia River Treaty. Bennett and his Progressive Conservative adversary, Davie Fulton, remained in heated political deadlock throughout the latter part of 1961. The two adversaries gave no quarter. Fulton baited Bennett with federal challenges to Bennett's plan to dam the Peace River. Bennett, in turn, made it plain once again that he would simply refuse to ratify the Columbia agreement—until the changes he wanted to see were made.

Bennett took every opportunity to singe Ottawa's beard, including holding a private discussion with United States President John F. Kennedy. In November 1961, during a banquet in Seattle, Washington, the B.C. premier met casually with the president and his secretary of the interior, Stewart Udall, to discuss issues related to the Columbia Treaty. From a protocol point of view, this was a highly unorthodox and undiplomatic encounter. But it demonstrated what Bennett had been saying all along: There was support for the sale of power from the Columbia project "at the highest political levels" south of the border.

Bennett's fortunes began to improve even more dramatically when the Diefenbaker Progressive Conservatives were ousted from office by a minority government headed by Lester Pearson in April 1963. It ended two-and-a-half years of bitter wrangling with Ottawa. Unlike Diefenbaker, Pearson agreed to allow British Columbia to negotiate the sale of downstream benefits with the Americans. It was a strategic difference which led, in early July, to a final Victoria-Ottawa agreement on the Columbia River Treaty process.

But Bennett's plans for quick implementation of his Two River Policy suffered a setback when, in late July, a decision by Chief Justice Sherwood Lett of the B.C. Supreme Court, triggered by a legal challenge by BCPC, declared that Bennett's expropriation of

B.C. Electric was *ultra vires*, that it was illegal and unconstitutional. Bennett's first reaction was to bluster about taking the case to the Supreme Court of Canada. At the same time, he let it be known that he was willing to renegotiate the terms of the BCE takeover. It was a risky strategy, but in typical populist fashion, Bennett, although shaken by the court's decision, carried his case to an even higher court. He called a surprise provincial election for September 30, 1963. There was only one real issue: public versus private power.

"On the Social Credit side, the election call was similar to a poker bluff," Tieleman wrote, "with the government knowing that if it won a strong mandate it could drive a very hard bargain in settling the dispute. Further, an electoral victory after the adverse B.C. Supreme Court ruling would mean increased legitimacy for [Bennett's] government at the expense of the judiciary."

Three days before the election B.C. Power Corporation tossed in the towel. Bennett's gamble paid off handsomely in two ways. The province got B.C. Electric for just over $197 million. And on election day, the Social Credit Party increased its share of the popular vote to forty-one percent, adding an extra seat in the legislature for a total of thirty-three, versus the combined opposition total of nineteen seats.

Although the Pearson government and Bennett had reached an accord on how to proceed toward a settlement of the interminable Columbia River Treaty talks, Bennett refused to cave in to federal control over the money the Americans would have to pay for the downstream benefits. The Liberal government proposed that the advance payment would go to Ottawa first, and then be distributed to British Columbia as the various capital construction projects began. Bennett utterly refused to accept this. Nobody was going to handle that money but himself. The Liberals then suggested Ottawa would withhold certain amounts to ensure the province did not default on payments connected with the international agreement. Again, Bennett refused. He was "infuriated." This last proposition, in his mind, would give the federal government power over a provincial government, with no recourse to arbitration. The international agreement that had taken so long to reach this stage was in serious risk of collapsing. To underline his displeasure, Bennett left for a vacation in Hawaii before any agreement was struck. His instructions to staff were that there was only one set of conditions he would agree to: all the money, his way, with no strings attached.

A furious series of negotiations ensued between the provincial and federal negotiators and finally, on Christmas Eve 1963, Bennett, perhaps in recognition of the season, made a small concession. It was agreed that if it was ever proven that British Columbia was at some point in the future to be in default, Ottawa could extract the amount of money in question from its subsequent federal transfer payment to British Columbia.

After years of exhaustive study and exhausting negotiation, all parties to the treaty appeared happy. Through sheer staying power, W. A. C. Bennett had forced the national governments of Canada and the United States to face the fact that if any agreement was to be reached, it would be on his conditions, and only his conditions.

Bennett had not just persevered. From the moment he took interest, he dominated the entire flow of the treaty process, tossing ultimatums left and right. Here was a provincial premier, ostensibly subservient to a federal government, in the midst of negotiating an international treaty with the world's foremost power, who refused to be marginalized. Bennett saw early on in his budding political career that the most essential element of power was power itself—the electricity that would help build a province.

Bennett would turn out to be the most effective political leader in B.C. history. His political fires were largely fuelled by his belief that he was plugged into the Lord. But even there he was more pragmatist than disciple; always willing to be guided by God's word, so long as the Lord agreed, as Keenleyside put it, "with [his] personal assessment of the desirability of taking a course [Bennett] favoured."

The story is often told about the day a visitor to B.C. Hydro was being shown through the senior management department of the utility's downtown Vancouver head office. Suddenly, the visitor was shocked to hear a loud, booming voice angrily berating an underling. As the bellowing continued, the visitor turned to his guide and inquired, "Who is that?"

"That is our chairman, Dr. Gordon Shrum," the guide replied with some embarrassment. "He is talking to our Kelowna office."

"Why does he not use a telephone?" the visitor asked mischievously.

B.C. Hydro's Dr. Gordon Shrum was, in some respects, a modern version of Adam Beck. Shrum seemed to carry the same fierce sense of mission for his utility. He had a remarkable ability to organize complex projects and bring them in on time and on budget. He was a renowned physicist, educator and administrator who believed there was little end to the wonders that science could deliver to mankind.

Following the appropriation of BCE, Bennett appointed Shrum chairman of the new crown corporation in 1961. When it was amalgamated with the B.C. Power Commission on April 1, 1962, Shrum became co-chairman, along with Hugh Keenleyside, of the new B.C. Hydro and Power Authority. Shrum remained as co-chairman until Keenleyside retired in 1969 and continued as sole chairman until nudged out of office at the end of 1972 by the NDP government.

In 1963, Bennett also appointed Shrum chancellor of Simon Fraser University—or at least chancellor of the concept he had for it. Shrum became responsible for the university's construction and design. The job took two years and five months and became a critical and organizational success.

Shrum was intensely loyal to Bennett and, along with Hugh Keenleyside, was instrumental in ensuring that Bennett's Two Rivers Policy became a reality. But like Adam Beck, Gordon Shrum seemed to have difficulty understanding that the quest for power was not always a godly crusade. Building and constructing were not benign deities. For every magnificent benefit that electricity delivered, there was a definable cost. For every dam built, there were fish spawning sites destroyed. For almost every piece of land flooded to build a reservoir, there were people whose lives were severely affected. For every new thermal generating plant built, more carbon dioxide was released into the atmosphere. For every marvellous new surge in electricity supply driven by nuclear fission, there were radioactive dangers to contemplate—both at the time, and well into anybody's future.

The story of electrical power in Canada is inevitably woven with the ambitions of strong-willed and, to a large extent, stubborn men; men often motivated by a singular sense of mission aimed too high to take into account all the social consequences that went into producing and delivering protons and electrons we occasionally did not need. For every good these men delivered through the wonder that was electricity, there were social costs we all had to pay.

To that extent, it may confirm what the second law of thermo-dynamics tells us, and what the Greeks have tried to teach us for centuries. The second law of thermodynamics, also referred to as the Entropy Law, tells us everything in the universe began with struc-ture and value and is irrevocably moving in the direction of random chaos and waste. Accordingly, whenever a semblance of order is cre-ated—the construction of a large hydro-electric dam meant to ease our burdens and light our nights, for instance—it is done at the expense of greater disorder.

The Greeks, in their mystical way, believed this to be true. His-tory was a process of continual degradation caused by our need to change things. As one myth has it, Man had started like gods, free from care and abundance, until Zeus caught up with us. Angry as he was with Prometheus's theft of fire, Zeus structured his revenge in the form of a beautiful evil in the likeness of a maiden called Pan-dora. She opened a box given her by the gods and out escaped every evil and plague mankind was to know. Only Hope remained trapped in the box.

Roughly put, the Greeks took from this that history was a process of continual degradation and that our jobs were not to celebrate mas-sive orchestrated changes but to try to preserve as much as we could. Like guardians of the Entropy Law, Plato and Aristotle believed the best social order was one that experienced the fewest changes.

W. A. C. Bennett had his own God, and it was not likely he gave the Greek philosophy of life much thought when it came to spurring economic development and change for British Columbia. Gordon Shrum would have recognized the second law of thermodynamics but maybe would have argued that what he and his premier were doing was making good use of Pandora's last comfort—providing hope for British Columbians. He would have had no time for the Greek's idea of a decaying, cyclical process to life. He was orches-trating change, always for the better.

Shrum was the ambitious and often impatient creator Bennett needed in his drive to develop public power for British Columbia. Bennett knew all too well, as biographer David Mitchell pointed out, that "power means control over people's lives." To the extent that he and Shrum orchestrated power in such a technologically and finan-cially conquering fashion, they were successes. But if there is a lesson the history of electrical power leaves us, it is that building power for "the people"—without full consideration of what it might do to the individual—can be a damaging, renegade form of energy. It can be as deleterious as it is protective.

In typical fashion, Bennett played a political stroke of genius by giving Shrum responsibility for constructing and bringing on stream the 2.4-million-kilowatt Peace River Power Project, while allowing Keenleyside, one of Canada's foremost diplomats, to supervise the building of the pivotal dam, eventually to bear his name, at the southern end of the Arrow Lakes on the Columbia. The personalities of the co-chairmen could not have been more different.

Keenleyside was a statesman and former ambassador to Mexico who left External Affairs in disillusionment. Among other undertakings, he went on to become an important member of the Canadian team negotiating the Columbia River Treaty. Keenleyside was a firm believer in public enterprise, especially public power. He was a meticulous man who believed in diplomacy over conflict and order over disorder. It is said he was so attentive to detail and correctness that if he was early for an appointment, he would get out of his car and pace back and forth outside until he could enter at the proper moment and be, absolutely, on time.

As co-chairman of B.C. Hydro, Keenleyside exhibited a sensitivity to a broad range of social issues, in particular the hazards of unchecked growth and expansion of electrical power. In his later life, he summed up his shame over being part of the mindless consumption rush to build more and more dams to produce more and more electricity, belatedly coming to agree with Charles Luce's comment that "the wisdom of three years ago is the idiocy of today."

Gordon Shrum, on the other hand, was a man who seemed to possess few doubts—about his objectives, about their impacts or about the ultimate costs and benefits. Progress seemed to be an unquestioned goal. Science would serve as the bible of direction. Shrum was demanding, domineering and, as the visitor to B.C. Hydro's head office discovered, loud. He seemed driven in everything he did.

The Peace River project was Shrum's personal priority. It was a mammoth technical challenge, the type Shrum loved to manage. The project—christened in September 1967 the "W. A. C. Bennett Dam"—came in at $750 million and stretched two kilometres across the Peace River. It created Williston Lake, a body of water covering

1600 square kilometres. The dam contained 43 million cubic metres of earth fill, enough, as Mitchell pointed out, "to build a nine-foot by twelve-foot wall from Vancouver to Halifax."

The 918-kilometre transmission line to Vancouver would bring "the greatest prosperity this province had ever known," as Bennett put it at the inauguration ceremony. Shrum then went on to compare Bennett favourably to King Khufu and the dam to the great pyramid of Gizeh. "The Pharaoh went broke building the pyramid," Shrum is quoted as saying. "We intend to make it pay."

Shrum and Keenleyside were civil to one another, but the diplomat's presence rankled the scientist. Shrum's autobiography contains a number of clearly competitive references. The fact is they did not particularly care much for each other, or for each other's ideas. They clashed during the time they shared the chairmanship of B.C. Hydro, in particular over the questionable benefits of emerging nuclear power generation.

Keenleyside spoke strongly against it, pointing out that it was both expensive and unreliable, and of all the areas in the world, British Columbia "was probably the area that needed it least." Shrum was a vocal exponent of nuclear power generation, even while other jurisdictions, like Ontario, were beginning to speculate over the new technology's rising costs. He was determined, as Keenleyside wrote, "that nuclear power should be brought into British Columbia to supplement hydro resources," even though the province's hydraulic resource potential was one of the most impressive in the world.

"At one time his enthusiasm carried him to the extreme of suggesting that a nuclear plant should be located under Vancouver's West End," Keenleyside wrote in his memoirs, "the most thickly populated area of its size on the continent."

Shrum's advocacy of a nuclear power generating station under Vancouver's populous West End was simply a reflection of the technical solution he had for overcoming the expensive cost of bringing electricity to consumers over long distances, from remote hydro-electric dams to the centre of the province's quickly expanding cities. The equation was simple: nuclear-generated power had been proven by science to be safe and could now be placed in the centre of its scope of customer demand, thus reducing costs of transmission and distribution.

Shrum also lobbied heavily for nuclear-generation facilities on

Vancouver Island. Although there was widespread opposition to the proposal at the time, Shrum persisted, pointing out in his autobiography that "it would have been the best thing in the world for the Island." One of the benefits cited if nuclear power generation was to be allowed along the largely unpopulated west coast of the island was that it would warm up the frigid Pacific waters.

But these were days when science had few limits and few detractors. A 1972 power study prepared for Shrum painted a moderately glowing picture of the benefits of nuclear power in British Columbia. The report concluded that the hazards of conventional nuclear power were "acceptable." But the cost—roughly twice the cost of thermal power generation—seemed to be the major drawback. Regarding the question of radioactivity, the report claimed there was not sufficient information to prove high doses of radioactivity caused genetic damage. In any case, the report went on, any genetic damage would "not show up for many generation's ahead" and by limiting it to contact with "small numbers of people there will no negligible risks to the race as a whole." The high cost aside, W. A. C. Bennett would have no part of nuclear-generated power in British Columbia.

Shrum seemed to enjoy attracting public controversy. In 1970 he was attacked by environmental critics for B.C. Hydro's use of herbicides to clear transmission rights-of-way. Environmentalists claimed B.C. Hydro was using chemicals like 2,4,5–T for clearing these corridors. They were suspected of causing birth defects in newborn children.

To prove his point, and to reaffirm his faith in science, Shrum went on television and drank the chemical from a glass. Outside of a bad after-taste, Shrum claimed he suffered no ill-effects. However, the fact that he was not a pregnant woman—and was already seventy-four years old at the time—did not seem to dissuade him of his belief in the benefits of modern science.

In the mid-1960s, Shrum had advocated the damming of the upper Fraser River basin. The move would bring even more electricity online for British Columbia. It would help prevent damage from persistent spring flooding. It would also, as the study into the plan reported, "put an end to all runs of anadromous fish dependent on spawning upstream of the dam in the Fraser Basin." It was a pretty extreme position to take in the name of technology and economic progress, even then. As he wrote in his autobiography: "From a strict dollars-and-cents standpoint, it would be better for the province to develop the hydroelectric potential of the Fraser and simply forget the fish."

The mere notion of Shrum's plan triggered an immediate reaction from fishers and members of the general public. A huge outcry grew over the thought of the massive damage dams on the Fraser would do to fish stocks. The Fraser was, and still is, one of the most important salmon-spawning rivers in the world. "I did not deny that it would reduce the number of fish," Shrum wrote in a curious defence of the plan, "I argued ... we could get more than enough money from our power dams to pay for the fish; we could retire all the Fraser fishermen for life."

Presumably the welfare of the people of British Columbia mattered deeply to Gordon Shrum, as it did to Hugh Keenleyside. But one tried to search out and balance a broad series of implications from rapid hydro-electric power development, identify the true costs and benefits of electricity beyond just its availability, and plan as prudently as possible for its future. The other was driven by a need to provide the marvels of electricity because each new expansive generating enterprise presented a new scientific or technological hurdle to be overcome in the interests of carving out a better life for mankind.

It was only W. A. C. Bennett's presence and sense of proportion that kept things in perspective. And even then, there were elements of his own dream of more power for British Columbia that would not only disfigure lush portions of the province's landscape and destroy fish and animal habitat, but also seriously and unfairly disrupt the lives of the very people power was meant to serve. For, up until the 1990s, one ingredient is immutably fixed in the story of the development of Canadian electrical power. In its march to that glorious destiny of "power at cost" or "power for the people," people were never allowed to stand in its way.

Deep in the craggy and remote southeast interior, more than two thousand of the six thousand British Columbians who lived along the Columbia River kept a nervous, two-decade-long vigil while the Columbia River Treaty negotiations played themselves out. The people who lived along the banks of the Columbia—from Revelstoke down to Castlegar, along the north-to-south wilderness route referred to as the Arrow Lakes—had for some time known their communities were earmarked for construction of storage dams necessary to feed the Columbia's water to the Americans. But in the greater scheme of things, the concerns of the citizens of the Arrow Lakes were of little affair to the negotiators on the International Joint Commission teams. They were of no concern to the president of the United States of America or to the prime minister of Canada. Lamentably, they were of little concern to the most important player in this melodrama, W. A. C. Bennett, the politician known for his protection of "the little guy."

The people of the Arrow Lakes district might just as well have been inhabitants of a distant planet, making way for the arrival and future settlement of the area by alien masters. The Columbia River Treaty, with its three huge storage dams to be built in British Columbia, would be negotiated, scrutinized, debated, passed, signed and ratified with no reference to the people of Arrow Lakes whatsoever. Public hearings on the impact of the treaty on the valley would be held only after the treaty was signed.

The Arrow Lakes district was a valley time forgot, a kind of "Rip Van Winkle valley," as James W. Wilson put in it his book, *People in the Way: The Human Aspects of the Columbia River Treaty*. Wilson had been B.C. Hydro's manager responsible for resettlement of the Arrow Lakes in the mid-1960s. He was so affected by their predicament that he wrote about his experiences and observations in 1973 and dedicated his book to them.

The Arrow Lakes was a valley that was for those who lived there not just a place, but "a chosen place." Before World War I, the valley had been considered a prized destination for pioneers looking for peace and tranquillity in British Columbia's rugged interior country. It was a valley of "velvet shadowed" summer evenings, where the pace of community life was so informal that by the time Wilson arrived, one of the problems Hydro faced was that there was little formal municipal organization—mayors and councillors, for instance—with which to discuss the government's and Hydro's plans.

Still, for many of those who lived along the two hundred kilometres of the Columbia's canyon, by the 1950s, Arrow Lakes was a place of subsistence living. According to Wilson, "there was precious little arable land" and the farms that dotted the mountainsides and the valley were, despite the odd herd of cattle and the proud vegetable gardens, patchy and "going to seed." It was "a sad little place of older people, most living on pensions, that time had by-passed." By the time serious talk began about damming the Columbia, the average age of valley settlers was fifty-three years and the average resident had lived there more than three decades.

As early as 1928, stories had circulated about Canadian and American engineers, technicians and diplomats discussing how to harness the power of the Columbia River. The main focus was the Arrow Lakes. It would take a few days for the message to reach them, but in the spring of 1944 they would learn that the two nations had agreed to ask the International Joint Commission (IJC) to study the river's development possibilities. For the next fifteen years, they heard sporadic rumours about where and when work might begin. Even when word filtered through about the engineering report that in 1959 was presented to the IJC, they heard little or nothing about the development options presented or the fierce diplomatic wrangling that took place at the negotiating table. They lived their lives, largely, as Wilson put it, "in a fog of ignorance."

The process B.C. Hydro used to acquire land and relocate more than two thousand Arrow Lakes residents before the dammed waters began to flood the valley was not marked by an excess of compassion or generosity. Neither term seemed to mean much to B.C. Hydro officials working on behalf of the Bennett government, just as when hydro officials in places like Saskatchewan, Manitoba, Ontario and Quebec received the go-ahead for hydro-electric dam construction plans there.

Word began to spread in early 1961 about the signing of a Columbia River Treaty. Thoughts of seeing the twentieth century finally arrive on their doorstep—in the form of new roads, new schools and maybe a hospital—ebbed and flowed with the unannounced arrival and eventual departure of surveyors and Hydro engineers, often only asking "How much do you want for your land?" and then departing. Perhaps the only thing of any value left behind was the promise from B.C. Hydro's co-chairman, Hugh Keenleyside, that residents would be dealt with "in a fair, sympathetic and generous manner," although that turned out to be worth little.

While Bennett fought his battles over control of the Columbia River Treaty, apprehension among the Arrow Lakes residents increased. The B.C. Power Commission refused to answer their questions about what might happen to them, their homes and their families. Even though the engineering plans revealed flooding from the dams along the Columbia River would displace as many as two thousand residents and destroy 1,300 properties, the Commission considered probing questions from Arrow Lakes residents to be "inadmissible" for consideration.

When meetings did take place between the citizens and B.C. Hydro representatives—on issues like land acquisition policy, financial compensation, replacement housing and land clearing—B.C. Hydro representatives generally conducted themselves like sixteenth-century explorers who had just stumbled upon Indians as they prepared to take over their land. Direct answers to questions about what was to become of them were not always forthcoming. As Wilson wrote: "Hydro's operational interest was in acquiring land and buildings, people being merely complicating circumstances."

B.C. Hydro's hard-nosed approach to negotiations over compensation or expropriation left a bitter taste among most Arrow Lakes residents. Hydro representatives had been instructed to "discuss" and "negotiate" with the residents but not to "bargain"—a term which would infer flexibility. A measure for the price one resident might demand for her home might be set on the cost of "replacement" but never on the "value" the resident might see in it. Hydro considered the dollar amounts offered for land and buildings to be confiscated "fair" and "generous," whereas the demands of the residents were often characterized as "unreasonable." It became a bit of a game that B.C. Hydro played well. It reminded Wilson of Lewis Carroll's Humpty Dumpty defence of his obstinacy: "When I use a word, it means just what I choose it to mean."

The priority was to get the inhabitants moved as cheaply and expeditiously as possible. The people of Arrow Lakes were standing in the way of Bennett's grand dream. But, as Wilson pointed out: "It is one thing to have visions and ideals for yourself; quite another to have them for others."

Many felt badly used and responded to James Wilson's surveys with expressions of "anger, frustration and hatred" aimed directly at the public utility. Many felt Hydro played games and provided better compensation packages for their neighbours than for them. Although most residents accepted the existence of the laws of state expropriation, and knew their only recourse was to bargain for proper compensation, the majority resented the fact that their arcadian valley was being sacrificed in the name of those two familiar but often indefensible abstractions: "social progress" and "the common good."

They had been arbitrarily uprooted from their pastoral lifestyle, torn away from family, friends and community. Their pristine lake would be turned into a muddy, unnatural reservoir to hold millions of hectares of water in storage for no other reason than that was what the Columbia River Treaty called for.

After all, this was an engineering project, not a social services project. The goal was not to protect citizens or see that they were well treated by the state. The important thing was not people, but getting the dams—near Mica Creek, at the outlet of the Arrow Lakes and on the Kootenay River near Duncan Lake—built on time and on budget. Under orders from Bennett, it was B.C. Hydro's responsibility to acquire land and buildings; people, as James Wilson put it so subtly, were just in the way.

The sense of outrage lingered among many residents of Arrow Lakes long after the rising waters hid their homes, farms and gardens. As late as 1997, one relocated Arrow Lakes resident—farmer Val Morton—was still demanding a review of the loss of his 128-hectare farm. Morton argued that B.C. Hydro officials had lied to him when they said his land was "needed" for the dam project. It turned out his land was "needed" for a planned provincial park, not as part of the flood site. More than thirty years later, at the age of seventy-three, Morton persists in trying to get his land back, now part of the McDonald Creek Provincial Park. Hydro officials to this day defend the expropriation under the sweeping regulation from the 1960s that allowed for land to be confiscated if the move would "benefit the public as a whole."

The crude designer towns planned to replace their former communities, complete with new roads, schools and recreation services, would never replace a willow tree planted as a sapling when a son went off to war. How do you replace the evening light reflecting off mountain tops, a barn, or even off a newly painted fence? How do you establish a "fair" price or the value of a garden that kept you busy and helped feed you for years? Several elderly residents claimed their dislocation from Arrow Lakes was so brutal in its way that it contributed significantly to the death of a spouse. Being expelled from their homes and their land was too much for some oldtimers of Arrow Lakes. They simply gave up and died.

One could argue, like many Bennett government and B.C. Hydro officials did at the time and still do, that the flooding of Arrow Lakes was all for "the public good." But the question leaps forward: Whose public good? And if the citizen to be relocated does not qualify as "public," who then are we talking about? And who decides which public gets the benefits of hydro-electric development and which public gets to carry the costs? As Wilson wrote so eloquently: "We cannot serve truly humane purposes unless the means we use to carry them out are also humane."

As a major public issue in a presumably democratic setting, the flooding of the Arrow Lakes was never the subject of multi-party scrutiny before a legislative committee. The financial estimates were laid before the legislature of the time, but not the estimates related to social costs.

The power of the state to arbitrarily seize or expropriate the private property of the Canadian citizen is extensive and frightening. But it is seldom "the state," as defined by government-in-council in action, which decides whose property should be confiscated in the public good. As the actions of Adam Beck in Ontario, Robert Bourassa in Quebec and W. A. C. Bennett in British Columbia revealed, the power to play Pharaoh in building dreams of electrical power to come is often singular and personal and has little to do with "democratic" action.

It is one thing to attempt to claim the high ground of "the common good" by driving citizens from their homes. It is another to plunder and confiscate land lived on for centuries in the name of the generation of electrical power. It is quite another to seize that land and refuse to recognize there are citizens living upon it, with rights and claims that pre-date those aspirations of political and electrical grandeur. That sort of ignorance is either the lowest abuse of power or, in the case of Canada's First Nations, the twentieth-century height of white man's racism.

As sad as the tale of the damming of the Arrow Lakes and the dislocation of its inhabitants might be, it pales in comparison with what hydro-electric projects have done to native peoples in Canada. Governments, politicians, hydro power officials and bureaucrats have too often joined together in their purblind excitement to manufacture and peddle Prometheus's gift, not really caring what impact their aspirations might have on aboriginal rights.

In provinces such as Quebec, Saskatchewan and Manitoba, not only were native rights to the land callously ignored, in some cases, their existence was denied. When their existence was acknowledged, it was often couched in highly patronizing terms. In the 1972 study of B.C. energy-development options—the same one that offered glowing praise for possible nuclear generation—the rationale for appropriating native settlements for power development was put in such a way that it would appear to almost be doing them a favour: "In due course these Indian people may join the main stream of the Canadian economy and free themselves from dependence on such marginal pursuits as river fishing ..."

The people of the Arrow Lakes claimed rights of private ownership in their contest with Bennett's dream. Possession of those rights did not stop them from being evicted from their lands with meagre compensation. At least there was compensation. But where native peoples have been concerned, most have had even stronger claims to the land and the waters upon it, claims that predated the white man's arrival on the continent. Royal recognition of their entitlement to the land was signed as early as the 1870s. In particular, the native peoples of western and northern Canada were told the treaties they signed, and the rights to the land they occupied, were reserved for them "as long as the rivers flow." Not only have those rights often been abrogated, some of those rivers no longer flow.

"Hydro projects designed to serve southern provincial interests, and even provide power for export, have largely failed to serve the interests of the northern Native people, the promises and the 'benefits' notwithstanding," James B. Waldram wrote in *As Long As the Rivers Run: Hydroelectric Development and Native Communities in Western Canada.* "For them, there has been and remains, nothing common about the 'common good'."

To add contemporary injury to historical insult, many native people who have been forced to live near the country's remote hydro megaprojects have had to pay more for their electricity (when they are allowed access to it) than do their white counterparts in the south—on whose behalf those once-free flowing rivers were barricaded or, in quaint terms of domination, "harnessed."

The tragic story of how we have used the glamour and allure of electricity to violate native rights, culture and ownership of the land is not restricted to one province. It is a shame that applies nation-wide. Much of our new-found sensitivity to the plight of native people living in the abusive path of electrical progress stems from Quebec's James Bay Power Project and that province's treatment of the Cree and the Inuit. With Robert Bourassa's support, Hydro-Québec stormed into the province's north country like Spanish conquistadors. They were collectively arrogant of the fact that in 1912, when the northern portion of what is now Quebec was originally ceded to the province, the law required the province to recognize aboriginal rights to the land.

The James Bay Power Project was not Quebec's first intrusion into native land. Beginning in 1940, the Aluminum Company of Canada had been allowed to construct hydro dams in the Montagnais Indian territory in the James Bay region east of lands claimed by the Cree. More than a dozen large power plants, and a number of reservoirs, were constructed right up to the late 1980s, even though the Montagnais claimed aboriginal title to the land.

Between the 1920s and the late 1950s, Ontario Hydro constructed hydro-electric projects on a number of northern rivers. Aboriginal claims were simply ignored. Native graveyards were flooded. Along the Winnipeg and English Rivers in northwestern Ontario, native bands were forced off their land. In the 1970s, the native communities of Grassy Narrows and White Dog were front-page news around the globe. The toxic devastation caused by mercury pollution discovered in the English-Wabigoon river system became an international cause for environmentalists at the time.

Between the early 1960s and the late 1980s, and with the full support of both Progressive Conservative and New Democratic governments, Manitoba Hydro pushed forward with a number of hydro-electric projects, including the Grand Rapids Dam and the Churchill River Diversion Project. These projects drove native bands from their land, flooded their hunting and trapping territory and ruined their traditional lifestyle with an impunity and arrogance that is, even today, simply appalling. The story of how the inhabitants of the community of South Indian Lake were treated barely three decades ago is as lamentable a tale as the accounts of the U.S. Calvary forcing the resettlement of the American Plains Indians a century earlier.

In the early 1970s, dam construction in Alberta was generally conducted on native land without prior negotiation with native groups. Grave sites were flooded. Wildlife habitat was seriously disrupted. In some cases, dams were constructed on native land simply with the consent of the Department of Indian Affairs, the federal agency supposedly responsible for protecting the rights of First Nations people.

In Saskatchewan, construction of the Island Falls Dam on the Churchill River was supposed to provide employment for native people at Sandy Bay. Instead, it destroyed their traditional economy and left the community poverty stricken. The Island Falls Dam was not even built to supply power for southern Saskatchewan. It was built to route electricity across the border to the Hudson Bay Mining and Smelting Company, located near Flin Flon, Manitoba.

When the Squaw Rapids Dam opened on the Saskatchewan River in 1963 it was called "a triumph of man over nature" by then NDP premier of Saskatchewan, W. S. Lloyd. No prior impact studies were conducted about the environmental effects of the dam or its consequences for Cumberland House, a native community located less than one hundred kilometres downstream. Not surprisingly perhaps, although the dam's impact on the native people downstream seemed of little concern to the Saskatchewan Power Corporation, discussions did take place about relocating and compensating some non-native farmers living in the reservoir, or forebay area, who might have their land flooded.

The Indian and Metis communities at Cumberland House were told, and they believed, that for them the project would mean cheap electricity, some construction jobs on the project and water levels on the Saskatchewan River—from where they derived much of their livelihood from fishing and trapping—that would remain stable, perhaps even improve. By 1964 it was clear the opposite was true. Irregular water flows flooded their land, killing fish, destroying waterfowl nests, muskrat and beaver lodges and drowning big game.

Their only recourse was to seek financial compensation from the Saskatchewan government and Saskatchewan Power Corporation. It would take until 1972—twelve years after construction on the dam began—before a confidential report acknowledged that native claims for compensation might be valid. But it would take the better part of a quarter-century before the people of Cumberland House would be able to get the Saskatchewan government and the Saskatchewan Power Corporation to even acknowledge publicly the downstream damage caused by the Squaw Rapids Dam project.

The situation faced by roughly five hundred Indian and three hundred Metis residents of Chemawawin, in northern Manitoba, was only slightly less appalling than the treatment Cumberland House natives received. In the Chemawawin case, Manitoba Hydro and the Manitoba government could not avoid providing the community with advance notice of the flooding to be caused by their proposed Grand Rapids Dam. Plans called for Chemawawin to be submerged by the dam's construction.

Before hydro development came along, the people of Chemawawin lived simple lives in mid-northern Manitoba, at a point where the Saskatchewan River emptied into the western end of Cedar Lake. Their economy was based on a fairly successful commercial fishing operation and proceeds from trapping and hunting. When Manitoba Hydro was finished, the people of Chemawawin would be forced to move to a town site called Easterville, further to the east on Cedar Lake. Inhospitable and rock strewn (it was nicknamed "the rock pile"), Easterville was a disaster by any stretch of imagination. The move wrecked the local economy and left the natives trapped in a continuous cycle of impoverishment, offset for short periods with non-productive make-work jobs.

The purpose of the Grand Rapids development was not to supply light and heat to hard-pressed citizens of northern Manitoba. Instead, the electricity would power the International Nickel Company's mining and milling operations at Thompson. Grand Rapids was also the first step in a romantic long-term plan that would, it was hoped, see the province of Manitoba become a major supplier of export electricity into the United States.

Coerced into resettling in Easterville, the natives agreed to accept "the rock pile" as their future home. Although legally responsible for the well-being of treaty Indians, the Department of Indian Affairs effectively abdicated its responsibilities to the natives during negotiations. The department did not even intervene in the early stages to ensure the Chemawawin residents had legal counsel to help them in this highly inequitable contest with the Manitoba government and its power utility. Consequently, they mistakenly placed their trust in what the province and Manitoba Hydro was telling them.

It would not be until 1985—twenty years after the Grand Rapids Dam had been officially opened by Conservative Premier Duff Roblin—that the Chemawawin Indians finally received title to the remaining 4,640 hectares of land they were promised. They would not receive their payment for compensation ($21.1 million) until 1991. But by then, the exhaustion of the generation-long fight with the Manitoba government made any sense of victory highly pyrrhic.

As the native band put it in their brief in a 1975 meeting with Manitoba Hydro: "When we look at the development, we can say that all governments of whatever political stripe have been callous and indifferent to the needs of Indian people when the choice has to be made between the welfare of Indian people and the short-term benefits of a society and a system which appears to measure benefits using money as its chief standard. If it had to be a choice between money and Indians, it seems the Indian always loses."

The Progressive Conservative government of Manitoba was, in the 1960s, prepared to launch still another hydro-electric folly. In the name of making Manitoba that "electric province" the government wanted it to be, the decision was made to divert the mighty Churchill River into the Nelson River and produce yet more electricity. As a consequence of this decision, the native community of South Indian Lake would be inundated with flood water.

South Indian Lake was a relatively isolated community located on the southeastern shore of Southern Indian Lake, about 1,200 kilometres by bush plane north of Winnipeg. It was the home of about a thousand treaty and non-treaty Indians and Metis. Like the native people of Chemawawin and Cumberland House, they subsisted on hunting, fishing and trapping. The community had also been able to establish a thriving commercial fishery.

When in 1966 news of Manitoba Hydro's plans first arrived in South Indian Lake, the idea of damming the mighty Churchill River, reversing its northward flow into the Nelson and increasing the height of Southern Indian Lake by as much as ten metres, was so incomprehensible to the natives that they ignored it.

Nevertheless, once again the Manitoba government would hurry the development to subdue another of its grand northern rivers, flood 1,500 square kilometres of boreal forest and destroy another native community in the process. And once again, the natives of the northern portion of the province were led to believe that they were being asked to make this immense sacrifice, all for their white Manitoba brethren to the south, anxiously awaiting new supplies of life-giving electricity.

But the main thrust of this project was not to light up new Winnipeg subdivisions. It was to sell the electricity to the United States. Manitoba natives were again being asked to sacrifice their livelihood and their culture so that someone in Minot, North Dakota, or Sioux City, Iowa, could use an electric toothbrush or pop-up toaster.

A University of Manitoba study tabled in January 1967 reported the flooding caused by the dam on the Churchill River would turn Southern Indian Lake into the "biggest man-made swamp in the world." The study also pegged the natives' financial loss related to the diversion project at a minimum of $11 million, not taking into account the severe disruption to their lives.

The Manitoba government refused to make the controversial report public. It preferred to use its own curious impact analysis, one that depicted the Churchill River Diversion Project as a boon to natives. The native people were depicted as technological relics headed for a predictable demise. They had no future. They were "anachronisms in the present age of technology." If they continued to live like they were, off the land, they were headed for economic and cultural disaster. By hastening the pace of disruption in their lives, the diversion project would actually be doing them a favour.

It took more than two years before the natives of South Indian Lake realized they faced a serious problem. They began organizing. They sought legal counsel. Few details about the utility's plans were revealed at the first meeting with Manitoba Hydro officials in April 1968. Public protests against the diversion project began in the south. The government was being pummelled daily by the news media and Manitoba Hydro came under attack for its lack of sincerity, particularly when it came to details about the project's impact on the natives. By 1969 the utility would be forced to concede that the diversion would be disaster for the community of South Indian Lake.

It was clear that at this point a vast number of Manitobans were opposed to the Churchill River Diversion Project. When lawyers for the natives sought an injunction against the granting of a licence to Manitoba Hydro, the Progressive Conservative government introduced a bill in the legislature allowing it to issue a licence to Hydro without a public hearing.

With all the confusion and obfuscation displayed by both the government and Manitoba Hydro, in May 1969 the residents of South Indian Lake made it clear they would not move. They had been lied to too often. Their sense of trust in government had been depleted. Citing "deceit, deception and manifold breaches of faith" perpetrated by the provincial government, they simply refused to move. The government dissolved the legislature and called an election.

The Conservatives were defeated in June 1969 by the New Democratic Party led by Edward Schreyer. The NDP had run on a platform opposing the high-level diversion project. But the general euphoria felt by those fighting the diversion plan was short-lived. In September 1969, after publicly cancelling the high-level diversion of the Churchill River, the Schreyer government announced it now intended to replace the plan with a new, low-level diversion scheme. The NDP agreed to lowering the flood level from ten metres to about four metres, displacing only about one-half the population of South Indian Lake. The Indians at South Indian Lake mobilized for legal action to stop the project from proceeding.

But in November 1972, the Schreyer government made a giant stride in public insensitivity, quite out of character for any truly social democratic party. It countered the native legal threat by changing the province's Water Power Act, allowing the minister responsible to issue a licence to Manitoba Hydro to begin construction without hearings or legislative review.

The Schreyer government claimed Manitoba was proceeding legally and according to the intent of a 1966 federal-provincial agreement on northern power projects. No one had the right to question Manitoba's right to proceed. According to the province's legal counsel, the project "was simply not negotiable."

The government went so far as to suggest to the natives that any negative effects of Manitoba Hydro's diversion project should be contrasted with the many benefits the flood waters would bring—colour TV, direct-dial telephone service, unlimited electric power for all those stoves and refrigerators, as well as "some job opportunities and construction work."

By 1975, the political energy behind South Indian Lake's effort to seek remedy through legal action began to ebb seriously. In July 1977, the native flood committee was finally able to strike an agreement with the federal government. Although a party to the deliberations, the Schreyer government refused to sign the document. It feared the arbitration measures in the agreement, meant to provide some sense of equity and fairness over issues in dispute, were too onerous and potentially too expensive for the province to abide by.

In September 1977, the Schreyer government was defeated in a provincial election. The new Progressive Conservative government headed by Sterling Lyon signed a revised Northern Flood Agreement. The arbitration measures that had seemed so onerous to the Schreyer government were not seriously objected to, or significantly altered, by the new provincial government. Still the community of South Indian Lake would not see the first part of a financial settlement for damages until 1985, almost two decades after the Manitoba government announced the start of the Churchill River Diversion project.

Ironically, by the time the province's grand vision of being the hydro-electricity capital of the continent caught up with reality, so much of the taxpayer's money had been spent that Manitoba Hydro could now claim the worst debt-to-equity ratio of all Canada's public power utilities (throughout the late 1980s and early 1990s it would hover at a very unhealthy 95:05). Also, by the early 1990s, the "electrical province" was stuck with substantial amounts of surplus electricity it was finding hard to sell.

In British Columbia, the Kemano I power project, completed in 1956 to provide electricity for the Aluminum Company of Canada's smelting facility at Kitimat, caused massive environmental and social damage. The project diverted one river and flooded seven lakes to establish a reservoir capable of containing nine hundred square kilometres of water. The Haisla Reserve Indian band was encouraged by Department of Indian Affairs to accept a one-time only compensation payment of $50,000 for the damage the project had on their territory and lifestyle.

The Cheslatta band, the most affected by the Kemano I project, were not given enough advance warning of the flooding and had to relocate from their homes in panic as floodwaters rose, engulfing their land and burial grounds and destroying their homes, their fishing stations and their trapping cabins. The Cheslatta were moved to a stark, windy plateau region which could not support their traditional economy. Tuberculosis and alcoholism replaced hunting and fishing as major preoccupations.

In 1995, the NDP government under the leadership of Mike Harcourt blocked the second phase of Alcan's electricity megaproject, the Kemano Completion Project. Alcan had been pressing ahead with plans for its $1.2 billion power dam development since 1987. At that time, agreement on water flows and fisheries protection (referred to by critics as a "closed-door deal") had been reached between the company, the federal government and Bill Bennett's Social Credit government. The company had been given permission to proceed with construction plans.

The project called for a 285-megawatt generating facility that would include a fifteen-kilometre tunnel drilled through the mountainous terrain in northern British Columbia. In typical hydroelectric mega-project terms, the tunnel would have drained away more than half the flow of the Nechako River (already reduced one-third by the original 1950s agreement).

The Kemano Completion Project was halted in 1991 after a legal challenge by native and environmental groups. A review of the project by the B.C. Utilities Commission revealed the project's planned diversion of the Nechako would seriously endanger salmon spawning and destroy the lucrative salmon fishery downstream in the Fraser River, into which the Nechako flows. Following the Harcourt government's decision to cancel the Kemano Completion Project, Alcan sought compensation for the $535 million it claimed it had already invested in the project. By April 1997, talks over compensation between Alcan and the provincial government had broken down. Alcan threatened a major law suit. The NDP government, now led by Premier Glen Clark, counter-threatened with legislation to short-circuit Alcan's legal action.

In early August 1997, the wrangling ended when Alcan agreed to proceed with a smelter project in return for the province's promise to provide cheap, publicly subsidized electricity from its growing power surpluses. British Columbia would sell 175 megawatts of electricity at discounted prices each year to drive the new smelter. In return, Alcan would proceed with a project that would create as many as two thousand jobs. The key to the deal was cheap electricity. Some estimates had Alcan saving as much as $300 million over the next twenty years.

Two ironic sub-issues resonate in this confrontation over the right to produce electricity in north-central British Columbia. First, this was not simply an issue about a company wanting to invest millions to provide itself with electricity for its smelters. Excess power from Kemano I had long been sold to B.C. Hydro. Some of it made its way into the hungry U.S. electricity market. Once again, this was a project that had little to do with providing British Columbians with access to power at reasonable cost, or providing protection against possible future interruptions in electricity supply.

Second, and despite the best intentions of the NDP government, a large part of the massive public outcry over potential damage to the Fraser River fishery came from sports and commercial fishers residing in the south. In particular, one vocal opponent was Rafe Mair of Vancouver radio station CKNW. Mair is an enthusiastic angler. His repeated condemnation of the Kemano Completion Project on his popular radio talk show is widely recognized as the media catalyst for stopping the multi-million-dollar project.

Native peoples looking on from those barren, windy plateaus of northern British Columbia could only hope that someday their white friends to the south might carry the same sense of public outrage and indignation over their plight as they would over that of a recreational salmon fishing opportunity on a warm, summer weekend afternoon in the Gulf of Georgia.

7 / Wrestling with the Ghost of Betty Furness

The electric light is pure information.

— Marshall McLuhan

BY THE SUMMER OF 1997 it appeared as if a certain amount of rational thinking had returned to the problematical world of Canadian electricity generation and distribution. On June 12, the Quebec government announced it had agreed to negotiate a revenue-sharing deal for future natural resource projects—including hydro-electric power development—with the Cree of northern Quebec.

After years of bitter acrimony, both sides called the decision "a major breakthrough." Premier Lucien Bouchard had travelled to tiny Waswanipi to meet with Cree leaders and discuss how negotiations might proceed. He claimed the occasion left him with "a sense of history" being made. The final agreement would provide the Cree with a substantial share of the revenue the province will eventually realize from resource development in northern Quebec, including forestry, mining and energy. In particular, the Cree would share in the revenues to be realized from the future sale of billions of dollars of electricity to the northeastern United States.

The Cree and Inuit have long maintained that the 1975 James Bay and Northern Quebec Agreement did not provide the native people with an adequate share of the revenue generated by northern resource development. The Cree leaders see revenue-sharing as the final key in providing native communities with the kind of compensation that would make them self-sufficient.

The agreement to proceed on negotiations toward revenue-sharing apparently does not signal a re-start of the Great Whale hydro-electric project. The Cree are adamant that they have no intentions of allowing Hydro-Québec to proceed with the Great Whale project. In August 1997, the six hundred Cree of the village of Whapmagoostin voted ninety-two percent against any plans Hydro-Québec might have to divert the Great Whale River into existing dam reservoirs. But the Cree do not object to discussions on future partnerships between themselves and the provincial utility for other hydro-electric ventures. Depending on the tabling of a strategic plan for provincial power development, future revenue-sharing projects could include the construction of a number of mini-dams to increase generating capacity.

Lucien Bouchard was not just bandaging old political wounds by flying north to lunch with Cree leaders. It certainly was not a moment struck suddenly with a profound sense of enlightenment and compassion toward the native peoples of northern Quebec—after decades of indifference, neglect and mistreatment. This apparent act of generosity and fellowship was simply an important part of the province's new strategy to grab a major share of the profits to be made from the North American energy market, estimated to be worth more than us$270 billion a year if full deregulation of the continental power industry were to take place. Instead of being stubborn impediments to the development and sale of the province's electricity resources, the native people of northern Quebec were now perceived as one of the access routes.

Quebec had already announced in October 1996 that it was now prepared to introduce legislation to open its electricity market to competition. It would tighten regulation of the electricity sector, but it would henceforth allow private and other public utilities to use Hydro-Québec's transmission grid for the wholesale wheeling of electricity in and out of the province. Quebec was responding quickly to the U.S. Federal Energy Regulatory Commission's new rules for access to the American electricity market. FERC's ruling was simple: If in the future a Canadian provincial utility wished to sell electricity into the United States, it had better open its own market to other power utilities. During the winter of 1996, Hydro-Québec was a hot hand for the Bouchard government to play in the continent's high-stakes power poker game; some might say "the only hand" it had left to play.

The province's economy was in a shambles, with unemployment comparable to Newfoundland's. Annual provincial deficits were coming in at roughly $4 billion, necessitating cuts in spending for health care, education and social programs. The provincial debt was creeping up on $80 billion and on a per-capita basis (roughly $10,000) was the highest in the country—not a small part of it attributable to previous hydro-electric expansion. Foreign investment was stuck at 1993 levels and Quebec's economic growth for 1997 was forecast at a minuscule 1.5 percent, barely ahead of Newfoundland's at 1.4 percent, but far behind Alberta's four percent.

Following tradition, and taking into account the bad economic news it faced, the Parti Québécois announced it was embarking on a new strategy to create jobs. Within political nano-seconds, Hydro-Québec proclaimed it now had plans for $1.7 billion worth of new power investment by the year 2000, much of it in northern Quebec. Labour organizations estimated this could mean thousands of jobs over the next decade.

Clearly, the only solution for the Bouchard government's economic woes was the one Quebec governments had turned to since the early days of *maîtres chez nous*. It would turn up the burners under Hydro-Québec and stake the province's future on deregulation of the American electrical power market. The province stood to make "enormous profits" from increased exports to the United States, according to Hydro-Québec management. If Quebec played its cards right, it was estimated the return for its efforts could eventually be worth as much as us$15 billion annually.

Although Hydro-Québec was burdened by long-term debt of roughly $36 billion, it still enjoyed some attractive competitive advantages. Its electricity rates were the cheapest on the continent; as much as thirty to forty percent lower than those of its chief export competitor, Ontario Hydro, and substantially lower than the rates of almost all major U.S. power utilities. In addition, Hydro-Québec was still purchasing 4,300 megawatts of Upper Churchill Falls power at one-quarter of a cent per kilowatt hour and selling it at rates of six cents and higher. In 2016 the price Quebec pays for Upper Churchill Falls electricity will drop to one-fifth of a cent per kilowatt hour. On price, Hydro-Québec would be in the continental driver's seat for years to come if it could crack the U.S. market.

In addition, Hydro-Québec had increased its generating capacity by more than twenty percent since the late 1980s. With roughly 31,000 megawatts of capacity now on hand, it was carrying embarrassing surpluses of energy. Its short-term contract sales had doubled since 1991 and revenue returns had reached over $600 million by 1996. The utility's ideal long-term target was to eventually sell one-half of its power into the United States.

In January 1997, the PQ cabinet approved the rates Hydro-Québec would charge for wholesale wheeling on the utility's transmission system. It also set the date for opening the provincial power grid to competition. In mid-March the grid was thrown open to American and Canadian competitors. FERC's basic condition for "reciprocal access" had been met by Quebec. In May 1997, FERC awarded Hydro-Québec the right to demand reciprocal transmission access to competitors' grids south of the Canada–U.S. border. It also recognized the authority of Quebec's new regulatory board to oversee transmission rates. The door to the U.S. market was really beginning to open.

The FERC decision cleared the way for the Quebec utility to transport its electricity to wholesale customers throughout the United States. Hydro-Québec was the first provincially owned utility to satisfy FERC reciprocity requirements. Earlier in the year, FERC had rejected similar applications from Ontario Hydro and B.C. Hydro on the basis the two provincial utilities had not gone far enough in opening their transmission grids to Canadian and American competitors.

Making revenue peace with the Cree and satisfying the U.S. power regulatory agency was only part of Quebec's grand new energy strategy. Recognizing the importance of natural gas as the major generation competitor of the future, in January, Hydro-Québec paid $309 million for a controlling, forty-percent interest in Noverco Inc., the parent company of Gaz Métropolitain Inc., North America's tenth-largest natural gas distributor. This was one of two major initiatives made by the province to recognize the growing convergence between electricity and natural gas.

The first initiative occurred in late 1996, when Quebec sought approval to build a natural gas pipeline from Sable Island off Nova Scotia—with its 500-billion-cubic-metre reserve of gas—to Montreal, a plan that could make the city and the province the strategic hub for distribution of Atlantic Canada's natural gas reserves into the United States.

These months of aggressive moves to gain economic advantage for Quebec seemed, at first blush, to herald a new wave of robust competition in the deregulating North American energy marketplace. But still, there were other strange structural undercurrents at work.

The FERC decision allowing reciprocal access to the Quebec transmission grid was a two-edged sword for the province and its public power utility. It freed Hydro-Québec to sell electricity into the rich northeastern and midwestern U.S. markets. But it also opened its transmission grid to any utility generator—public or private—wanting to sell electricity on the open market. This included, of course, provinces such as Newfoundland which could now by-pass the major barrier to electricity export that the Quebec transmission grid had represented since the implementation of the Upper Churchill Falls power agreement in 1976.

In early June 1997 it was reported that "secret talks" were now underway between Quebec and Newfoundland over Churchill Falls power. Newfoundland had plans to develop the Lower Churchill Falls in Labrador. If a proper investment and construction package could be put together, the FERC decision meant Newfoundland could now use Hydro-Québec's transmission system to sell any new electricity it generated into the United States market.

Unlike the days of the late 1960s, Hydro-Québec was now eager to profit from any new power construction ventures along the Churchill River system. But the tables had turned on Quebec. The original agreement had long been a target of anger and frustration for successive Newfoundland governments. It had been a running political sore for Newfoundland since 1976. Twice Newfoundland went to the Supreme Court of Canada to have the terms changed or the agreement nullified. On both occasions the high court ruled that it was a legitimate business deal and ruled in Quebec's favour, the last time in 1988.

In September 1996, an angry Newfoundland Premier Brian Tobin threatened to "pull the plug" on the Churchill Falls agreement by passing unilateral legislation—much like Canada had done during the 1995 fish war with Spain—allowing Newfoundland to shut down the Churchill Falls generating facility until the deal was renegotiated. Whether Tobin could actually get away with it was problematic. But his threat did bring the issue back to the front pages of the nation's major newspapers and Quebec back to the negotiating table—just as FERC was musing over Quebec's efforts to obtain an electricity export permit.

To get a piece of the action from any future development of the

Lower Churchill, Quebec would be forced to renegotiate the usurious 1969 Upper Churchill Falls agreement. If Premier Bouchard's grand scheme to access new revenue from the sale of hydro-electricity and natural gas into the United States was to be realized—and Quebec was to become a major continental energy hub—a more equitable compensation for Upper Churchill Falls power would have to be part of the overall bargain.

"God bless FERC," Brian Tobin was quoted as saying when word began leaking out about serious discussions now taking place between the two provinces. The momentum for a new deal had clearly swung to Newfoundland's side. If a suitable compromise could not be reached, Newfoundland would be free to find a new partner, develop the Lower Falls site, and sell its newly generated electricity, not just in the United States, but as a competitor to Hydro-Québec in its own provincial market.

Putting aside for the moment the object lesson of how deeply and fundamentally the world of continental deregulation and the terms of the Free Trade Agreement were eating away at any future plans the Bouchard government had for economic stability to underpin separation or even sovereignty association, another obvious reality was being forged. Nowhere in Quebec's sudden and commanding march for control of a very large portion of Canada's electricity exports was there discussion about turning this potential source of immense wealth for the province and its citizens over to the private sector.

The PQ government had promised during the negotiations for revenue-sharing with the northern Cree that in September 1997 it would table a new, long-term strategic plan for building its new electrical empire in the twenty-first century. To listen to Premier Bouchard talk, it would be the rekindling of Robert Bourassa's stalled plans for the James Bay Power Project—without the Great Whale hydro-electric megaproject portion. During the 1980 referendum, Bourassa had promised that James Bay would be the "first step on the path that would turn Quebec into one of the wealthiest societies in North America." In 1997, Bouchard was picking up the cadence for Bourassa's march to affluence and prosperity, and it would be public ownership of Hydro-Québec, not private ownership, which would, in his eyes, take Quebec there.

Quebec was actually defying the continental forces of privatization and deregulation of the electricity-generation business. In some respects it was increasing regulation. By putting the *Régie de l'energie* in place in 1996 to regulate transmission of electricity along the province's grid, the Bouchard government was adding a necessary regulatory ingredient to ensure fairness in the marketplace and a decent rate of return to Quebec. The move also provided opportunities for private-sector generating companies to compete with Hydro-Québec, although on a limited basis. But both sectors would be monitored by the new regulatory process.

To critics of public enterprise, and the editorial forces favouring privatization of public power utilities such as the *Report on Business*'s Terence Corcoran, the direction which Quebec was beginning to take was downright discouraging. The hyperbolically inclined business reporter whined that the government's move created a new board "that will have more regulatory clout over the province than colonial governor Sir John Sherbrooke." Given the randomness and damaging uncertainty that had existed in the power sector over the preceding two-and-a-half years, there were many who applauded the move.

What perhaps made Corcoran even more upset is that Bouchard had the people of Quebec behind him. As far back as April 1996, a public committee looking into the issue reported that the vast majority of Quebecers favoured keeping Hydro-Québec a provincially owned entity. The panel reported that those polled saw little or no justification for privatization and fully expected that if it did come about, consumer electricity rates would just increase. Even the province's main business lobby group, Conseil du patronat, could only count on forty-three percent support for complete privatization when it polled members in late 1995.

If Corcoran was dejected by prospects such as these in Quebec, he must have been apoplectic over events in Ontario. Where the Bouchard government seemed to have grabbed the initiative in preparing for future competition in the electrical generation and distribution business, the Harris government came across as confused and ideologically uncertain about the future of both continental energy and the role of Ontario Hydro.

To the mid-point of the summer of 1997, the Harris government seemed to be sleep-walking in step with its favourite laissez-faire political philosophy. Deep down, the Harris government was intent on turning over to the private sector as much of Ontario Hydro as it could justify. But it lacked the political courage to make this happen. Brave only goes so far in politics. It understood and admired the ideological liturgy of Social Darwinism, but after two years of testing the privatization waters, it just did not trust that privatization could be made to happen in its first term in office, if the Progressive Conservative Party had aspirations for a second term.

But where privatization of the provincially owned power utility was not even being discussed in Quebec—and there certainly was no talk in that province about breaking up Hydro-Québec—in Ontario, Hydro's status was still the subject of some confused, and confusing, public debate.

The real confusion began in May 1997, when the Harris government announced it was preparing to break up Ontario Hydro into at least two corporate parts. The surprise for ideologues was the rider attached to the announcement: The rendered corporate parts would remain publicly owned. In mid-June 1977, to more scratching of heads, Ontario Hydro announced it had hired three prominent Progressive Conservative Party loyalists to lobby the Harris government, on its behalf, not to break up the corporation. The evidence seemed to say that the issues surrounding Ontario Hydro's status had changed. Privatization was, for the moment, no longer high on the Harris government's list of priorities.

The bad news was it was now intent on preparing a "white paper" on the future of Ontario Hydro, one that would propose that the troubled utility should be broken up into smaller crown-owned companies. If that did not confuse Ontario ratepayers who had been listening to the Harris government's paeans to the benefits of privatization for two years now, the announcement by the Power Workers' Union, at roughly the same moment, that it was launching an advertising campaign to promote the *merger* of Ontario Hydro with Manitoba Hydro and Hydro-Québec must have. The Power Workers' move was further evidence that the Harris government was probably marching in the wrong direction on industry reorganization. The trend was to larger, amalgamated power corporations, not bits and pieces of them.

The union, like Lucien Bouchard, had one thing right about the future of North American electrical utilities: Bigger would be better. The most successful power utilities of the future would not be a handful of spirited private-sector companies fighting valiantly and fairly for your business, driving down prices and increasing services with their competitive zeal. The successful utilities would be mega-utilities—private and public. And there would be very few of them.

When serious competition is introduced into a marketplace the natural reaction is not to have the number of competitors increase; maybe in the short term it is, but certainly not in the long term. While the Harris cabinet was fretting over how best to break up Ontario Hydro during the early summer of 1997, U.S. newspapers were reporting almost daily about "a massive merger wave" taking place. As is often the case, the Americans were setting the logical pace. Applying the rule of business survival best known to large corporations, American utilities were attempting to eat each other up in multi-billion-dollar efforts to be big and more "competitive."

The Harris government was running against the wind where structural change in the American electricity market was concerned. In 1996, US$45 billion worth of merger activity took place. The number of mergers was increasing annually. In fact, as the government was mulling over its white paper to break up Ontario Hydro, the utility's once proud status as the continent's largest generator of electricity was being surpassed. Thanks to mergers, in only two years a number of American power utilities had now outgrown Ontario Hydro in both generating capacity and revenue. One, the Houston-based Enron Corp., now had revenues just slightly less than the combined revenues of Ontario Hydro, Hydro-Québec and Manitoba Hydro.

The confusion in the minds of Ontarians was understandable. Although two-thirds of the population did not support it, the call for privatization of Ontario Hydro and the opening of the market to competition had been as constant and persistent these past two years as the Energizer Bunny—and just as boring. But if that call for privatization now made little sense, the idea of busting up the province's power utility, when the Americans were doing the opposite, made no sense at all.

To be sure, of all Canada's major power utilities, Ontario Hydro had the most to atone for. It was fat, looked broke and seemed terribly short on vision. Word was spreading that the corporation was nowhere near as committed to sustainable development as corporate brochures claimed; that budgets and organization for this important initiative were being quietly pared back.

In January 1997, Ontario Hydro revealed that it would not be moving ahead with its vaunted Renewable Energy Technologies (RETs) program. The program had originally been budgeted to cost $110 million over five years and would pay for a serious search for renewable forms of energy generation. In its Web-site notice of cancellation follow-up in July, Ontario Hydro denied that the RETs program was dead. It said it just was not about to move ahead with a sustainable-development initiative, regardless of the fact many would say it was long overdue. Certainly the forty-seven companies who went out of their way to join in the bidding for RETs contracts thought so. In late July, a lawyer for the companies disgruntled by the program's cancellation launched a class-action lawsuit against Ontario Hydro for compensation to cover the money they spent in preparing renewable-energy proposals.

The reason Ontario Hydro was copping out of the search for sustainable-energy options was simple: It was too costly. The ten RETs proposals finally chosen had come in at an average price of ten cents per kilowatt-hour, or a little less than twice the price of its fossil-fuel generation costs. In this highly sensitive time of global warming and the urgent need for sustainable-development solutions, Ontario Hydro was choosing the bottom line over environmental protection. It was saying that our first go-around on sustainable-energy development was not "cost effective." It was an appallingly callous move on the utility's part, a corporation known as one of the major sources of pollution in the province of Ontario.

To make matters worse, the same month Ontario Hydro released an internal report that revealed the corporation had been dumping hundreds of tonnes of metals—in particular, copper, zinc, arsenic, iron, lead and tin, most of it from the Pickering nuclear station, since as early as 1971. Although there was debate over whether the dumping of the metals had an adverse effect on drinking water or human health, president and CEO Allan Kupcis admitted at a news conference the report showed a lack of respect for the environment in the corporation's nuclear division.

Ontario Hydro seemed once again to be in danger of becoming the target of increasing public ridicule. In many eyes, and despite the remedial measures taken in 1993, it had again taken on the characteristics of a bloated corporate dinosaur, deadened to public priorities like environmental protection. In the past, major errors in demand forecasting had led to misguided spending and debt accumulation, and all that meant for the province was a plummeting credit rating and many deferred or curtailed social programs. The arrogance and insensitivity, the decades of unquestioned power, the nuclear generating problems and the yet undefined costs of disposal, the profligacy, the pollution, the expensive surplus electricity it was carrying (as much as one-third even at peak capacity) were all sins requiring immense expiation. Evidently, the high priests of 700 University Avenue were in no mood for atonement.

But even with all the public antagonism over the corporation's apathy and arrogance, it was still seen with some favour by the majority of Ontarians. The utility had kept its promise to freeze electricity rates until 2000. It was paying down some of its debt. Its cash flow was increasing, although timidly. The lights were on. Perhaps most significant, in an age of dying attachment to public institutions, it was still seen by most Ontarians—warts, sins, transgressions and all—as "ours."

That familial affection was well-tested in August with the bombshell announcement that Ontario Hydro's nuclear generation program was in corporate meltdown and that it might take as much as $8 billion to remedy the problems—providing the problems surrounding the seven nuclear reactors could be repaired. Although the internal report blamed management for the sorry state of the utility's nuclear division, the question in the minds of most Ontarians was public safety. Given the litany of nuclear failures to date, was it possible to depend on Hydro's nuclear technology?

The public uproar over public safety and whether one could trust Ontario Hydro was a very real and pressing one, so much so that it provided a clear opportunity for the Harris government to press ahead with its plans to sell off the troubled utility. The pieces to this political puzzle had been in place long before the internal report surfaced about how badly the nuclear division was being managed. But the immediate sense of public concern that followed the tabling of the scathing report did no harm to the Harris government's intentions.

The Harris government had come puffing into office in June 1995 promising that it would look at major changes in Ontario Hydro, including the strong possibility of privatization. Within weeks, the utility's chairman, Maurice Strong, told a gathering of the Canadian Electrical Association that Ontario's electricity system was "obsolete," that "the status quo was not an option" and that one serious option was to restructure the corporation and privatize it in whole or in part. The same month, Strong and the rest of Ontario Hydro's board of directors released copies of a report prepared by independent financial advisers and investment bankers that Ontario Hydro should be restructured and privatized. Strong was replaced as chairman of Ontario Hydro by one of the members of the Bay Street investment group—William Farlinger, former chairman of Ernst & Young —which had recommended privatization. Farlinger had also been the head of Harris's transition team. The *Globe and Mail* called him "a doctrinaire privatization advocate."

At the same time, the Harris government announced a special advisory committee, headed by former Liberal finance minister Donald Macdonald, had been struck to investigate how best to bring competition to Ontario's electricity market. It came up with a report that in typical Canadian fashion said, privatization if necessary, but not necessarily privatization.

In the spring of 1996, Macdonald's seven-person advisory committee recommended that competition should be injected into the province's electricity-generating business and Ontario Hydro should be half-privatized. For what appeared to be nostalgic reasons, the hydro-electric facilities at Niagara Falls should remain in public ownership. All remaining hydro-electric and fossil-fuel generating stations would be offered for sale to the private sector. The Macdonald committee suggested the Ontario public would get to keep ownership of the debt-laden and accident-prone nuclear-generation facilities. And the Burghers of Bay Street could take the rest.

Macdonald told the press the day his committee's report was made public that although there was little absolute data to prove that private competition would set the pace in reducing rates or getting rid of the utility's long-term debt for Ontarians, he felt "instinctively" that would be the case. A few days after the report was tabled, the National Utility Service reported that Canadians already enjoyed the second-lowest electricity rates among fifteen major countries. Although Ontario had the second-highest rates in Canada, they were still as much as thirty percent lower than the average rates in the United States—the continental competitors the utility (or its private-sector offspring) would someday be up against.

By August, government polling feedback confirmed there was

little public appetite for privatization of Ontario Hydro. Less than one-quarter of those polled thought it a good idea, although a significantly higher number agreed that competition in the electricity sector would be a good thing for consumers. Privatization began to head for the back burner, to be replaced by an even louder call for "competition."

"The establishment of the competitive marketplace does not speak to ownership at all," Allan Kupcis would state in a March 1996 interview. "It talks to unbundling of the utility and the recognition that the generation component is just an electron factory. It's a commodity. And you produce it. The middle—the transmission system—is just the toll highway. Once you have unbundled ... you say: 'Boy, this is not an integrated utility any more'."

Throughout 1996 and early 1997, Kupcis and William Farlinger embarked on a series of speech appearances. The major themes were a need for more "customer choice" and "freedom of choice" and how Ontario Hydro was readying itself for "competition"—especially "customer-driven competition." It was "getting the jump on competition" and "competing in our customers' best interests." Ownership seemed no longer to be an issue worth debating within the curved walls of Ontario Hydro's Toronto head office.

By the end of 1996, it seemed the Harris government was no longer in a hurry to dump Ontario Hydro. It was as if the Progressive Conservatives had given it their best ideological try and had been played to a draw. There was talk the utility could use tighter regulation—a self-evident statement of no small dimensions. In mid-November, the minister responsible for energy and the environment, Norman Sterling, pounded home the theme, like Farlinger and Kupcis, about the benefits of increased competition in the electricity industry, and indicated that competition meant major changes and that these unstated changes would inevitably be "unsettling" for some people. But that was it. Sterling's prescription for application of the "Common Sense Revolution" plans to Ontario Hydro now seemed innocuous enough. The goal no longer was to disembowel. It was to "bring Hydro back to its proper role, providing reliable and affordable electrical power to Ontario," which some would argue—sustainable development aside—it had been doing for some time.

Even the privatization ardour of William Farlinger appeared to cool. His speeches throughout 1996 read like chants to the gods of increased competition. For a moment, it looked as if he was extolling the virtues and benefits to be realized by a strong, competitive, publicly owned Ontario Hydro. Rarely was the P-word mentioned. Given Farlinger's original enthusiasm for private-sector ownership of the utility, it seemed to be one of the most unusual conversions on the road to electricity's Damascus ever recorded. But was it?

By the end of January 1997, in a speech to the Economic Developers Conference of Ontario ("Team Canada—Ours to Recover"), Farlinger gave a slightly clearer idea of what kind of thinking was going on behind the privatization scene. Although he did not support the idea that publicly owned power monopolies should be simply converted into privately owned monopolies, as Nova Scotia had done to much disappointment, he did believe that "competition will make privatization happen." Ah, yes. It was a semantical ellipse that said little, yet explained everything.

His long-term view of what might happen to Ontario Hydro called for electricity generation and the retail distribution business to be separated from the transmission of electricity. This seemed essentially the kind of structural or organizational rendering that Ontario Hydro was going through. With generation being engulfed by competition from various elements of the private sector, and retail distribution within the province in the hands of 306 largely surly and unco-operative municipal utilities, that left only one logical role for Ontario Hydro. The natural successor company might then be, according to Farlinger, a transmission company.

Still, beyond the lack of enthusiasm most citizens had for selling off their power utility holus-bolus, a number of other factors were evidently making the Harris government slow its plunge into hydro privatization. First, the last two years gave sceptics time to massage the numbers. Many, even on Bay Street, were beginning to see the cost-benefit effect of selling off Ontario Hydro did not make political sense. There was an ugly reality to appreciate about these takeovers. As author Walter Stewart pointed out in *Uneasy Lies the Head,* the most likely buyers of crown corporations ready for the privatization heap were firms that were already too large. In this case, they would not be acting for the good of the little ratepayer and taxpayer. The conglomerates that would eventually take over crown corporations would be less concerned about delivering electricity and making jobs than they would in creating their own wealth. What good would be served, Stewart asked, by having huge conglomerates take over a crown corporation "and write the expense of the [takeover] off their income tax?" It was like conglomerates being allowed to finance their growth from the government's Consolidated Revenue Fund.

Second, a move to sell the utility to private investors would bring in some short-term cash for a provincial government wrestling with deficits in the billions of dollars range. But it would also result in "stranded assets" worth as much as $16 billion—primarily the risky nuclear components the private sector would be loath to touch. If Hydro was sold off—or at least the attractive parts of it—$16 billion was the estimated size of the tab that would be left with Ontario taxpayers. Arguments made by unions and public advocacy groups that privatization would cost Ontario ratepayers, rather than save them money, were making headway in the news media. The message was evidently getting through to the Progressive Conservative caucus.

Third, there was the presence of those 306 municipal utilities, many of whom still believed Ontario Hydro belonged to them. These co-operatives were the political grassroots in a reactionary, conservative province. If the rates they paid for Hydro's electricity were to nudge upward, or if a privatized version of Ontario Hydro were to cause them competitive indigestion in any way whatsoever, they would be on the Harris government like locusts on a cornfield in a hot, dry summer.

Finally, the increasing public criticism over any number of controversial political initiatives taken by the Harris government—from cuts in health care, education and social services to Toronto's amalgamation—seemed to make it much less enthusiastic about meeting all its political and ideological agenda targets at once. Prudence might dictate that privatization of Ontario Hydro could well be a second-term item.

In fact, in February the Progressive Conservative caucus decided that of its four major privatization targets—Ontario Hydro, TVOntario, the Ontario Liquor Control Board and the Toronto Transit Commission—only TVOntario was still on its list for review. (Even that one would get sidelined in the summer when TVO executives pitched the government a plan that might allow them to take over the network—a sort of publicly funded, public-privatization that could only happen in Canada.) Even though a privatization "secretariat" had been set up by the Harris government in March, the consensus seemed to be that its focus, for the moment, would be on smaller departmental operations and services.

While the Harris government hemmed and hawed, Ontario Hydro was boldly pressing ahead with its plan—at least until the August 13 release of the internal report on the state of its nuclear division—to gain greater access to the U.S. electricity market. It pledged to FERC in late February that in exchange for a power marketer licence to sell electricity into the United States, the Canadian utility was now prepared to allow U.S. electricity producers to compete for sales within Ontario, even if it meant shutting down some of its own capacity. The offer was not considered good enough by the Americans.

FERC objected to Ontario Hydro's monopoly control over the transmission of electricity, principally the fact that U.S. producers could transmit power through, but not into, Ontario. That meant Ontario's municipal distribution utilities would not be able to buy electricity directly from U.S. producers.

At the end of April, Premier Harris appeared to back off rather testily on his government's privatization quest. "We did not commit to privatizing anything," said Harris, despite what his former campaign manager, Tom Long, had told the right-wing Fraser Institute in September 1995—that "the Harris government is committed to privatization."

Harris claimed that, all along, what his government had been committed to was simply putting government agencies and crown corporations to "a private-sector test." Apparently, the results were positive, according to the premier. By being as prudent as they had been and taking the time necessary for Ontario Hydro to pass the test, Ontario had a more efficient electrical utility than when the Conservatives had entered office. It appeared the issue was closed.

Within weeks, the government's Planning and Priorities Board gave energy minister Norman Sterling the go-ahead to begin the break-up of Ontario Hydro. A white paper would be issued in June, explaining what the Harris government was proposing for Ontario Hydro. Public discussions would be held over the summer and the enabling legislation introduced during the fall sitting of the legislature. The new message was clear: If not privatization, then a break-up would do.

The plan for dismantling Ontario Hydro was reportedly being pressed forward by major business and industrial power users and the province's municipal utilities. Ontario Hydro could be split into two publicly owned companies, one responsible for transmission of electricity and another for generation and distribution. The transmission company—considered to be a classic example, like the country's highway system, of a "natural monopoly"—would most likely be regulated by the Ontario Energy Board.

Although it was assumed these moves were made to meet the forces of deregulation head-on, and once-and-for-all open the Ontario market to the advantages of competition in electricity generation, no parts of the provincial utility would be sold off to private investors, according to the announced plan.

A day later, the energy minister seemed to reverse himself, claiming that although there were no plans to sell Ontario Hydro at the moment, that could change a few years down the road. At this point it was still hard to say what the future might be for the province's $40 billion crown-owned public utility.

Where the problem of what to do with Ontario Hydro was concerned, the Harris government seemed, not unlike the Progressive Conservative, NDP and Liberal governments before it, a bit like Gordius and a bit like Alexander the Great. Gordius was the father of Midas. Whereas the son was a monarch best known for very dumb decision-making when it came to his love of gold, Gordius, the father, was the Chauncey Gardener of mythology.

Gordius—or "Gordus," depending on your fable—was a farmer who became king of Phrygia simply because he drove his wagon into the town square at the moment the people were searching for a king an oracle had prophesized would arrive in a wagon. The knot he used to tie his wagon was so well fastened that it was said that whoever was capable of untying it would become Lord of Asia. Alexander the Great tried, but he failed. Not one given to frustration and deliberating over complex solutions to challenges such as this, Alexander solved the problem by cutting the Gordian knot with his sword.

It was clear that, by the summer of 1997, the Harris government had finally begun, in its own way, to put the wheels of change into motion for the province's electrical power industry. The decision had been made to move on Ontario Hydro. But from most perspectives, the wagon was still tied securely in the town square. Alexander, in the form of Mike Harris or Norman Sterling, was nowhere in sight.

"This is what everyone's wondering: which way is it going to go?" asked Ralph Torrie, of Torrie Smith Associates, an Ontario-based consultancy firm well known for its analyses of current energy issues and sustainable-development options. In March 1995, Torrie Smith Associates prepared a paper for Environment Canada on sustainable development and electric power planning. The report concluded that Ontario Hydro's planning path had been, and continued to be, "clearly unsustainable." Reliance on fossil fuels caused substantial air pollution. Dependence on nuclear power generation was characterized as a Faustian bargain, its immense financial and social costs yet to be computed. And hydro-electric development had been highly damaging to aquatic life and fish stocks.

"Many of the actions that are being taken by the Harris government can be viewed as necessary from strictly a business point of view—regardless of any privatization moves. But they can also be viewed," said Torrie, "as preparation for the auction block."

Torrie felt public utilities had probably reached a point where they might not be necessary, or even be a particularly good idea any more. "If you look at the history of public power in this country, I don't see how you can come to any other conclusion except that it was a resounding success—up to a certain point. I would have voted for public power in 1906 in Ontario. And if someone asked me in 1950 to look back on it, I would say it is one of the great Canadian success stories.

"We had the cheapest electricity in the world. Practically everyone had access to it. It was an amazing accomplishment ... But the complaint I have about the current debate is that there is no distinction made between whether or not the time has come to privatize—and how we should be restructuring the electric utility business—versus whether or not we are now talking about throwing out the whole Canadian tradition of public ownership—which is what I call the baby-in-the-bath-water approach."

Other Ontarians fear that break-up of Ontario Hydro could end up costing Ontario ratepayers and taxpayers billions of dollars and put the reliability of their electricity service in jeopardy. Others are simply nostalgic about what might be considered a rather romantic institutional past. And then there are those who have become fed up with the arrogant and irresponsible way Ontario Hydro still conducts business. "I am a left-wing kind of person and I would love to be an unqualified defender of public enterprise, but I am sorry. Ontario Hydro is just a terrible example of a public enterprise," said author Paul McKay in late 1995. McKay is an exponent of independent, small-scale power, especially environmentally friendly hydro-electric installations. He is also a former special adviser to the minister of energy and environment during the Rae administration.

"Ontario Hydro is a lousy example of public ownership—on a grand scale. At the same time, my kind of left-wing perspective has prompted me to look at the private-enterprise side of the industry in the United States, and the electric business and energy business in general, and I see that it is equally appalling. The problem is that both have mucked it up so badly that it will take a long time and a lot of hard work to figure a way for us out of this mess."

Ralph Torrie used America's mixed ownership experience as a basis for judging utility effectiveness. Having both investor-owned and publicly owned utilities makes it possible to compare performance. His conclusion is that publicly owned utilities have outperformed investor-owned utilities. "I am not convinced that public utilities have screwed up any more than private ones have. The difference is when a private company screws up, it's a triumph of the marketplace's 'invisible fist.' It is the market doing what it is supposed to do— when IBM goes awry, or General Motors screws up, or Olympia & York ...

"But let a publicly-held company get it wrong and suddenly it is an example of government doing what it shouldn't be doing, which is getting involved in the economy at all. It is a real double-standard and I have never seen any convincing evidence that says business failure has been more severe in the public sector than it has been in the private sector, have you?"

There are those who argue that the days of publicly owned cor-porations, holding near-monopoly status, are inexorably numbered, by force of technology if nothing else. It is a change that is long overdue. Competition in the electricity-generating business provided by gas-fired turbine technology will inevitably provide consumers with cheaper electricity rates and more choice, so they argue. Even now, small-scale gas-turbine generators are being offered on the North American market. They can now be installed for as little as us$400 per kilowatt, making the technology seem attractive for small businesses like restaurants, hotels and convenience stores.

But based on North American consumer experience in a broad range of recent deregulation revisions—in the banking business, in the airline industry and in telecommunications, for instance—the evidence that, with increased competition, choice automatically increases to dazzling proportions and prices fall with remarkable consistency is not irrefutable.

Remember, this time the locus of change envelops one of the most important elements in our lives. We are not talking here about choosing which bank to deposit money into, which airline to fly or which telephone company to use. We are talking about electricity—the element most important to us beyond oxygen, food and water. Will tomorrow's suppliers of our Promethean gift bless us with the same degree of reliability and consistency that our publicly owned utilities have over the decades? Will "greater consumer choice" be there when we need it, and will that "choice" continue to be there for us after the inevitable megamergers take place?

Trouble signs are already on the horizon. If one listens to the lobbyists for independent power producers, open competition will spawn more eager and trustworthy energy companies—using gas-fired turbines, wind and solar power, hydrogen fuel cells and small-scale hydro—than we can count, all independent and all competing for your electricity dollar. But as Allan Kupcis pointed out in the spring of 1997, there is no guarantee it will happen that way: "The current independent generators that exist in Ontario—and they are up to about seven or eight percent of our total generation—have been able to build [generating facilities] because they had twenty-to-thirty-year contracts with Ontario Hydro to provide power at a guaranteed rate, with inflation clauses built in. That's all risk-free."

The unsettled state of the continental energy industry, along with the surpluses in electricity most Canadian power utilities are cursed with, has changed the way both the utilities and investment banks look at the contracts for independent power. "You take a twenty-year purchase contract with Ontario Hydro being the buyer and any [financial] backer without question will give you the money," said Kupcis. "But that's gone. There is no power entity that is going to write you a twenty-year contract."

For the consumer waiting for more "choice," Kupcis is one important herald to pay attention to. There are others who indicate there will not be as many independent power producers as deregulation exponents would have us believe. As in the Canadian telecommunication industry when it was deregulated in the late 1980s, the future electric survival formula will follow a predictable path to fewer, not more service, suppliers.

Dick Gathercole, executive director of the B.C. Public Interest Advocacy Centre in Vancouver, recalls the situation in California: "The independent power producers a few years ago said, 'We can make millions and millions of dollars if you just unleash us to compete in the California market.' Well, essentially they have been unleashed for years. They just couldn't get a contract because they could not produce power to compete with power generated with natural gas on-site."

The deregulation of telecommunications, on the other hand, triggered a nova-like expansion of "resellers" of telecommunication bandwidth—purchased from the provincial telephone monopoly utilities—for business and residential users. It was to be a virtual boon to all telephone subscribers—more choice and lower prices. Within a few years, the original resellers were all but gone: some broke, some bankrupt and some bought out by larger telcos. Only this time, some of the large telcos had head office addresses south of the Canada–U.S. border.

"The telephone companies said: 'We want competition,'" said Gathercole. "But their concept of competition was that their team had five times as many players as the other team. Then you get rid of the referees. And they thought competition was just great as long as they were competing with Ted Rogers, because they could wipe the floor with Ted. But now they are not competing with Ted Rogers any longer. Its AT&T, and eventually it will be British Telecom. Now they are pretty nervous."

What seems clear from the telecommunication deregulation experience is that competition focuses on the major users, providing them with price-cut benefits, but provides very little benefit, if any, to smaller users.

"What you are seeing in telecommunications now is that prices for local service, particularly outside the urban areas, have gone up," said Gathercole. "Prices for frequent or big long distance users have gone down. I could even make a convincing argument for the fact that your basic telephone subscribers are now subsidizing the big business users, based on how costs are allocated.

"It's like gas, too. The projection when deregulation took place was that gas prices would go down by at least one-third. But gas has remained stable or has gone up. The only reason it has not gone up faster is because the commodity cost of gas was low. But now gas prices have started to go up, because you have the big players controlling it."

When electricity consumers take into account that the demand for natural gas will inevitably go up once gas-fired generation begins to infringe on hydro, coal and nuclear as generating options, prices for natural gas will inevitably go up for small consumers.

And so what is the issue? Privatization versus public ownership of power utilities? More consumer choice versus service and reliability? Cheaper prices for electricity versus more expensive prices? Monopoly control by public ownership or monopoly control via private ownership?

In a deregulated environment, the natural tendency for the "big players," with the deeper capital pockets and need for increasingly larger revenue return for their investors, is to seek to control as much of the marketplace as is possible. Whether operating as publicly regulated but investor-owned monopolies, or like Canada's major banks, as a market-controlling quasi-cartel, the experience has seldom, if ever, led to more choice and cheaper prices. The opposite is usually true; check your bank statement and add up your charges for fees on services that were once free.

"I spent the last fifteen years fighting B.C. Hydro on rates and things like that," said Dick Gathercole. "And I am a great supporter of B.C. Hydro. Why? Because if you are going to have just one big system or utility, it is better to have it in the public sphere.

"If you start breaking up B.C. Hydro, aside from the fact it might fit someone's personal vision, where is the advantage?" Gathercole asks. "You cannot convince me and my clients at this stage that you are going to end up with cheaper electricity than B.C. consumers are getting now. Maybe some customers might end up with cheaper electricity, but not all. And then when you compute the costs and downsides from environmental damage..."

Gathercole chaired the British Columbia Energy Council in 1994. The council prepared a major energy policy paper for Mike Harcourt's NDP government. Entitled *Planning Today for Tomorrow's Energy: An Energy Strategy for British Columbia*, the council's report recognized that the days of electricity generation, transmission and distribution being viewed as a natural monopoly were over. Monopolies could still be justified in transmission and distribution, the report stated, but new electricity-generation technology meant the days of monopoly control in generation were ending.

The council recommended that competition be introduced in the wholesale sector, allowing for producers to sell their electricity to a utility, using the transmission lines of that or another utility. But the council was opposed to retail wheeling, the sale of electricity directly from a producer to a consumer. It is retail wheeling that is the growing focus of the energy debate going on in the United States. It comes mainly from states panicking with high, uncompetitive electricity rates.

But retail wheeling would be in direct conflict with the emerging concept of sustainable development: meeting the needs of the present generation without diminishing the ability of future generations to meet their needs.

"Retail wheeling would result in utilities and private power producers competing for sales and electricity generation," the report stated. "Although it might, in certain short-term cases, provide electricity rate relief for some consumers, in the long term [retail competition] would be one of the most costly avenues for the future of electricity to travel in—technologically, socially and environmentally."

It was no accident that in British Columbia the preoccupation of a council in search of an energy strategy would be focused on sustainable development rather than debate the issue of utility ownership. Not surprisingly, any comparison between how Ontario perceives the future of its power utility and how it is perceived in British Columbia is very much grounded in political ideology. One set of provincial politicians seems intent on turning back the clock to 1905 and the days of the Electric Ring. The other seems to be grappling, in its halting and bureaucratic way, with whether or not we have a future at all.

In British Columbia, like in Quebec, there was no way B.C. Hydro, for all its historic faults, was going on the privatization block, at least not while the New Democratic Party was in power. It was not simply a matter of left-wing belief in the greater good of public enterprise or ownership of the means of production. There was a time when privatization of B.C. Hydro had been seriously considered. When the NDP under Mike Harcourt's leadership was elected to office in November 1991, one of its first moves was to study the costs and benefits of privatizing B.C. Hydro.

The glory days of W. A. C. Bennett and the Columbia River Treaty notwithstanding, the monopoly utility had been a political aggravation to many British Columbians for decades. As the powerful economic handmaiden of Social Credit governments, B.C. Hydro displayed a lamentable track record in a province more environmentally and socially conscious than most. The Harcourt government was elected on a strong platform of conservation and environmental protection and a dedicated belief in the principles of sustainable development. On the other hand, for almost three decades B.C. Hydro conducted itself less as an electric utility and more as a deranged provincial construction company.

The Columbia River Treaty called for three major dams to be built in the river basin—the Duncan, the Keenleyside and the Mica. The initial dam work triggered a construction binge that resulted in twenty-nine hydro-electric generating stations, one conventional thermal station and two combustion turbine stations generating, in total, more than 10,700 megawatts of power. It also meant forty-two massive reservoirs flooded over 267,000 hectares of valuable forest, farm and recreation land, caused the wholesale destruction of fish and other aquatic life and forced the dislocation of thousands of very unhappy citizens.

By the time this megaproject mania came to a screaming halt with the completion of the Revelstoke Dam in 1984, in the eyes of many British Columbians at least, the love affair with their provincial electrical utility had ended. When Revelstoke came on-stream, its power was completely surplus to B.C. needs. For the next four years its electricity had to be sold on the spot market at a price roughly half of what it cost to produce. By the early 1980s, B.C. Hydro had an overall capacity surplus of sixty percent of its total system, long-term debt would rise to $8.5 billion in 1985, and it was projected that British Columbia would not have to undertake another major hydro-electric project until the millennium.

But much of the damage had already been done. Precious fish-spawning rivers and streams had been dammed shut to migrating salmon, steelhead and trout. Along the way it was discovered the Keenleyside Dam was also causing serious damage to salmon spawning. The force of the outflow water spilling into the basin at the foot of the dam caused gas bubbles to form, killing even more fish downstream. The careless application of herbicides kept the transmission lines free of underbrush, but raised serious questions about their toxic effects on humans and animals. The cost of the human dislocation in the Peace-Williston and the Columbia Basin—in lost land, jobs and lifestyle opportunities—was largely ignored. Not unlike the native people of northern Saskatchewan and Manitoba, many British Columbians would not receive proper compensation for the impact of hydro-electric development and flood control for decades. It would not come until the Harcourt administration put together a multi-million-dollar compensation program in 1993.

Even taking into account this squalid corporate history, what the Harcourt government's probe into the pros and cons of privatizing B.C. Hydro concluded was that the utility was more valuable to the province if left in public hands. An outright sale of the utility might net roughly $4 billion, and help reduce the province's long-term debt, but there were just too many advantages to public ownership.

Ratepayers enjoyed the third-lowest rates in the country. Those rates were one-half the U.S. average and one-third of what one would pay in New York. B.C. Hydro had lower per-unit costs of operation than most other utilities. Where environmental-damage issues were concerned, remedies and solutions could come more quickly through the correcting hand of government. The decision was inevitable: Better the devil you control than the devil you do not.

In fact, one very important new initiative evolved out of B.C. Hydro's checkered plight in the 1980s. In 1989, B.C. Hydro embarked on a program called "Power Smart," in recognition of the massive savings in electricity to be realized from "demand-side management" (DSM). DSM is a means of pulling consumers and manufacturers away from wasteful use of electricity. It is a recognition of a basic truth governments and electrical utilities were very slowly beginning to comprehend about the industry—that conservation is the cheapest form of electricity.

Originally, Power Smart encompassed more than two dozen programs aimed at reducing the future demand for electricity by encouraging more efficient ways of using it. Eventually, B.C. Hydro's Power Smart program became a North American model for energy conservation. The program endorses and encourages a wide variety of energy-saving ideas and techniques—from smarter construction of new homes, offices and hotels to encouraging the manufacture of more energy-efficient appliances and electric motors. In a number of cases, Power Smart led to the introduction of new, more energy-efficient standards in manufacturing.

By 1995 the program had, for example, replaced 41,000 older, less efficient refrigerators, and its accumulated power savings reached 1.75 million kilowatt hours annually—enough to supply electricity for a city the size of Nanaimo. Together with B.C. Hydro's Resource Smart program, enough electricity has been saved to meet the electricity needs of a quarter-million homes. By 1996, more than thirty utilities worldwide had bought into the Power Smart concept.

For a while, Ontario Hydro was blowing its own horn for its emphasis on sustainable-energy development under the banner of its "Renewable Energy Technologies" program. But given the news about the corporation's real intentions for RETs, many outside and inside the corporation are rightly sceptical about the utility's plans for sustainable-energy development. Many claim the sustainable-development program has been downgraded in importance since Maurice Strong left the chairman's post. And even if the corporation were to spend the $22 million a year on the RETs program it originally proposed, that barely represents 0.244 percent of annual corporate revenues. It hardly seems a bold commitment to renewable energy development.

A B.C. Hydro spin-off program—"BC21 Power Smart"—is a year-long project that will retrofit more than eighty thousand B.C. homes with energy- and water-saving products and devices at no cost to the consumer. The $20 million energy-saving program includes a personalized, home-by-home energy assessment. Teams will "audit" homes and provide them with a variety of solutions to improve energy efficiency: hot-water-tank blankets, low-flow faucet aerators and showerheads, toilet-flush reducers and weather-stripping.

Less than two years into its mandate, the NDP government set some serious new goals and objectives for B.C. Hydro, initiatives that pointed the utility more in the direction of social responsibility and less in simply supplying electricity. It was a sincere political effort to modernize the public utility.

The utility's corporate goals now included—in addition to providing low-cost electricity and service reliability—a leadership role in sustainable development, more equitable employment practices, a new relationship with aboriginal citizens and their communities, job creation and targets to increase revenue from export of its electricity surpluses.

While the forces for utility privatization were turning up the heat in Ontario, the Harcourt government was trying to make B.C. Hydro into a better corporate citizen and a stronger public corporation. In 1995, then-minister responsible for B.C. Hydro Glen Clark made it clear to his critics that the Harcourt government had no intention of privatizing B.C. Hydro. As Clark put it to the press: "The privatization of B.C. Hydro is not on the table in any way, shape or form."

What was open to change was the utility's near-monopoly control over the generation of electricity in British Columbia. B.C. Hydro generates about seventy-eight percent of the electricity consumed in the province. This is supplemented by Alcan at its Kemano plant, West Kootenay Power & Light in southeastern British Columbia, some self-generated industrial and some small local hydro. In September 1995, the British Columbia Utilities Commission rejected open competition for B.C. Hydro at the retail level—on the basis it would increase damage to the environment and restrict social planning options—but recommended the utility should move toward wholesale competition, relying for the moment on new gas-fired generating technology to provide new supplies of electricity.

In April 1996, after replacing Mike Harcourt as NDP leader and surviving a rancorous provincial election, Clark used the tabling of a critical report about B.C. Hydro's IPC International Power Corp. to promise to make the beleaguered utility even more accountable to the legislature. In accepting criticism for his role in the way the Raiwind joint venture turned out, Clark promised to give the crown corporation secretariat new powers to monitor B.C. Hydro. He also pledged to strike an all-party legislative committee to act as a further public-accountability watchdog.

The media furor over the IPC affair did the Clark government few political favours. It raised doubts among many British Columbians about whether the people running their public power utility (not to mention the provincial government) knew what they were doing. It naturally allowed for the question to be asked: Would British Columbia's electricity future be more assured if put in private-sector hands?

The most vocal questioning group, of course, was the Independent Power Association of B.C., smaller independent producers demanding a larger share of the province's power-generation market. The second-loudest cry came from large industrial users. They claimed their electricity rates were too high and that the extra costs would make them uncompetitive in the North American marketplace. However, it is well known that U.S. industrial rates are at least twenty-five to thirty percent higher than B.C. rates. A number of studies have also revealed that with the odd exception, such as aluminum smelting, the cost of electricity was nowhere near as large a bottom-line survival factor as many industry spokespeople like to make out.

They were making the electricity-costs-too-much noise not for competitive reasons, but to keep the pressure on governments and their utilities to shave a few cost points. The issue was not the uncompetitive cost of B.C. electricity. It was modern, and completely understandable, corporate mendacity. In December 1996, industrial power users in British Columbia claimed they could save $200 million a year if they were allowed to buy electricity on the open market.

"What they are looking for is short-term advantage," said Dick Gathercole. "If you said, 'Okay, you can stay with B.C. Hydro or you can go elsewhere' most would stay with B.C. Hydro because they need the security of supply and the support services behind it. They don't really want to take the risk."

What many large industrial and commercial users want is electricity both ways. They want access to the grid so they can buy on the spot market when it is to their advantage, but they want B.C. Hydro to be there when spot market prices begin rising or there is disruption in the supply of their electricity.

"During the market structure review [the industrial users] took a position *against* retail access," adds Gathercole. "The only thing different now is that spot prices are a little lower ... so now they are talking about their competitors having access to cheaper electricity from the Pacific Northwest, and it isn't true, at least not yet."

Of course, a third resounding voice for open competition, or retail access, was the large private power generators like UtiliCorp's West Kootenay Power & Light and Alcan's Kemano. In late 1996 West Kootenay Power asked the BCUC for open access to B.C. Hydro's transmission system for its wholesale, industrial and large commercial customers—a clear move toward retail competition. B.C. Hydro's Brian Smith replied that the utility had no intention of opening up its transmission lines to allow customers to buy on the open market.

"They want to get access to B.C. Hydro's customers. They want to get access to B.C. Hydro's system," said Gathercole. "They are one of the groups who talk about privatization and breaking up B.C. Hydro and having local distribution companies. Essentially, their long-term goal is to gain control of the system and sell into the U.S. market. There is a big market there, and prices are quite high, so in the long run that is what they are looking for."

The Independent Power Association's call for privatization of B.C. Hydro and increased competition was logical from its point of view. Who would not like to see B.C. Hydro broken up and the job of new electricity generation handed over to Independent Power Association (IPA) members? But it proved once again there was no clear definition of what "privatization" might be. It meant different things to different people or organizations.

The model the IPA proposed was a strange one indeed. The IPA suggested generation should be open to competition, but B.C. Hydro's large generation facilities on the Peace and Columbia Rivers should remain in public hands for public-policy reasons related to the Canada–U.S. agreement. But the Peace and Columbia river basins represented three-quarters of all Hydro's installed generating capacity. Did that mean "privatization" or "competition" was a good deal for only one-quarter of the provincial output?

What about transmission and distribution? The IPA claimed these were "natural monopolies" and should be privatized. But the traditional definition of natural monopoly meant that this portion of an industry was best left to the public, not the private, sector to manage. A natural monopoly, it is almost universally agreed, is a market in which society is better off with control vested in only one firm. It is usually a market characterized by high fixed costs and necessary economies of scale. But B.C. Hydro's transmission and distribution system had been in place for decades.

In this publicly confusing time in British Columbia, here was an organization talking about an outright takeover of B.C. Hydro's transmission and distribution systems and asking for "competition" in a power-generation market that only added up (or subtracted down) to less than one-third of provincial output. It was, as Alice might have said, curious indeed. The IPA was clearly being as opportunistic as only good business predators can be. But its loud public haranguing helped stoke the fires of confusion among many British Columbians about who should be in charge of delivering on their electricity needs.

In early December 1996, the Clark government announced it had finally reached an agreement with the Bonneville Power Administration for the return of downstream power benefits from the Columbia River Treaty. Beginning in 1998, the province of British Columbia would have an extra 1,400 megawatts of electricity, a boost in surplus power equal to ten to fifteen percent of the province's current capacity.

The agreement changed the whole energy equation in British Columbia from what to do with the errant provincial utility to what to do with a huge, rich power legacy from the days of W. A. C. Bennett. It gave the Clark government an enormous economic and public-policy tool to work with.

In terms of new export potential, the downstream benefit package provided British Columbia with instant competitive advantage. "It certainly gives the province some choice," said Marvin Shaffer, the province's principal negotiator in the most recent Columbia River Treaty negotiations over downstream benefits. "It is a lot of power, coming back to where it is needed—the Vancouver area and southwestern B.C.—to meet future domestic growth. It gives the province some choice of whether it develops more power resources in the province or what it sells in the United States.

"Right now I think it is fair to say the province is pretty bullish on exports. If the markets in the United States are there, the preference would be to sell, at least initially, most of the power there, then allow these other attractive projects, like cogeneration on Vancouver Island, to be developed. It isn't necessary that B.C. Hydro do it all. It could be independent producers."

Domestically, the arrival of this extra power meant it could be made available for industrial and commercial users at whatever price is deemed appropriate by the province. In late June 1997, the Clark government announced it was prepared to use this new infusion of power as an inducement to attract new, electricity-intensive industry to British Columbia. Under the Jobs for Power Act, it began offering discounted electricity in exchange for the promise of new jobs. As well, the downstream benefits all but eliminated any need for B.C. Hydro to spend large sums of capital on new, major generation projects in the future, perhaps ever again.

The utility's hydro-electricity dominance meant it would remain the biggest player in the province's electricity game. But the switch to alternative-energy-generation forms—from cogeneration to gas-fired technologies, from wind, solar and small hydro to hydrogen fuel cells being developed with much international attention by Ballard Power Systems of Burnaby, B.C.—clearly meant that it was now the logical time to modernize B.C. Hydro and reorganize the public corporation to fit the new realities of the North American power market.

The focus of electricity generation in British Columbia had switched from monopoly to competitive without having to go through the chaotic step of privatization. That issue was no longer in debate. There was now room enough for some independent generators. But the provincial government held the hammer. Electricity prices could now be kept stable for some time to come, falling in real terms, as they had in British Columbia for the past few years.

Revenue from export sales, in particular from the Columbia downstream benefits, would begin to fill public coffers, perhaps eating away at provincial deficits and the debt. The province's credit rating would inevitably improve. With B.C. Hydro in charge of the transmission and distribution system, a high degree of reliability (power is available to the average B.C. Hydro customer an exceptional 99.971 percent of the time) and security of electricity supply for consumers was guaranteed. To give it all away now, just to be able to say the erratic, unpredictable and often costly forces of the marketplace should prevail, would have been an act of folly and public disservice not seen since Ontario Hydro decided it would fight the threat of competition from natural gas with the Live Better Electrically campaign.

In mid-January 1997, employment and industry minister Dan Miller announced the NDP government would introduce by the end of the year a policy to end B.C. Hydro's virtual monopoly over the traditional integrated power market. The feeling seemed to be there was no longer any time to lose. The continental power business was changing very fast. At the end of March, just before the BCUC was about to begin hearings on B.C. Hydro's monopoly status, Miller announced the BCUC hearings would be deferred. In its place, Miller appointed the BCUC's chairman, Simon Fraser University economist

Mark Jaccard, to head a task force on electricity market reform. Jaccard was an advocate of reform in the power industry in general. He favoured competition in electricity generation and was someone who had the respect of most of the players in the game, including industrial customers and independent power producers.

In the past, as the BCUC chairman, Jaccard had faced off in bitter public disputes with B.C. Hydro's senior management. He had argued that the days of production monopolies had ended. That did not mean privatization was the replacement. Jaccard may have been dedicated in his task to break up its monopoly status, and even prepared to do public battle with senior management over the issue of who regulates B.C. Hydro, but he still saw a major role for Hydro after electricity reform was completed.

The task force that Jaccard chaired would not be required to table a detailed finding until November 1, 1997. A final report was required by the end of December. But it was clear from the terms of reference the Clark government set that B.C. Hydro would remain a publicly owned utility—at least for as long as the NDP remained in government. The task force's mandate required that it "take into account" the following objectives: "job creation and economic development"; "greater choice" for consumers; "reasonable access" for electricity producers to the system; "continued incorporation of environmental and social considerations in the management and regulation" of the province's electricity industry, "access to export markets for B.C. electricity," and "continued stewardship of the province's hydropower endowment."

More tellingly, the mandate "bound" the task force by the following constraints. It required that their findings could not adversely affect electric-sector employees, meaning no wholesale loss of jobs at B.C. Hydro could take place—a hint that break-up of the utility was not an option. It required there be no adverse effects on "classes" of electricity customers, indicating there could not be a move to unequally applied rates. It also required there be no negative impact on the hundreds of millions of dollars B.C. Hydro provided to the province each year. Finally, the terms of reference commanded that "public ownership of the assets of B.C. Hydro" would continue.

As a government document, the task force's terms of reference were, as one senior industry analyst put it, "the strongest statement of provincial energy policy that we have had in eight years."

The development of British Columbia's electric-power policy would now begin to reflect what was happening in Quebec. In fact, the two governments will probably mimic each other as change evolves in the Canadian electricity industry. That, in and of it itself, is not surprising because the two governments have long held similar ideological perspectives, particularly on the role of public institutions.

So it was no surprise to learn in June that B.C. Hydro, like Hydro-Québec only the month before, had reversed itself and would now agree to open its transmission grid to competitors—Canadian and American—seeking to sell electricity in the province. It signalled the first major step toward change for B.C. Hydro. It also indicated how prepared the Clark government was to restructure its utility for energy competition in the continental marketplace.

In all likelihood, the coming reorganization for B.C. Hydro will result in a holding company model, with two or three separate corporations reporting to the holding company and responsible to it. The corporations responsible for transmission and distribution of electricity will be publicly owned and perform as monopoly utility operations. Generation of electricity, in both jurisdictions, will be thrown open to competition. But this important generative function will now be subject to a much tighter regulatory regime, primarily for environmental and social-policy reasons. Even Prometheus, as considerate as he was, needed monitoring.

The move to the break-up of traditional, vertically integrated public power monopolies was well underway by the mid-summer of 1997. The difference between the three major jurisdictions—British Columbia, Quebec and Ontario—will be that the first two will not have to put up with pretences about privatization of their power utility. While changing the nature of the business in their provinces, both governments will maintain control and ownership of major elements of the electricity industry.

Ontario will try to square an awkward circle. It will keep talking about maintaining public ownership of the soon-to-be-segregated elements of Ontario Hydro, but as soon as the political winds shift in their favour—as soon as the province's municipal utilities acquiesce, or a way can be found to quietly bury the multi-billion-dollar cost of stranded nuclear assets in non-radioactive taxpayer soil—the Harris government will once again try to prove that political dogma makes more sense than common sense.

8 / The Words of the Prophets

*The Greeks associated greater change and growth with
greater decay and chaos. Their goal, then, was to hand down
to the next generation a world as much preserved from 'change'
as possible.*

— Jeremy Rifkin, *Entropy: A New World View*

AS WE MOVE TO CLOSE OUT 1997, the best that can be said is that
the Canadian public power utility business now resembles a working model of the second law of thermodynamics. Nothing is predictable, everything seems to be in chaos and no one really knows
where the industry is headed and what it might look like when it
gets there. In that sense, Canada is right on track with the rest of
the changing electricity world.

For many observant consumers, the industry—as exemplified by
our decades-long relationship with large, vertically integrated provincial monopolies—is moving much too hastily away from the
familiar and often comforting sense of order and predictability into
disorder, randomness and unknown costs in power supply, in reliability and in environmental degradation.

Except in Ontario, where the Harris government keeps trying to
manufacture an economic past that never did exist, privatization was,
by the autumn of 1997, hardly an issue any more. In most electricity
jurisdictions the idea that private ownership must prevail over public
was now perceived as a rather quaint and somewhat naive concept—
sort of like Margaret Thatcher's 1950s-style hairdos—that had been
run down in the mad scramble of power utilities to make and sell
more and more electricity to pay the bills for the sins of their past.

The primary issue now was competition. Even that term came
full of contradictions and wrought with confusion. Competition was

supposed to mean more companies supplying more choice for the consumer shopping for electricity. But south of the 49th Parallel, where the term had its longest and most popular play, a form of mini-merger mania was going on. Electricity competition was becoming an oxymoron because in the end it was likely only a handful of dominant energy companies would survive. And they would not be inclined to compete very strenuously among themselves. This situation would then make the future utility market in America look uncomfortably like the one that was just in the process of being overthrown—large energy megacorporations, each controlling its designated area of the market.

Even deregulation meant something and meant nothing. Yes, the hidebound and not very effective regulatory regimes of the past were being disassembled by new legislation and the threat of new technologies and new market forces. And in the short run it would mean more players entering the marketplace with more and presumably cheaper electricity for some consumers. But almost anyone connected with this industry in major transformation was using the term deregulation in a benign form, as if this latest economic crusade would simply push those tyrannical monopolies out of the way and provide us with a cornucopia of electrical beneficence.

Electricity deregulation is a movement with a very ugly downside potential for the long term. Because some electricity prices would likely drop with increased competition, it could trigger an energy or consumption binge that could all but destroy serious conservation efforts—efficiency improvements, demand-side management or the introduction of new, more environmentally friendly, or renewable, generating technologies. At its worst, deregulation could continue to place increasing stress and pressure on the environment.

Taking events a step further into the future from 1997, one could even suppose deregulation's ultimate irony: It could begin to spawn demand so damaging to the environment that we might be forced to apply strict regulations on electricity generation in the future simply because we were running out of future. The net effect of introducing deregulation into electricity markets would be that we would eventually need regulation more than ever.

To pile irony upon irony and contradiction upon contradiction, by the summer of 1997 our Canadian "deregulating marketplace" was now —to all intents and purposes—being regulated by the Federal Energy

Regulatory Commission (FERC), an American agency located somewhere along the banks of the Potomac River between Maryland and Virginia. By mid-summer, FERC was having a more pronounced effect on the future plans of Canada's power utilities than was the most aggressive and powerful provincial government.

FERC was like some continental Rapunzel, residing in a faraway castle, toying with her suitors, coquettishly dangling her hair and her rules of engagement from high upon the castle's towers. FERC kept pulling the tresses up and down to tease her admirers and force them into making concessions to win her affection or favour.

Hydro-Québec was the first to succumb to her enchantment and pledged it was prepared to change the way it had done the electricity business in Quebec for decades, if only she would open the gates of the American marketplace and let it come in. Hydro-Québec proved it was aggressively diversifying its business and its approach to public power by agreeing to open its transmission grid to competitors, signing reciprocal trade deals with natural gas suppliers and even buying into gas companies. FERC smiled upon the Quebec utility and agreed to issue it a permit for the right to export power into the United States.

British Columbia, which had almost been as quick as Quebec lining up at the bottom of the castle tower, was heading, as former BCUC chairman Mark Jaccard once put it, toward "competition without privatization." B.C. Hydro had been spurned by Rapunzel earlier in the year when it first attempted to obtain a permit to sell electricity directly to American customers. It was turned down, not because B.C. Hydro was a public entity, but because its transmission grid was not considered sufficiently open to competitors. Ownership was not the issue. Equal access was.

In August 1997, B.C. Hydro received permission from the BCUC to set new tariff rates and eliminate differential pricing on its transmission grid, a major irritant to FERC. Differential pricing meant power companies paid higher prices for transporting power longer distances. B.C. Hydro—like its counterparts in Ontario and Quebec—was desperate to gain access to the American market, arguing it could lose more than $100 million annually in sales if FERC permission was not granted. But as many critics pointed out, eliminating differential pricing could result in higher costs for domestic electricity users. It was also argued that B.C. Hydro and BCUC were using the wrong yardstick: They were willing to accept direction from FERC rather than regulate the province's industry in the interests of users and the residents of the province.

Because FERC had earlier refused Ontario Hydro direct access to U.S. customers—other than contracted utilities—Ontario Hydro now claimed $235 million in annual export revenue had been placed in jeopardy. Ontario Hydro took FERC to court, arguing for a stay in her previous decision because it violated trade laws between Canada and the United States.

Ontario Hydro was getting nervous. If it accepted FERC's demand for wholesale access to its transmission grid, it could seriously put at risk the vast majority of its traditional business. The almost $6 billion in wholesale electricity it sold each year to the 306 municipal utilities could, in theory, be up for competitive grabs if open access was allowed. Consequently, its aspirations for open access to U.S. markets—but not allowing the same in Ontario—stuck Ontario Hydro between and rock and a hard place. To get a piece of the U.S. action, and not even that large a piece at this point, it might have to take a chance on losing large chunks of its own market. But that was what competition was all about, right?

The current state of Canadian electrical power utility business was utterly unpredictable and disordered. The last decade had plunged the industry into a worldwide tumult of change "whose possible consequences no one can yet clearly foresee," as Walt Patterson of the Royal Institute of International Affairs put it. Patterson was speaking as a senior fellow in the institute's energy and environmental program. He told an electrical industry audience in Brighton in February 1997 that, to the extent he could foresee anything, even into 1998, "I would say that the opportunities may well be to get out while the getting is good, and the challenges may well be to batten the hatches and wait until the chaos subsides.

"At the moment all the signs suggest that 1998 is going to be a very uncomfortable year for those in the electricity business, including both suppliers and customers. The last pillars of the traditional institutional infrastructure are to be uprooted and cast aside; but no one yet appears to be absolutely clear what will take their place."

Defining the future direction of Canada's three largest public power utilities was almost as futile as trying to predict the precise direction all the balls on a billiard table would head in just before the break.

In October 1996, Ralph Torrie prepared a major discussion paper for presentation to the National Round Table on the Environment and the Economy. In it Torrie sketched out a scenario of what might lie ahead for the Canadian power sector, and for consumers and taxpayers. Citing an earlier study prepared for Natural Resources Canada, and collating it with data available and studies he and his associates had compiled, Torrie painted a sobering picture of the future.

First, within ten years most provinces will have competitive markets for electricity that may even include retail competition. Second, open access to transmission grids, combined with surplus generating capacity that currently exists, could keep prices flat, or even declining, for the next decade. Third, when new capacity is required, it will likely be fired by natural gas. With the odd exception, small renewable forms of energy generation "will not be competitive, and neither will new coal, hydro electric, or nuclear units. There will be pressure to increase [existing] plant utilization and to extend the life of older coal-fired plants." Fourth, provincial power utilities with very high debt ratios and high-priced electricity will not be able to compete with the new low-cost suppliers, and "transitional arrangements" will be needed "to recover stranded costs, including the possibility of government bailouts where the Crown has backed the utility's bonds." Finally, the competitive marketplace will eliminate central planning of new generation resources. There will be no Integrated Resource Plans. Generating companies "will not pursue demand management as an alternative to generation" and "will not voluntarily use a higher cost process to reduce environmental impact" of their chosen technologies. The reason? It would put them at a disadvantage compared to their competitors.

As Torrie put it in the discussion paper: "[T]he utilities, the government agencies considering restructuring options and most private analysts tend to agree that the move to a competitive market means a set-back for demand-side management, small scale renewables, research and development, integrated resource planning, social costing, environmental research, greenhouse gas emissions (in most provinces) and small-scale cogeneration."

If remaining utilities were to be privatized, according to Torrie, the negative results in environmental and social responsibility terms would only be magnified. Given the questionable regulatory regimes that have been in place to monitor Canadian public power utilities, there is "an understandable concern that privatization will remove what government leverage does exist to achieve environmental and sustainable development progress in the power sector."

The concerned citizen might then ask: Okay, I'll have more choice, and maybe slightly cheaper electricity for a while, but who will be in charge of protecting the environment? Who will be in charge of organizing and implementing new renewable-energy strategies? Who will be responsible for the tens of billions of dollars in stranded assets left by those indebted public utilities? Who will I call if my power goes out? Who do I call if the air gets too thick to breathe? Who indeed? Adam Smith?

Torrie responded with three of his own seminal questions: "Is retail wheeling worth the extra environmental and regulatory risks it carries? Are we trading a relatively short-term financial gain for longer-term environmental pain? Are we 'throwing out the baby with the bath water' by linking privatization of public power with the introduction of a competitive market in electricity?"

On the day that Ontario Hydro announced it was hiring three well-known Progressive Conservatives to lobby the Ontario Progressive Conservative government of Mike Harris not to implement plans to break up the province's power utility, it was reported in one news-paper that two billion people—roughly one-third of the world's population—still lacked access to electricity.

An optimist would see that statistic as a terrific marketing and sales opportunity. A pessimist would perhaps see it as Odin, the Norse god, might have looked upon the news. Odin was unlike Zeus or even Prometheus. He did not throw thunderbolts and he did not steal. He was a solemn, pensive god. While the heroes in Valhalla enjoyed their feasts, Odin ate nothing. Two ravens perched on his shoulders. One was named Thought and the other Memory. Each day they would fly off and bring back news of all that man had done. While the other gods feasted, it was Odin's responsibility to ponder what his ravens told him, because his job was to postpone as long as possible man's day of doom.

Odin would have no doubt taken badly the news Thought had delivered that day. He would in all likelihood have appended it to what Memory told him about what had happened years before. First, that between 1967 and 1992 generation of electricity around the world more than doubled, most of it derived from the burning of dirty fossil-fuels like coal and from nuclear fission. Second, that over the thirty-year period from 1990 to 2020, greenhouse gas emissions from Canadian sources alone, largely in the form of carbon dioxide, were projected to grow by about 133 percent. Third, Odin would not have been pleased to hear that China—soon to be the world's largest emitter of greenhouse gases—was in the process of adding 15,000 to 20,000 megawatts of electricity to its system annually between 1995 and 2000.

China's latest electricity growth project—some of it from the completion of the mammoth Three Gorges Dam project, but much of it fired by coal-burning and nuclear reactors like the CANDU—would be the equivalent of building as many as two power utility companies the size of B.C. Hydro every year for five years. Given the news his ravens delivered, Odin would undoubtedly have been more melancholy about his job than usual.

As Swedish futurist and former undersecretary of state for the environment, Måns Lönnroth, put it in his 1989 glimpse over the horizon into electricity's distressed and distressing future: "Two issues are likely to dominate the future debate over electricity and the environment: the role of nuclear power and the climatic effects of [carbon dioxide]."

Some of us would like to think that the slow but steady erosion of Ontario's experience with nuclear power generation—and having witnessed America's about-face on the nuclear power development issue—mimics what is going on around the world. Many believe that the only problem we have now is how to get rid of the radioactive spent fuel and decommissioned plants and equipment. But those people are basking in a deceiving interlude because many developing nations fully intend to rely on nuclear power and fossil-fuel generation—unless given viable alternatives—to serve growing consumer demand in their countries.

As Walt Patterson put it during a May 1997 industry congress in Montreux, Switzerland: "The electricity industry worldwide now faces the most severe environmental challenge it has ever had to meet ... It is to make electricity services universally, reliably and affordably available, without doing serious damage to the planet."

Given the western world's growing enchantment with the presumed benefits of the competitive marketplace, and the value of individual initiative and enterprise, someday, someone, somewhere—perhaps with a Commerce degree, a belief in the stability and value of nuclear power and a pocket calculator in hand—will want to make sure those two billion electrically disenfranchised earth inhabitants become part of the global electric marketplace. Given what we know today, it could spark an environmental disaster of inestimable proportions. But perversely enough, for the moment, that is the good news.

The bad news is that we may do more damage to ourselves as a species, faster and more effectively, through the rampant emission of greenhouse gases into the atmosphere than we will from the spectre of nuclear power failures. Because next to transportation—in all its forms and variations of exhaust discharge—the manufacture of electricity is the number two source of carbon dioxide emissions into the environment. As Patterson stated to industry representatives at Montreux: "Emissions from electricity generation are your problem. Unless you do something about them, the anticipated increase in electricity use in the coming century may make the whole problem insoluble."

Canadians, as we have already noted, are close to the top of the list of the world's "eco-pigs." In fact, Canada consumes energy at a rate four times higher than is environmentally sustainable. Much of the abuse we hand out to Mother Earth is through the consumption of electricity. As Dr. John Robinson, head of the University of British Columbia's Sustainable Development Research Institute, put it when the Earth Council released its report on energy utilization in the spring of 1997, the planet's ecosystem would be in danger of collapse if the rest of the world consumed at the same rate and level that Canadians do. "We don't know how close to the edge we are," Robinson was quoted as saying, "but there is an edge and we'd better start thinking seriously about moving back from it."

When it comes to issues like the environment, Canadians are a walking, talking contradiction. When asked what is most important in our lives—in terms of the Big Questions—Canadians put down "protecting the environment." They put it ahead of economic growth. In a study conducted by Environics Research Group for the United Nations and released in June 1997, seventy-three percent of Canadians polled said protecting the environment should be given priority even at the risk of slowing down economic growth.

Yet, if we were asked to contribute an extra ten dollars to our monthly electricity bill to be used, exclusively, for the development of renewable energy sources, or to identify savings in untapped efficiency improvements—in Ontario alone, that would come close to half-a-billion dollars a year—the howls of outrage and righteous indignation would echo through the heavens. Neither Thought nor Memory would have to bother passing *that* message along to Odin.

If we truly want to help save the environment, we have our wires crossed. Saying you love the planet is one thing. Being prepared to pay for that salvation is another. In the context of electricity, price makes us stupid. As author Mark Sagoff wrote in the June 1997 issue of *The Atlantic Monthly*, current fossil-fuel prices are very low in North America and as a result "remove incentive for fuel efficiency and for converting to other energy sources." Electricity, either as a commodity or a service, is unbelievably cheap in both relative and real terms. In the short term, it may well get even cheaper. It certainly will not climb to the point necessary for us to voluntarily demand a serious move toward renewable energy sources or search for new avenues of conservation and efficiency.

One of our problems in Canada seems to be that we have an abstract view of the environment. We most often think of it as freshwater flowing in northern rivers, tall trees with leaves trembling in the wind, a loon's call from a pristine lake, magnificent mountains and clean, smog-free air. The reality is more concrete; all of these splendorous visions we now put at huge risk if we allow random market forces and unregulated competition to prevail where sustainable development should be our only goal.

In the light of the immense damage we already do to the environment, with our gluttonous consumption of electricity, to follow advice offered by Ontario's Macdonald Advisory Committee on competition in Ontario's electrical system ("A Framework for Competition") that "full retail competition be phased in as soon as practicably possible" passes beyond the individually absurd into collective lunacy and on to the globally suicidal.

Deregulating the electricity marketplace to its fullest—getting rid of government or regulatory oversight and allowing market forces to prevail—will have two highly probable results, as Ralph Torrie pointed out in 1996. First, because the market is free of regulatory control, integrated resource planning, or a government's or a utility's ability to investigate all the options for future power generation and place the highest priority on renewable forms of generation, is no longer possible. Second, demand-side management, or the ability to identify efficiencies in electricity use rather than build new generation capacity, as important as it is to our future, is virtually impossible to achieve without stringent regulation.

The notion that privatized utilities and non-utility generators of electricity would practise DSM and discourage the use of electricity they so eagerly produce for that open marketplace is, as Flavin and Lenssen put it in 1994, "counterintuitive." Why? Because they lose money on DSM. Their profits, and the size of the dividends they pay to their shareholders, are linked to sales of electricity. As Flavin and Lenssen pointed out in their "State of the World" paper, in almost juvenile explanation: "The economic interests of electricity consumers are at odds with the interests of shareholders to whom utility executives are responsible." Other more fierce critics of deregulation of the electricity marketplace and open competition might add that unregulated generators could also be at odds with the survival of the planet, if left to their own devices.

Open access and immeasurable competition will, in the case of electricity, only lead to a wasteful increase in consumption. Three other things happen as sure as Memory and Thought perch on Odin's shoulders: Conservation goes out the window, the serious search for new, energy-saving solutions comes to a halt and the amount of carbon dioxide being released into the atmosphere increases.

After deregulating its electricity market, Norway experienced roughly that result. Competition for consumers increased. Consumption increased. The ardor for renewable, alternative generation options cooled. And efforts at sustaining development through demand-side management applications—one of the sanest, no-cost ways of checking consumption growth and finding new sources of electricity—faded away as a meaningful priority.

And yet, Canadians are being asked to follow that very model to the same result. We are even told by some advocates—like independent power associations, large non-utility power generators and industrial users of electricity—that we should be *excited* by the prospect of open competition for electricity.

Unfortunately, demand-side management—the search for efficiencies within present production and use of electricity—is anathema to deregulation of the market. Telling a home owner she could save serious money by purchasing only energy-efficient appliances or installing extra-insulated windows; or offering a developer certain tax relief for constructing an energy-efficient condominium, is a long way away from trying to seduce both into buying yet more electricity. The two are truly incompatible.

That is the basic dilemma we are faced with as the industry goes through these traumatic throes of change in the years ahead. But if we fail to untie this Gordian knot, we will pay an awful price. As Måns Lönnroth put it as early as 1989, "the only way to avoid either a very large scale nuclear power program or major climatic changes is through increasing the *efficiency* with which energy is used in industrialized countries ... Energy efficiency is the only strategy through which the environmental pressures can be relieved."

For the moment, the mechanism for easing the strain we place upon the environment in our thirst for electricity is not to be found in that attractive list of renewable energy sources—wind, solar, biomass, geothermal, small hydro, tidal power or even self-contained, on-site gas-fired generation. Each technology is handicapped, to some extent, in its capacity for generation by cost, the vagaries of the climate, environmental impact or the mechanical and financial realities of life—just ask those forty-seven groups who tried to get Ontario Hydro interested in their RETs projects!

For instance, the latest panacea applauded by the marketplace proponents seems to be small-scale, gas-fired turbine generation, suitable for commercial operations, hospitals, schools, even homes. But this is not cheap, plug-in, worry-free technology. It is the opposite: complex, expensive to operate and requiring a lot of supervision as well as back-up support. Expensive cabling and synchronizing equipment is needed. Permits are needed to control emissions. In residential areas, exhaust stacks will probably be required. Maintenance must be paid for. If your unit is part of the electricity grid, you will be required to throttle back during off-peak hours, reducing your efficiency and raising your unit costs of operation. If you are not on the grid, and failure strikes, you are on your own. That's the beauty of competition, free enterprise and more consumer "choice."

However, a 1996 study conducted by Ontario Energy/Environment Caucus ("Power to Change—Restructuring the Electricity Sector in

Ontario") estimated the potential electricity capacity needed from a variety of renewable sources to eliminate reliance on nuclear and coal-powered generation. Of the many alternatives chosen—from cogeneration to wind, from small hydro to landfill gas—the single largest source of estimated new capacity for Ontario (10,000 megawatts) was "energy efficiency"—finding ways to save electricity rather than building new capacity.

In the early 1990s, an internal review at Ontario Hydro indicated that as much as 1,000 megawatts could be saved at the utility just by identifying efficiencies in its own electricity consumption. After all, Ontario Hydro then used about fourteen million megawatt-hours (fifty percent more than the City of Toronto). But 1,000 megawatts in efficiency represented about thirty percent of the capacity of the Darlington nuclear generating facility. Find roughly 2,000 megawatts more and you could buy eight to ten years of no new generating capacity construction.

After the first OPEC oil shocks in 1973, conventional wisdom had it that we had no option but to find alternative energy sources to oil. Throughout the 1970s and 1980s, we frantically pursued new, additional ways to make electricity—nuclear, coal, gas, liquid fuel from coal, solar and wind. Billions and billions of dollars were poured into the search for new supplies of electricity.

Conservation, on the other hand, was considered a negative thing; a matter of doing without. It conjured up images of being forced to put on a sweater and shiver in the dark and cold. Conservation and energy saving were not sexy and did not receive the plaudits they would someday deserve.

"But what happened is that energy conservation and efficiency improvements ended up delivering more new supply, if you like, than all those new sources added together," said Ralph Torrie in the spring of 1997, "all the new nuclear, oils, gas, coal, hydro, all the renewables, all that stuff; if you added all these new sources up, between 1973 and today, they would not add up to as much energy as we gained from improved energy productivity."

Torrie and others, like former BCUC chairman Mark Jaccard, believe that "the cheapest resource of all is conservation." In 1989, a study of energy efficiency conducted in the United States discovered that simple consumer conservation efforts would realize a minimum twenty-seven percent saving in electrical consumption. An earlier study conducted by Ralph Torrie and colleague David Brooks in 1988 estimated primary energy usage could be reduced by fifty percent by the year 2000 through the discovery of efficiencies.

"There is still a huge, untapped efficiency improvement potential out there," claimed Torrie. "But it is amazing how difficult it is for people to think of that as a major, giant resource. [Yet] that is where the largest growth has been in the last twenty years, and still we don't think of efficiencies as one of our options."

People talk about windmills and solar cells as alternatives, but the demand side is hard to visualize. Even the concept of hydrogen fuel cells is an abstract one until we are told the technology may one day power our cars and trucks and buses. Geothermal power is easy once we are told it is heat or water from beneath the earth's surface. Small hydro is immediately imaginable and so is tidal power, even biomass (burning plant matter like tree bark and chips from the pulp and paper preparation process). But efficiency is not a stick with something whirling around on top like a windmill, so we tend to treat it as if was invisible; as if it was not an alternative solution. We treat it as if it is not even there.

"Well, it really is there," said Torrie. "And for us it is a good thing it was there because that is what saved our ass—single handedly— since the OPEC oil crisis. It is one of the biggest business stories of the 20th century—the energy productivity improvements in the industrialized economies. But it is invisible, and it still does not get acknowledgement for the power it represents."

Progressive law schools teach that technology always leads the law. We invent different products and ways of satisfying our needs as individuals and as a society. We incorporate them into our lives. We construct institutions to support and foster them. And while doing that, we formulate laws that serve to protect and perpetuate those institutions. But it is all based upon the application or introduction of new technology, or technique.

There is nothing immutable about this process. The only constant is change. There is nothing inherently wrong with change. It is not always progress, but it can become that if we pay attention; to precedents history provides, to the structure and impact of the change confronting us, and to the need to preserve those parts or elements that have already proven beneficial, for all society, not just a few.

Except for the basic physics, everything about electricity is about to change—how it is generated, how it is delivered, how it is used and paid for, and how its use will ultimately affect the future of this planet. To assume in this entropic environment, as many privatization and deregulation advocates do, that there are some unchanging theories to be applied to solve any shortcomings—like the belief in the guaranteed marvels of competition and the open marketplace—is the height of human arrogance and folly.

The issue that seems to have been central to the debate over this wide-ranging environment of change—the role and effectiveness of large, vertically integrated, mostly monopoly and mostly public utilities—is no longer debatable. Those institutions, like laws, are being bent out of shape by the force of technology and at least a generation or more of public criticism over the way in which they have conducted their business.

But that does not mean their usefulness is over. They have a very important transitional role to play in this next stage of the evolution of electricity. We do not re-write the Criminal Code when we find elements of it no longer in tune with society's mores, beliefs or needs. We keep what is useful and amend that which requires amendment. It is our deliberate, institutional way of both responding to change and preserving those functions that perform well for us.

It is not change we should be concerned about. It is how we orchestrate that change that counts. The changes on the horizon of electricity can even be seen as exciting. Those large, often inert monopoly utilities will be forced to change their structures and the way they operate. In the era of what Walt Patterson calls "the advent of the active buyer," we will probably be introduced to "power brokers" or "power aggregators" who will negotiate electricity supply on behalf of a number of clients: large corporations, small businesses, hospitals, colleges, even small towns and neighbourhoods, perhaps even groups of neighbours on a particular street. Energy service companies will compete for business with customized electricity "packages" designed to fit the exact electricity needs of buyers.

As gas-turbine generation expands and cogeneration opportunities multiply, these technological innovations may lead to the establishment of "mini-utilities," as Lönnroth termed them. These mini-utilities could be linked, much as Local Area Networks (LAN) in computer management style, exchanging information, like bond traders, on electricity availability, price and delivery schedules, much like the larger utilities do at the moment.

These structural changes could lead us in the direction of what Flavin and Lenssen called "the distributed utility." The traditional utility model, based on the archaic assumption that large, central stations are the most economical way to provide power, will give way to a "distributed" power system that relies on a broad mix of large and small generating facilities. This shift might mimic the structural change in a company's use of computers. Where once the company relied on two or three mainframe computers as its sole computing source, today its system is probably composed of thousands of personal computers, all linked in a network. Each computer is not of equal capacity. Some are small and provide certain optimum service for their cost. Others rival or exceed the capacity of the older mainframes. But they are all essential parts of a more powerful and more efficient managed network.

As Lönnroth pointed out, these innovations do not spell the death knell for central-system utilities. For householders and other small users, self-generation, or being plugged into an electricity LAN made up of your nearest neighbours, will be a long way off. For both categories of consumer—large companies and residential consumers —the traditional power utility must be there as a back-up, an alternative power provider and a guarantor of system reliability.

Those large public utilities, in particular those relying on nuclear and fossil-fuel generation, must make way for replacement by renewable sources. New technologies will be, and are being, introduced that will inevitably begin the dismantling of the large utilities over time. But if we are mindful of lessons of the past, they will still be allowed to perform a valuable service—if left in well-regulated, public hands—of providing the reliability and quality of service the new competitive entrants cannot.

In many cases the utilities will be the operators of the transmission grid over which electricity from a number of sources will be carried. Ideally, they will act as environmental gatekeepers, giving the highest priority of carriage to electricity generated by renewable energy and funding, perhaps through a user fee, efforts to conserve energy through the discovery of new technical efficiencies. In this, utilities can play an important leadership role.

In fact, if given creative policy directions and provided with strong regulatory guidance, the traditional utilities might become the mechanism by which integrated resource planning is achieved, despite the chaos of competition. Provincial governments could require their utilities to adopt full IRP as their operating goal, giving them responsibility for implementing and supervising a system of incentives and regulations for investing in DSM or renewable research and development.

The utility's new gatekeeper role could include the administration of IRP concepts such as environmental costing (adding in the cost of pollution when weighing the comparative costs of differing generation systems), supervising the implementation of a program of "set-asides" (establishing a minimum portion of the total electricity market to be set aside for electricity from renewable energy projects) and "green pricing" (offering consumers a chance to put their money where their environmental mouth happens to be by asking them to pay a slightly higher electricity rate, providing that money goes into the search for efficiencies or R&D on renewable energy).

Competition from new-technology entrants should not be feared by traditional utilities, as Walt Patterson told an industry audience in May 1997. "The electricity industry's worst enemy to 2020 and beyond may prove to be lack of imagination ... Why not, for instance, decide that the industry's long-term objective is to be 'sustainable electricity?' After all, no one would advocate the opposite. Then you can take the lead to establish successful criteria for 'sustainable electricity' and to devise pathways toward it. The public will cheer you on."

The publicly owned, properly regulated power utility can be—should be—our development platform, or bridge, to electricity's future. If that future is going to be as tumultuous and as unconventional as most forecasters anticipate, it would only be prudent to introduce a large element of stability and control into the equation. Relying on competition and market uncertainty to take us through decades of turmoil would be unbelievably irresponsible.

In this light, we should be rightly nervous of the louder prophets of deregulation, privatization and invisible hands. Their words, as the poets sing, are best left to subway walls and tenement hallways. We need a strong hand of leadership and regulation over electricity. That should be the essential job for governments—providing strong and unequivocal direction for the future electricity industry. The alternatives are too perilous, considering the risks the marketplace offers. We are not debating here the manufacturing, marketing and sale of shoes or weed eaters.

In a larger sense, we are not even talking about electricity as the central focus of our thoughts and needs any more. We are talking about stewardship of the environment—and a public responsibility to see that that very important mandate is carried out with efficiency and with certainty. The future of the electricity "industry" is no longer just about making, buying and selling moving protons to make lights go on and water warmer.

As Patterson told his industry audience (a message just as appropriate for provincial governments as for their utility charges) think less about the moment as a matter of electricity: "Think of environment and sustainability not as threats but as opportunities ... Environment should be a truly long-term focus of your business, as it evolves away from old models, now inadequate, to new models that meet the global challenge. Electricity really can be part of the solution, not just an increasingly beleaguered part of the problem."

Bibliography

BOOKS

Armstrong, Christopher, and H. V. Nelles., *Monopoly's Moment: The Organization and Regulation of Canadian Utilities, 1830–1930* (Temple University Press, 1986).

Baker, M., Miller Pitt and R. D. W. Pitt, *The Illustrated History of Newfoundland Light & Power* (Creative Publishers, 1990).

Bocking, Richard C., *Canada's Water: For Sale?* (James Lewis & Samuel, 1972).

Bourassa, Robert, *Power From the North* (Prentice-Hall, 1985).

Brodeur, Paul, *Currents of Death: Power Lines, Computer Terminals, and the Attempt to Cover Up Their Threat to Your Health* (Simon and Schuster, 1989).

Brodeur, Paul, *The Great Power-Line Cover-Up* (Little, Brown and Company, 1993).

Christensen, Bev, *Too Good To Be True: Alcan's Kemano Completion Project* (Talonbooks, 1995).

Denison, Merrill, *The People's Power: The History of Ontario Hydro* (McClelland & Stewart, 1960).

Dewar, Elaine, *Cloak of Green* (James Lorimer & Company, 1995).

Fleming, Keith R., *Power at Cost: Ontario Hydro and Rural Electrification, 1911–1958* (McGill-Queen's University Press, 1992).

Freeman, Neil B., *The Politics of Power: Ontario Hydro and Its Government, 1906–1995* (University of Toronto Press, 1996).

Hailey, Arthur, *Overload* (Doubleday, 1979).

Halberstam, David, *The Fifties* (Villard Books, 1993).

Hamilton, Edith, *Mythology* (Little, Brown and Company, 1942).

Hughes, Thomas P., *Networks of Power: Electrification in Western Society, 1880–1930* (The Johns Hopkins University Press, 1983).

Keene, Roger, *Conversations with W. A. C. Bennett* (Methuen, 1980).

Keenleyside, Hugh L., *Memoirs of Hugh L. Keenleyside: On the Bridge of Time*, Volume 2 (McClelland & Stewart, 1982).

Lévesque, René, *René Lévesque: Memoirs*, translated by Philip Stratford (McClelland & Stewart, 1986).

Macdonald, L. Ian, *From Bourassa to Bourassa: A Pivotal Decade in Canadian History* (Harvest House, 1984).

Maiden, Cecil, *Lighted Journey: The Story of B.C. Electric* (British Columbia Electric Company, 1948).

McCutcheon, Sean, *Electric Rivers: The Story of the James Bay Project* (Black Rose Books, 1991).

McKay, Paul, *Electric Empire: The Inside Story of Ontario Hydro* (Between the Lines, 1983).

McKay, Paul, *The Roman Empire: The Unauthorized Life and Times of Stephen Roman* (Key Porter Books, 1990).

Mitchell, David J., *W. A. C. Bennett and the Rise of British Columbia* (Douglas & McIntyre, 1983).

Munson, Richard, *The Power Makers: The Inside Story of America's Biggest Business ... and Its Struggle to Control Tomorrow's Electricity* (Rodale Press, 1985).

Nance, John J., *What Goes Up: The Global Assault on Our Atmosphere* (William Morrow and Company, 1991).

Negru, John, *The Electric Century: An Illustrated History of Electricity in Canada* (Canadian Electrical Association, 1991).

Nelles, H. V., *The Politics of Development: Forests, Mines & Hydro-Electric Power in Ontario, 1849–1941* (Macmillan of Canada, 1974).

Plewman, W.R., *Adam Beck and the Ontario Hydro* (Ryerson, 1947).

Posluns, Michael, *Voices From the Odeyak* (NC Press Limited, 1993).

Rae, Bob, *From Protest to Power: Personal Reflections on a Life in Politics* (Viking, 1996).

Regehr, T.D., *The Beauharnois Scandal: A Story of Canadian Entrepreneurship and Politics* (University of Toronto Press, 1990).

Reisner, Marc, *Cadillac Desert: The American West and Its Disappearing Water* (Douglas & McIntyre/Penguin, 1986).

Richardson, Boyce, *Strangers Devour the Land: The Cree Hunters of the James Bay Area Versus Premier Bourassa and the James Bay Development Corporation* (Macmillan of Canada, 1975).

Rifkin, Jeremy, with Ted Howard, *Entropy: A New World View* (Bantam, 1980).

Shrum, Gordon, *Gordon Shrum: An Autobiography*, with Peter Stursberg (University of British Columbia Press, 1986).

Smith, Philip, *Brinco: The Story of Churchill Falls* (McClelland & Stewart, 1975).

Stewart, Walter, *Uneasy Lies the Head: The Truth About Canada's Crown Corporations* (Collins, 1987).

Sturgis, James Lawrence, *Adam Beck* (Fitzhenry & Whiteside, 1978).

Tuchman, Barbara W., *The March of Folly: From Troy to Vietnam* (Alfred A. Knopf, 1984).

Waldram, James B., *As Long As the Rivers Run: Hydroelectric Development and Native Communities in Western Canada* (University of Manitoba Press, 1988).

Wilson, James W., *People in the Way: The Human Aspects of the Columbia River Treaty* (University of Toronto Press, 1973).

Worley, Ronald B., *The Wonderful World of W. A. C. Bennett* (McClelland & Stewart, 1971).

Wyatt, Alan, *Electric Power: Challenges and Choices* (The Book Press, 1986).

REPORTS, STUDIES, AND BRIEFS

A Framework for Competition: The Report of the Advisory Committee on Competition in Ontario's Electricity System to the Ontario Minister of Environment and Energy, May 1996

AMPCO Position on Electricity Market Restructuring, Association of Major Power Consumers of Ontario, July 1995

Annual Corporate Reports, the British Columbia Hydro and Power Authority

Annual Corporate Reports, Hydro-Québec

Annual Corporate Reports, Ontario Hydro

Annual Corporate Reports, the Manitoba Hydro-Electric Board

A Report on the Effects of the Reporting, Legislative and Regulatory Requirements of B.C. Hydro, A. L. Peel & Associates, August 1994

A Strategy for Sustainable Development and Use for Ontario Hydro: Report of the Task Force on Sustainable Energy Development, Ontario Hydro, October 1993

An Overview of Short Term Electricity Trade, B.C. Hydro and Powerex, February 1991

An Introduction to B.C. Hydro's Integrated Resource Plan, B.C. Hydro, 1994 Electricity Plan

Business Strategies for Sustainable Development in the Canadian Energy Sector, Torrie, R., prepared for the National Round Table on the Environment and the Economy, October 1996

Comparative Cost of Financing Ontario Hydro As a Crown Corporation and a Private Corporation, Gordon, M., April 1995

Competition, Convergence and Customer Choice (Executive Summary): Finding New Paths to the Customer By Restructuring Ontario's Electricity Sector, Corporate Strategic Planning, Ontario Hydro, June 1995

Creating a Sustainable Energy Future, Flavin, C., in *State of the World 1988* (W.W. Norton & Company, 1988).

Damming James Bay: I. Potential Impacts on Coastal Climate and the Water Balance, Rouse, Wayne R., Ming-Ko Woo, and Jonathan S. Price, The Canadian Geographer, 1992

Economic Development and Environmental Preservation: The Case of the James Bay Hydro-Electric Power Projects, Quebec, Hamley, William, International Journal of Canadian Studies, Fall 1991

Electric Load Forecast 1994/95–2014/15, B.C. Hydro, December 1994

Electric Power in Ontario: Regulation for the 21st Century, presentations to a seminar organized by the University of Toronto Electric Power Project in collaboration with Ontario Hydro, June 1995 sessions:

I "Industry Restructuring and Regulation: A Political Analysis"—Daniels, R., and M. Trebilcock.

II "Regulating Transmission and Distribution"—Halpern, P., and L. Booth.

III "Power Trading: Towards a National and International Market"—Howse, R.

IV "Restructuring and the Regulation of Conventional Pollutants"—Dewees, D.

V "Negotiating the Workplace: An Analysis of the Impact of Alternative Human Resource Management Techniques on Power Industry Productivity"—Warrian, P.

VI "Financing: Crown Versus Investor-Owned Corporations"—Gordon, M.

VII "Costing Environmental Risks: Nuclear and Fossil Generation"—Dewees, D.

VIII "Industry Rationalization: Distribution Costs and Appropriate Regulatory Structures"—Yatchew, A.

X "The Costs of Dislocation: Labour Adjustment Policies in the Electric Power Industry"—Warrian, P.

Electricity and Industry in Ontario: Costs, Competitiveness, and Sustainable Development, Torrie, R., and R. Skinner, for the Green Energy Coalition, June 1994

Exporting Disaster: The Cost of Selling CANDU Reactors, Martin, D.H., Campaign for Nuclear Phaseout, November 1996

Global Warming: A Briefing for the National Roundtable on the Environment and the Economy, Torrie, R., January 1997

Hydroelectric Power Generation and Sustainable Development—A Contradiction of Terms?, Boothroyd, P.

Hydro in Ontario: A Future Role and Place, Ontario Hydro Task Force, 1972

Impacts of Growth in Resource Use and Human Population on the Nechako River: A Major Tributary of the Fraser River, British Columbia, Canada, Hartman, G.F., GeoJournal, October 1996

Looking Forward with Ontario Hydro: "For the People," The Society of Ontario Hydro Professional and Administrative Employees

Making the Connection: The B.C. Hydro Electric System and How it is Operated, B.C. Hydro

Managing Instead of Building: B.C. Hydro's Role in the 1990s, Jaccard, M., J. Nyboer, and T. Makinen, B.C. Studies, Autumn/Winter 1991/92

Nuclear Sunset: The Economic Costs of the Canadian Nuclear Industry, Martin, D.H., and D. Argue, for the Campaign for Nuclear Phaseout, February 1996

Ontario Hydro and the Electric Power Industry: Vision for a Competitive Industry; Helping Ontario to Thrive to and beyond 2000, Financial Restructuring Group on behalf of Ontario Hydro, June 1995

Ontario Hydro's Fatal Condition: Implications for Canadian Public Policy, Adams, T., Canadian Business Economics, Spring 1993

Ontario Hydro and the Electric Power Industry: Challenges and Choices, Working Draft of the Report of the Financial Restructuring Group, June 1994

Planning Today for Tomorrow's Energy: An Energy Strategy for British Columbia, B.C. Energy Council, November 1994

Power and Dignity: The Social Consequences of Hydro-electric Development for the James Bay Cree, Niezen, R., Canadian Review of Sociology and Anthropology, November 1993

Providing Energy in Developing Countries, Lenssen, N., in *State of the World 1993* (Earthscan Publications, 1993).

Provincial Power Study: British Columbia Energy Board, Vols 1 & 2 plus appendices, April 1972

Public Attitudes Towards B.C. Hydro, Goldfarb Corporation, 1988

Reshaping the Power Industry, Flavin, C., and N. Lenssen, in *State of the World 1994* (W.W. Norton & Company, 1994).

Restructuring the Electricity Industry in Ontario, Vol. 1 & 2 of the Phase III Report of the Ad Hoc Task Force of the Municipal Electric Association, September 1994

Statement on the Comparative Gains and Losses to the People of Ontario from Privatizing the Generating Plant of Ontario Hydro, Gordon, M., August 1995

The British Columbia Electricity Market Review: Report and Recommendations to the Lieutenant Governor in Council, British Columbia Utilities Commission, September 1995

The Cost of New Electricity Supply in British Columbia, B.C. Hydro, June 1994

The Coming Reformation of the Electric Utility Industry, Lönnroth, Måns, Electricity, 1989

The Dismal Economics of CANDU, Lermer, G., Options Politiques, April 1996

The Future of Ontario's Energy System: Phase 2—Adding Value, Power Workers' Union, October 1995

The Future of Ontario Hydro, Power Workers' Union, August 1995

The Political Economy of Nationalization: Social Credit and the Takeover of the British Columbia Electric Company, Tieleman, H. William, a Master of Arts thesis, Faculty of Graduate Studies, Department of Political Science, University of British Columbia, 1984

The Select Committee on Ontario Hydro Affairs: Report on Proposed Uranium Contracts, The Legislative Assembly of the Province of Ontario, Second Session: Thirty-first Parliament, March 1978

The Way Ahead: B.C. Hydro Corporate Strategic Plan, B.C. Hydro, 1993

Towards Energy Sustainability: Implementing the B.C. Energy Council's Energy Strategy for British Columbia, Ministry of Energy, Mines and Resources, Province of British Columbia, May 1995

Sustainable Development and Electric Power Planning—A Review of the Issues, Torrie, R., J. Smith, R. Skinner, for Environment Canada, March 1995

Sustainable Development and Ontario Hydro: A Review of the Task Force Report and General Comments, Torrie, R., for Northwatch Coalition, May 1994

Index

Adams, Tom, 59, 61, 78, 81, 83
Aluminum Company of Canada (Alcan), 164, 170, 171, 199
Armstrong, Christopher, 50, 51, 53
Arrow Lakes, B.C., 158–62
Association of Major Power Consumers of Ontario, 20
Atomic Energy Control Board, 81
Atomic Energy of Canada, 81, 82

Batchelor, Charles, 39
Beck, Adam, 50, 62, 64–76, 135
Bell, Gordon, 57
Bennett, Bill, 171
Bennett, W.A.C., 18, 25, 131, 136–40; Two River Policy of, 141–51
Bonneville Power Administration (U.S.), 17, 28, 132, 202
Bouchard, Lucien, 27, 173, 174, 178, 179
Bourassa, Robert, 94–98, 105–08, 110, 112–14, 117–19, 125, 135
B.C. Electric Company (BCE), 18, 137, 142–44, 146, 148, 150, 152
B.C. Hydro: efficiency and profitability, 25–26; financial health of, 131–32, 196; flooding of Arrow Lakes, 157–62; formation under W.A.C. Bennett, 146–48; IPC scandal, 126–28, 130–31, 132–34; "Power Smart" program, 197–98; privatization controversy, 194–205; rates, 197; sale of downstream benefits to U.S., v, 202–03; under Shrum and Keenleyside, 151–57. See also Bennett, W.A.C.; Columbia River Treaty; Two River Policy
B.C. Power Commission, 148, 152, 160
B.C. Power Corporation, 143, 146, 150
B.C. Utilities Commission, 171, 199, 208
Brooks, David, 218
Bruce nuclear plant, 60, 61, 63, 90
Burrard Thermal Plant, 143

Canadian Electrical Association, 183
Canadian General Electric, 66, 79
CANDU, 81–82
Chalk River, Ont., 82

Chuchman, George, 14, 15
Churchill Falls, Nfld., v, 26, 99, 105, 132, 175, 177, 178
Churchill River, Man., 167, 168, 170
Clark, Glen, 126, 127, 133, 171, 199
Cliche Inquiry, 112
Columbia River Treaty, v, 25–26, 28, 135, 136, 141, 144, 149, 157–59, 196, 202
Columbia River, 139–40
Coon-Come, Matthew, 120, 124
Coulombe, Guy, 116, 118

Darlington nuclear plant, 57, 86, 87
Davis, William, 87, 88
Denison, Merrill, 67, 75
Denison Mines, 88–89
Department of Indian Affairs, 166, 170
deregulation and privatization, 206–09, 214–15; Argentina, 15; Brazil, 15; Britain, 14; British Columbia debate, 194–205; California, 23; Canada, 13–14; Chile, 15; Norway, 14, 215; Ontario (current debate) 25, 179–91, 206 (fictional account), 2–10; United States, 15–16; versus public ownership, 191–94
Dickinson, Arthur, 20, 86
Diefenbaker, John, 144, 145, 149
Douglas Point nuclear plant, 82–83, 84–85, 90
Drew, George, 76
Duncan Dam, B.C., 196
Duplessis, Maurice, 100, 101

Edison, Thomas, 37, 38, 39, 40, 42, 45
Electric Development Co., 66, 68
electric power monopolies, development of, 43–54
"Electric Ring," 67–69, 195
electricity: alternative generation, 216; development, 31–33, 37–41; efficient use, 217–18
Energy Probe, 59, 61, 78, 81, 83
environmental degradation, 29, 123–24, 196–97, 212–14. See also methylmercury; Native peoples and hydro

DELUSIONS OF POWER

Farlinger, William, 184, 185, 186
Federal Energy Regulatory Commission
    (U.S.), 16, 174, 176–78, 188, 207, 209
Federal Power Commission (U.S.), 47
Fisk, Jim, 43
Flavin, C., 215, 220
Fleming, Keith R., 18, 70
Fraser River, 156–57, 171, 172
Freeman, Neil, 68, 73, 77, 84, 88
Frost, Leslie, 81
Fulton, Davie, 144–45, 149
Furness, Betty, 79

Gaglardi, Phil, 138
Gathercole, Dick, 193, 194, 200, 201
Gathercole, George, 85
Gaz Métropolitain Inc., 176
Godbout, Adelard, 101
Gordon, Myron, 22, 27, 28
Gould, Jay, 43
Grand Coulee Dam, 139
Grauer, Dal, 143–44, 147, 149

Hadekel, Peter, 98, 117
Hamel, Philippe, 101
Harcourt, Mike, 129, 131, 132, 171, 194, 196, 199
Harris, Mike, 179, 188, 189, 211
Holt, Herbert, 101
Hudson Bay Mining and Smelting Com-
    pany, 165
Hughes, Thomas P., 38, 41, 42, 43, 51
Hydro-Québec: as flagship of provincial
    development, 18–19, 99–101, 104; cancella-
    tion of Great Whale, 92–94, 122, 125;
    debts of, 120, 121–22, 175; exports to U.S.,
    116–19, 174–77; founding of, 101–02;
    launch of James Bay Project, 94–97,
    106–10, 113; negotiations with Newfound-
    land, v, 99, 105–06, 177; profitability of,
    26–27; under Lucien Bouchard, 173–79;
    under René Lévesque, 102–04, 116. See
    also Bourassa, Robert; James Bay Power
    Project; Native peoples and hydro

Independent Power Assn., 201–02
Insull, Samuel, 45–46, 48, 50
International Joint Commission, 139–40,
    158–59
IPC International Power Corp., 126, 127,
    129, 130, 133, 134, 199
Island Falls Dam, Sask., 165

Jaccard, Mark, 204, 208, 217

James Bay and Northern Quebec Agree-
    ment, 111, 121, 124, 173
James Bay Power Project, 94–99, 107–13;
    environmental impact of, 123–24; Great
    Whale, 19, 29, 92–93, 99, 109, 119, 120–21,
    123–25, 173–74; La Grande, 94–95, 107,
    110, 113, 119; Nottaway–Broadback–
    Rupert, 115, 119–20, 121
Jehl, Francis, 38, 39
Jobs for Power Act (B.C.), 202
Johnson, Lyndon Baines, 135, 136
Joron, Guy, 113, 115

Keene, Roger, 140
Keenleyside, Hugh L., 146, 147, 149, 151, 152,
    154, 155, 157, 159
Keenleyside Dam (B.C.), 196
Kemano project, 170, 171, 172, 199, 200
Kootenay River, 161
Kupcis, Allan, 59, 60, 63, 182, 185, 192

Lajambe, Hélène, 121–22
Laurendeau, André, 103
Laxton, John, 127, 130, 133
Lenssen, N., 215, 220
Lesage, Jean, 102
Lett, Sherwood, 149
Leuchtenburg, William E., 67
Lévesque, René, 18, 100, 102–105, 107,
    112–14, 117
Lönnroth, Måns, 212, 216, 219, 220
Lyon, Sterling, 170

Macdonald Committee, 184, 214
Mackenzie, William, 66
Mackintosh, Alex, 57
Mair, Rafe, 172
Malouf, Albert, 110–11
Manicouagan-Outardes, 100
Manitoba Hydro, 131, 166, 167, 168, 169
Marchand, Jean, 103
McCutcheon, Sean, 95, 97, 100, 107, 110
McKay, Paul, 53, 76, 78–80, 84, 89, 191
McTaggart, Andrew, 143
methylmercury, 92, 97, 121
Mica Dam, B.C., 161, 196
Miller, Dan, 203
Mitchell, David J., 18, 136, 137, 138, 139, 140,
    143, 144, 145, 148, 153
Morgan, J.P., 39, 40, 43
Morton, Val, 161
Munson, Richard, 37, 41, 43, 45, 48, 49
Murphy, John, 21

Native peoples and hydro development, 20, 29; in Alberta, 165; in British Columbia, 170–72; in Manitoba, 164, 166–70; in Ontario, 164; in Quebec, 92, 93, 97, 109–11, 120–21, 164, 173–74; in Saskatchewan, 165–66; recognition of land rights, 162–63
Negru, John, 33, 36
Nelles, H.V., 50, 51, 53, 65
Nelson River, 167
New England Power Pool, 116
New York Power Authority, 93, 113, 116, 118, 125
Newfoundland, v, 99, 105–06, 132, 177–78
Niagara Falls, 66, 77
Nicholls, Frederic, 66
Norris, George, 47, 48, 49

Odeyak, the, 124–25
Ohio Power, 33
Ontario Hydro: as major employer, vi; competitiveness, 27–28; debts, v, 23–24; fictional account of privatization, 2–10; formation under Adam Beck, 65–76; generating capacity, 29; investment in hydro-electric power, 77–78; investment in nuclear power, v, 81–91, 183; "Live Better Electrically" campaign, 78–79; privatization controversy, 25, 179–191, 206; Ralph Nader's opinion of, 54; rates, 23; Renewable Energy Technologies program, 182; revenues, 24; under Maurice Strong, 55–64
Organization of Petroleum Exporting Countries (OPEC), 15, 86, 106, 113
Ottawa River, 77

Parizeau, Jacques, 19, 92, 93, 99, 122, 125
Patterson, Walt, 209, 212, 213, 219, 221, 222
Peace River, 140–43, 149, 154
Pearson, Lester Bowles, 135, 149, 150
Pellatt, Henry M., 66
Pelletier, Gérard, 103
Pickering nuclear plant, vi, 12, 84–85, 90, 182
Plewman, William R., 76
Porter Commission (Ont.), 87, 89
Post-War Rehabilitation Council, 148
Power Commission Act (Ont.), 69
Power Corp. of Canada, 128, 143
Power Workers' Union, 14, 21, 180
privatization. See deregulation
public power utilities: future, 209–12, 218–22; regulation, vii–ix

Rae, Bob, 57, 62, 63, 64, 135
Raiwind Power Project, 126, 130, 199
Revelstoke Dam, 196
Rio Algom Mines, 88–89
Robinson, John, 213
Roblin, Duff, 167
Rockefeller, John D., 43
Rogers, Ted, 193
Rolphton demonstration project, 82
Roman, Stephen, 88–89
Roosevelt, Franklin D., 45, 48, 49

Sagoff, Mark, 214
Saskatchewan Power, 165–66
Saskatchewan River, 165, 166
Schreyer, Edward, 169–70
Shaffer, Marvin, 202
Sheehan, John, 127, 130
Sherman Antitrust Act (U.S.), 44, 47
Shrum, Gordon, 151–57
Smallwood, Joey, 105–06
Smith, Brian, 131, 132, 133, 201
St. Lawrence River, 77, 78, 102
Sterling, Norman, 185, 188, 189
Stewart, Walter, 82, 186–87
Strachan, Robert, 146
Strong, Maurice, 55–57, 62–64, 183–84, 198

Tennessee Valley Authority, 17, 49
Three Gorges Dam project, 212
Three Mile Island, 12, 89
Tieleman, William, 147, 148, 150
Tobin, Brian, 177, 178
Torrie, Ralph, 190, 191, 210, 211, 214, 217, 218
Trudeau, Pierre, 103, 107
Two River Policy, 139, 142, 143, 145, 149, 152

Udall, Stewart, 149
Ungava Bay, 95
United States, energy policy, 15, 17
Upton, Francis, 39

W.A.C. Bennett Dam, 154
Waldram, James B., 163
Water Power Act (Man.), 169
Watt, Charlie, 124
Wenner-Gren, Axel, 141–42
West Kootenay Power, 199, 200
Westinghouse, 42, 79–80
Whitney, J.P., 69, 72
Williston Lake, B.C., 154
Wilson, James W., 158, 160, 161, 162